TENDER DARKNESS

A Mary MacLane Sampler

EDITED, WITH AN INTRODUCTION &
NOTES, BY ELISABETH PRUITT
FOREWORD BY
MICHAEL R. BROWN

PETRARCA PRESS
AUSTIN · TEXAS
2014

First edition.

Printed in the USA.

This paper is PH-balanced.
It should undergo lessened crumbling,
yellowing, or other deterioration over time.

BIBLIOGRAPHIC DATA

MacLane, Mary, 1881-1929
Tender darkness: a Mary MacLane sampler
Rev. of Tender darkness: a Mary MacLane anthology
1st ed. / p. cm.
Includes bibliographic references (p.).
Lib. of Congress Control No. PENDING
1. Feminism - United States - Literary collections
2. Women - United States - Literary collections
ISBN 978-1-883304-07-2 - Paperbound
ISBN 978-1-883304-08-9 - Casebound

Table of Contents

Foreword

THIS BOOK'S first edition, published in the final days of 1993, returned Mary MacLane to an audience that never should've been without her unique art. Since then, various reprinters have tramped along this book's blazed course, then struck off to their various compass-points. She hasn't gone out of print since.

Measuring this against those - Penelope Rosemont's rollicking 1997 piece of surreal Wobblyism, Julia Watson's studious consideration of that same year, Melville House's widely-noticed reprints of 2013, a Danish translation of her tremendous debut, *I Await the Devil's Coming*, in 2014, a Spanish translation of the same for 2015 - this book's path through the author's works remains worthwhile.

Its purpose remains to make available, affordably and accessibly, the best of MacLane's literary craft. With last month's release of a 600-page anthology of her writing - *Human Days: A Mary MacLane Reader*, edited by myself - her oeuvre is no longer scattered, and it shows as surprisingly recondite and anything but simple.

Tender Darkness, some 400 pages shorter, may be considered the quickest entry to this author's special world.

The works herein are the same as in the first edition, in improved texts. The bibliography (which remains the most detailed index of secondary MacLane sources to date) is lightly edited. The notes, taken from *Human Days*, are considerably expanded and now focus on the breadth of MacLane's reading and consequent quotes, references, and allusions. The Introduction is retained, very lightly edited, so that the words that introduced a new generation to an always-fresh talent may be seen again.

Michael R. Brown
Butte County, California
November 2014

Introduction

THE WORLD FOR Mary MacLane was one-half wonder, one-half adventure. She found inspiration all around her, from the great plateaus and mountains of her native Butte to the rarified gentry of Newport in its Gilded Age glory days. She captured the fancy of millions in this country and abroad, was elevated to near-mythic status in her own time, and was gossiped about incessantly, imitated constantly, and condemned mercilessly. She was hailed by some of the finest authors and critics of her day as a literary genius, and was endlessly celebrated (when she was not being reviled) by the lowest of the yellow press. She was the prototype of today's media icons. And yet this unique individual - pioneering free spirit, bon vivant, gambler extraordinaire, newswoman, writer for and star of the silent screen - has somehow remained out of print and unavailable to readers in her own country for more than seventy-five years.

She wrote her first book in 1901, at the age of nineteen. It created a nationwide sensation when published a year later, sold almost 100,000 copies in short order, and made her a rich woman. *The Story of Mary MacLane* was like a flame suddenly springing up in a closed tinderbox. In a time in which women, like children, were to be seen and not heard, Mary MacLane gave her sex a voice. And what a voice it was. With a frankness and sophistication far beyond her years, she wrote openly of such diverse things as drugs, death, the Devil (whom she blithely announced she wished to marry, should he ever appear), truth, bisexuality, and beauty. Her writing rings true today, and actually says more to us now than it did to her own generation. As we approach the end of the Twentieth Century in America, many of us have been forced to realize that the traditional values and attitudes no longer hold true. The rules no longer apply. And Mary was fighting to rewrite the entire rulebook in America of 1901 - fighting to live her life, and to write about it, on her own terms.

While she was greatly misunderstood in her time, there can be no doubt that she was a figure of major importance. *The Chicagoan* eloquently eulogized "this errant daughter of literature" upon her death in August 1929 as "the first of the self-expressionists, and also the first of the flappers. She represented the missing link between the shaved bare leg of the present and the bashful ankle of the past. She should be as important to any student of modern manners as the Java ape-man is to anthropologists. She throws the subject into perspective, for she broke loose upon a startled world as far back as 1902.

"How did it happen that a revolution in manners, a transvaluation of values in the female code of behavior, started, or seemed to start, with an unruly young woman who couldn't bear the sight of the tooth-brushes hanging up in the family bathroom at Butte, Montana? What seed fell upon that austere provincial soil to produce this amorous diarist with a narcissus complex? What mystic or glandular voices spoke to Mary, bidding her go forth into the world as the Jeanne d'Arc of the Warm Mammas?

"The New Woman has had many famous prophets, from Susan B. Anthony to Henrik Ibsen, but the origin of her wild young sister, the New Female, has not yet been carefully traced. The career of Mary MacLane is Chapter I in *The History of Flapperism*, ready-made for any ambitious sociologist. This is a work that is crying to be written - yea, crying out loud."

But *The History of Flapperism* was never to be written, and Mary MacLane was gradually forgotten. For a scant two months after she died, so too died the decade she helped create: the Roaring Twenties, collapsing in on itself one awful October day known forever after as Black Thursday. But no matter. Now, in this book, after too many years in the shadows, Mary MacLane lives again.

The present volume affords a broad overview of MacLane's most productive years. Included are the complete text of her first book (printed for the first time in its original, unexpurgated form); a 1902 interview with the enigmatic writer; seven of her colorful newspaper feature articles (two of them written, in the first flush of her success, for Joseph Pulitzer's flagship Manhattan daily, the rest in 1910, when MacLane had returned to Montana after almost a decade of East Coast lionizing); notes; and a detailed bibliography.

I am indebted to many people and institutions for their kind assistance. To Carole Bell, Rosemary C. Hanes, and Pat Rigsby of the Library of Congress; Francena Brumbaugh of Stanford University; Harry Clancy; Ellen Crain of the Butte-Silver Bow Public Archives; Ann Deromedi and JoAnn Myers of the Thermopolis (Wyoming) Public Library; Anne Drew and John Hughes of the Butte-Silver Bow Public Library; Martha Finnerty; Jacqueline Fretwell of the St Augustine (Florida) Historical Society; the George Washington University Library; Bob Hemmingson of the Fergus Falls (Minnesota) Public Library; Willis Kim of the University of California at Berkeley Library; Margaret Kulis of the Newberry Library; Paula Lee and Richard Popp of the University of Chicago Library; Phil Lipson; Ronald S. Magliozzi of the Museum of Modern Art; Carolyn J. Mattern; Ada McAllister; the New York Public Library; the Otter Tail County (Minnesota) Historical Society; Lucille Nichols Patrick; the Rockland (Massachusetts) Public Library; Richard A. Schrader of the University of North Carolina at Chapel Hill Library; Dr Mary Smith; Bruce Stuppi; Dr Virginia Terris; Tracy Thornton of the *Montana Standard*; the University of San Diego Library; Dave Walter and Rebecca Kohl of the Montana Historical Society; and Leslie Wheeler - my grateful thanks. And to Margery Wood and Elizabeth Wood, my very special appreciation.

Elisabeth Pruitt
Belmont, California
June 1993

I AWAIT THE DEVIL'S COMING

(Pub. as "The Story of Mary MacLane")

- 1902 -

To The Devil
Of the Steel-Gray Eyes, Who One
Day may Come - Who knows? -
I Dedicate, with the Mad Love of
A Young Weary Wooden Heart,
This, My Book.

*

Butte, Montana
November, 1901.

I, of womankind and of nineteen years, will now begin to set down as full and frank a Portrayal as I am able of myself, Mary MacLane, for whom the world contains not a parallel.

I am convinced of this, for I am odd.

I am distinctly original innately and in development.

I have in me a quite unusual intensity of life.

I can feel.

I have a marvelous capacity for misery and for happiness.

I am broad-minded.

I am a genius.

I am a philosopher of my own good peripatetic school.

I care neither for right nor for wrong - my conscience is nil.

My brain is a conglomeration of aggressive versatility.

I have reached a truly wonderful state of miserable morbid unhappiness.

I know myself, oh, very well.

I have attained an egotism that is rare indeed.

I have gone into the deep shadows.

All this constitutes oddity. I find therefore that I am quite, quite odd.

I have hunted for even the suggestion of a parallel among the several hundred persons that I call acquaintances. But in vain. There are people and people of varying depths and intricacies of character, but there is none to compare with me. The young ones of my own age - if I chance to give them but a glimpse of the real workings of my mind - can only stare at me in dazed stupidity, uncomprehending; and the old ones of forty and fifty - for forty and fifty are always old to nineteen - can but either stare also in stupidity, or else, their own narrowness asserting itself, smile their little devilish smile of superiority which they reserve indiscriminately for all foolish young things. - The utter idiocy of forty and fifty at times! -

These to be sure are extreme instances. There are among my young acquaintances some who do not stare in stupidity, and yes, even at forty and fifty there are some who understand some phases of my complicated character, though none to comprehend it in its entirety.

But, as I said, even the suggestion of a parallel is not to be found among them.

I think at this moment, however, of two minds famous in the world of letters between which and mine there are certain fine points of similarity. These are the minds of Lord Byron and of Marie Bashkirtseff. It is the Byron of *Don Juan* in whom I find suggestions of myself. In this sublime outpouring there are few to admire the character of Don Juan, but all must admire Byron. He is truly admirable. He uncovered and exposed his soul of mingled good and bad - as the terms are - for the world to gaze upon. He knew the human race. And he knew himself.

As for that strange notable, Marie Bashkirtseff, yes, I am rather like her in many points, as I've been told. But in most things I go beyond her.

Where she is deep, I am deeper.

Where she is wonderful in her intensity, I am still more wonderful in my intensity.

Where she had philosophy, I am a philosopher.

Where she had astonishing vanity and conceit, I have yet more astonishing vanity and conceit.

But she, forsooth, could paint good pictures, - and I - what can I do?

She had a beautiful face, and I am a plain-featured insignificant little animal.

She was surrounded by admiring, sympathetic friends, and I am alone - alone, though there are people and people.

She was a genius, and still more am I a genius.

She suffered with the pain of a woman, young, and I suffer with the pain of a woman, young and all alone.

And so it is.

Along some lines I have gotten to the edge of the world. A step more and I fall off. I do not take the step. I stand on the edge, and I suffer.

Nothing, oh, nothing on the earth can suffer like a woman young and all alone!

- Before proceeding farther with the portraying of Mary MacLane, I will write out some of her uninteresting history.

I was born in 1881 at Winnipeg, in Canada. - Whether Winnipeg will yet live to be proud of this fact is a matter for some conjecture and anxiety on my part. - When I was four years old I was taken with my family to a little town in western Minnesota, where I lived a more or less vapid and lonely life until I was ten. We came then to Montana.

Whereat the aforesaid life was continued.

My father died when I was eight.

Apart from feeding and clothing me comfortably and sending me to school - which is no more than was due me - and transmitting to me the MacLane blood and character, I can not see that he ever gave me a single thought.

Certainly he did not love me, for he was quite incapable of loving any one but himself. And since nothing is of any moment in this world without the love of human beings for each other, it is a matter of supreme indifference to me whether my father, Jim MacLane of selfish memory, lived or died.

He is nothing to me.

There are with me still a mother, a sister, and two brothers.

They also are nothing to me.

They do not understand me any more than if I were some strange live curiosity, as which I dare say they regard me.

I am peculiarly of the MacLane blood which is Highland Scotch. My sister and brothers inherit the traits of their mother's family which is of Scotch Lowland descent. This alone makes no small degree of difference. Apart from this the MacLanes - these particular MacLanes - are just a little bit different from every family in Canada, and from every other that I've known. It contains and has contained fanatics of many minds - religious, social, whatnot. And I am a true MacLane.

There is absolutely no sympathy between my immediate family and me. There can never be.

My mother, having been with me during the whole of my nineteen years, has an utterly distorted idea of my nature and its desires, if indeed she has any idea of it.

When I think of the exquisite love and sympathy which might be between a mother and daughter, I feel myself defrauded of a beautiful thing rightfully mine, in a world where for me such things are pitiably few.

It will always be so.

My sister and brothers are not interested in me and my analyses and philosophy, and my wants. Their own are strictly practical and material. The love and sympathy between human beings is to them, it seems, a thing only for people in books.

In short, they are Lowland Scotch and I am a MacLane.

And so, as I've said, I carried my uninteresting existence into Montana. The existence became less uninteresting, however, as my versatile mind began to develop and grow and know the glittering things that are. But I realized as the years were passing that my own life was at best a vapid, negative thing.

A thousand treasures that I wanted were lacking.

I graduated from the High School with these things: very good Latin; good French and Greek; indifferent Geometry and other mathematics; a broad conception of History and Literature; peripatetic philosophy that I acquired without any aid from the High School; genius of a kind, that has always been with me; an empty heart that has taken on a certain wooden quality; an excellent strong young woman's-body; a pitiably starved soul.

With this equipment I have gone my way through the last two years. But my life, though unsatisfying and warped, is no longer insipid. It is fraught with a poignant misery - the misery of Nothingness.

I have no particular thing to occupy me. I write every day. Writing is a necessity - like eating. I do a little housework, and on the whole am rather fond of it - some parts of it. I dislike dusting chairs, but I have no aversion to scrubbing floors. Indeed, I have gained much of my strength and gracefulness of body from scrubbing the kitchen floor - to say nothing of some fine points of philosophy. It brings a certain energy to one's body and to one's brain.

But mostly I take walks far away in the open country. Butte and its immediate vicinity present as ugly an outlook as one could wish to see. It is so ugly indeed that it is near the perfection of ugliness. And anything perfect, or nearly so, is not to be despised. I have reached some astonishing subtleties of conception as I have walked for miles over the sand and barrenness among the little hills and gulches. Their utter desolateness is an inspiration to the long, long thoughts and to the nameless wanting. Every day I walk over the sand and barrenness.

And so then my daily life seems an ordinary life enough, and possibly, to an ordinary person, a comfortable life.

That's as may be.

To me it is an empty damned weariness.

I rise in the morning; eat three meals; and walk; and work a little, read a little, write; see some uninteresting people; go to bed.

Next day, I rise in the morning; eat three meals; and walk; and work a little, read a little, write; see some uninteresting people; go to bed.

Again I rise in the morning; eat three meals; and walk; and work a little, read a little, write; see some uninteresting people; go to bed.

Truly an exalted, soulful life!

What it does for me, how it affects me, I am now trying to portray.

January 14

I have in me the germs of intense life. If I could live, and if I could succeed in writing out my living, the world itself would feel the heavy intensity of it.

I have the personality, the nature, of a Napoleon, albeit a feminine translation. And therefore I do not conquer; I do not even fight. I manage only to exist.

- Poor little Mary MacLane, - what might you not be? What wonderful thing might you not do? But held down, half-buried, a seed fallen in barren ground, alone, uncomprehended, obscure - poor little Mary MacLane! -

Weep, world, - why don't you - for poor little Mary MacLane.

Had I been born a man I would by now have made a deep impression of myself on the world - on some part of it. But I am a woman, and God, or the Devil, or Fate, or whosoever it was, has flayed me of the thick outer skin and thrown me out into the midst of Life - has left me a lonely damned thing filled with the red, red blood of ambition and desire, but afraid to be touched, for there is no thick skin between my sensitive flesh and the world's fingers.

But I want to be touched.

Napoleon was a man and though sensitive his flesh was safely covered.

But I am a woman, awakening, and upon awakening and looking about me, I would fain turn and go back to sleep.

There is a pain that goes with these things when one is a woman, young and all alone.

- I am filled with an ambition. I wish to give to the world a naked Portrayal of Mary MacLane: her wooden heart, her good young woman's-body, her mind, her soul.

I wish to write, write, write!

I wish to acquire that beautiful benign gentle satisfying thing - Fame. I want it - oh, I want it! I wish to leave all my obscurity, my misery, - my weary unhappiness behind me forever.

I am deadly, deadly tired of my unhappiness.

I wish this Portrayal to be published and launched into that deep salt sea - the world. There are some there surely who will understand it and me.

Can I be that thing which I am - can I be possessed of a peculiar rare genius, and yet drag my life out in obscurity in this uncouth warped Montana town!

It must be impossible! If I thought the world contained nothing more than that for me - oh, what should I do! Would I make an end of my dreary little life now? I fear I would. I am a philosopher - and a coward. And it were infinitely better to die now in the high-beating pulses of youth than to drag on, year after year, year after year, and find oneself at last a stagnant old woman, spiritless, hopeless, with a declining body, a declining mind, - and nothing to look back on except the visions of things that might have been - and the weariness.

I see the picture. I see it plainly. Oh, kind Devil, deliver me from it!

Surely there must be in a world of manifold beautiful things something among them for me.

And always while I am still young, there is that dim light, the Future. But it is indeed a dim, dim light, and ofttimes there's a treachery in it.

So then yes. I find myself at this stage of womankind and nineteen years, a genius, a thief, a liar - a general moral vagabond, a fool more or less, and a philosopher of the peripatetic school. Also I find that even this combination can not make one happy. It serves, however, to occupy my versatile mind, to keep me wondering what it is a kind Devil has in store for me.

A philosopher of my own peripatetic school - hour after hour I walk over the desolate sand and dreariness among tiny hills and gulches on the outskirts of this mining town; in the morning, in the long afternoon, in the cool of the night. And hour after hour, as I walk, through my brain some long, long pageants march: the pageant of my fancies, the pageant of my unparalleled egotism, the pageant of my unhappiness, the pageant of my minute analyzing, the pageant of my peculiar philosophy, the pageant of my dull, dull life, - and the pageant of the Possibilities.

We three go out on the sand and barrenness: my wooden heart, my good young woman's-body, my soul. We go there and contemplate the long sandy wastes, the red, red line on the sky at the setting of the sun, the cold gloomy mountains under it, the ground without a weed, without a grass-blade even in their season - for they have years ago been killed off by the sulphur smoke from the smelters.

So this sand and barrenness forms the setting for the personality of me.

I feel about forty years old.

Yet I know my feeling is not the feeling of forty years. These are the feelings of miserable, wretched youth.

Every day the atmosphere of a house becomes unbearable, so every day I go out to the sand and the barrenness. It is not cold, neither is it mild. It is gloomy.

I sit for two hours on the ground by the side of a pitiably small narrow stream of water. It is not even a natural stream. I dare say it comes from some mine among the hills. But it is well enough that the stream is not natural - when you consider the sand and barrenness. It is singularly appropriate.

And I am singularly appropriate to all of them. It is good, after all, to be appropriate to something - to be in touch with something, even sand and barrenness.

The sand and barrenness is old - oh, very old. You think of this when you look at it.

What should I do if the earth were made of wood, with a paper sky!

I feel about forty years old.

And again I say I know my feeling is not the feeling of forty years. These are the feelings of miserable, wretched youth.

Still more pitiable than the sand and barrenness and the poor unnatural stream is the dry, warped cemetery where the dry, warped people of Butte bury their dead friends. It is a source of satisfaction to me to walk down to this cemetery, and contemplate it, and revel in its utter pitiableness.

"It is more pitiable than I and my sand and barrenness and my poor unnatural stream," I say over and over, and take my comfort.

Its condition is more forlorn than that of a woman young and alone. It is unkempt. It is choked with dust and stones. The few scattered blades of grass look rather ashamed to be seen growing there. A great many of the headstones are of wood and are in a shameful state of decay. Those that are of stone are still more shameful in their hard brightness.

The dry, warped friends of the dry, warped people of Butte are buried in this dusty dreary wind-havocked waste. They are left here and forgotten.

The Devil must rejoice in this graveyard.

And I rejoice with the Devil.

It is something for me to contemplate that is more pitiable than I and my sand and barrenness and my unnatural stream.

I rejoice with the Devil.

The inhabitants of this cemetery are forgotten. I have watched once the burying of a young child. Every day for a fortnight afterward I came back, and I saw the mother of the child there. She came and stood by the small new grave. After a few days more she stopped coming.

I knew the woman and went to her house to see her. She was beginning to forget the child. She was beginning to take up again the thread of her life where she had let it go. The thread of her life is involved in the divorces and fights of her neighbors.

Out in the warped graveyard her child is forgotten. And presently the wooden head-stone will begin to decay. But the worms will not forget their part. They have eaten the small body by now, and enjoyed it. Always worms enjoy a body to eat.

And also the Devil rejoiced.

And I rejoiced with the Devil.

They are more pitiable, I insist, than I and my sand and barrenness - the mother whose life is involved in divorces and fights, and the worms eating at the child's body, and the wooden headstone which will presently decay.

And so the Devil and I rejoice.

But no matter how ferociously pitiable is the dried-up graveyard, the sand and barrenness and the sluggish little stream have their own persistent individual damnation. The world is at least so constructed that its treasures may be damned each in a different manner and degree.

I feel about forty years old.

And I know my feeling is not the feeling of forty years. They do not feel any of these things at forty. At forty the fire has long since burned out. When I am forty I shall look back to myself and my feelings at nineteen - and I shall smile.

Or shall I indeed smile?

January 17

As I have said, I want Fame. I want to write - to write such things as compel the admiring acclamations of the world at large; such things as are written but once in years, things subtly but distinctly different from the books written every day.

I can do this.

Let me but make a beginning, let me but strike the world in a vulnerable spot, and I can take it by storm. Let me but win my spurs, and then you will see me - of womankind and young - valiantly astride a charger riding down the world, with Fame following at the charger's heels, and the multitudes agape.

But oh, more than all this I want to be happy!

Fame is indeed benign and gentle and satisfying. But Happiness is something at once tender and brilliant beyond all things.

I want Fame more than I can tell.

But more than Fame I want Happiness. I have never been happy in my weary young life.

Think, oh *think* of being happy for a year - for a day! How brilliantly blue the sky would be; how swiftly and joyously would the green rivers run; how madly, merrily triumphant the four winds of heaven would sweep round the corners of the fair earth!

What would I not give for one day, one hour, of that charmed thing Happiness! What would I not give up?

How we eager fools tread on each other's heels, and tear each other's hair, and scratch each other's faces, in our furious gallop after Happiness. For some it is embodied in Fame, for some in Money, for some in Power, for some in Virtue - and for me in something very much like love.

None of the other fools desires Happiness as I desire it. For one single hour of Happiness I would give up at once these things: Fame, and Money, and Power, and Virtue, and Honor, and Righteousness, and Truth, and Logic, and Philosophy, and Genius. The while I would say, What a little,

little price to pay for dear Happiness.

I am ready and waiting to give all that I have to the Devil in exchange for Happiness. I have been tortured so long with the dull, dull misery of Nothingness - all my nineteen years. I want to be happy - oh, I want to be happy -

The Devil has not yet come. But I know that he usually comes, and I await him eagerly.

I am fortunate that I am not one of those burdened with an innate sense of virtue and honor which must come always before Happiness. They are but few who find their Happiness in their Virtue. The rest of them must be content to see it walk away. But with me virtue and honor are nothing.

I long unspeakably for Happiness.

And so I await the Devil's coming.

January 18

And meanwhile - as I wait - my mind occupies itself with its own good odd philosophy, so that even the Nothingness becomes almost endurable.

The Devil has given me some good things - for I find that the Devil owns and rules the earth and all that therein is. He has given me, among other things - my admirable young woman's body, which I enjoy thoroughly and of which I am passionately fond.

A spasm of pleasure seizes me when I think in some acute moment of the buoyant health and vitality of this fine young body that is feminine in every fiber.

You may gaze at and admire the picture in the front of this book. It is the picture of a genius - a genius with a good strong young-woman's body, - and inside the pictured body is a liver, a MacLane liver, of admirable perfectness.

Other young women and older women and men of all ages have good bodies also, I doubt not - though the masculine body is merely flesh, it seems, flesh and bones and nothing else. But few recognize the value of their bodies; few have grasped the possibilities, the artistic graceful perfection, the poetry of human flesh in its health. Few have even sense enough indeed to keep their flesh in health, or to know what health is until they have ruined some vital organ, and so banished it forever.

I have not ruined any of my vital organs, and I appreciate what health is. I have grasped the art, the poetry of my fine feminine body.

- This at the age of nineteen is a triumph for me. -

Sometime in the midst of the brightness of an October I have walked for miles in the still high air under the blue of the sky. The brightness of the day and the blue of the sky and the incomparable high air have entered into my veins and flowed with my red blood. They have penetrated into every remote nerve-center and into the marrow of my bones.

At such a time this young body glows with life.

My red blood flows swiftly and joyously - in the midst of the brightness of October.

My sound sensitive liver rests gently with its thin yellow bile in sweet content.

My calm beautiful stomach silently sings as I walk a song of peace, the while it hugs within itself the chyme that was my lunch.

My lungs, saturated with mountain ozone and the perfume of the pines, expand in continuous ecstasy.

My heart beats like the music of Schumann, in easy graceful rhythm with an undertone of power.

My very intestine even basks contentedly in its place like a snake in the hot dust, vibrating with conscious life.

My strong and sensitive nerves are reeking and swimming in sensuality like drunken little Bacchantes, gay and garlanded in mad revelling.

The entire wonderful graceful mechanism of my woman's-body has fallen at the time - like the wonderful graceful mechanism of my woman's-mind - under the enchanting spell of a day in October.

"It is good," I think to myself, "oh, it is good to be alive! It is wondrously good to be a woman young in the fullness of nineteen springs. It is unutterably lovely to be a healthy young animal living on this charmed earth."

After I have walked for several hours I reach a region where the sulphur smoke has not penetrated, and I sit on the ground with drawn-up knees and rest as the shadows lengthen. The shadows lengthen early in October.

Presently I lie flat on my back and stretch my lithe slimness to its utmost like a mountain lioness taking her comfort. I am intensely thankful to the Devil for my two good legs and the full use of them under a short skirt, when, as now, they carry me out beyond the pale of civilization away from tiresome dull people. There is nothing in the world that can become so maddeningly wearisome as people, people, people!

- And so Devil, accept, for my two good legs, my sincerest gratitude. -

I lie on the ground for some minutes and meditate idly. There is a worldful of easy indolent beautiful sensuality in the figure of a young woman lying on the ground under a warm setting sun. A man may lie on the ground - but that is as far as it goes. A man would go to sleep, probably, like a dog or a pig. He would even snore, perhaps - under the setting sun. But then, a man has not a good young feminine body to feel with, to receive into itself the spirit of a warm sun at its setting, on a day in October. - And so let us forgive him for sleeping, and for snoring.

When I again rise to a sitting posture all the brightness has focused itself to the west. It casts a yellow glamor over the earth, a glamor not of joy, nor of pleasure, nor of happiness - but of peace.

The young poplar trees smile gently in the deathly still air. The sage brush and the tall grass take on a radiant quietness. The high hills of Montana, near and distant, appear tender and benign. All is peace - peace. I think of that beautiful old song -

Sweet vale of Avoca! how calm could I rest
In thy bosom of shade -.

But I am too young yet to think of peace. It is not peace that I want. Peace is for forty and fifty. I am waiting for my Experience.

I am awaiting the coming of the Devil.

And now, just before twilight, after the sun has vanished over the edge, is the red, red line on the sky.

There will be days wild and stormy, filled with rain and wind and hail; and yet nearly always at the sun's setting there will be calm - and the red line of sky.

There is nothing in the world quite like this red sky at sunset. It is Glory, Triumph, Love, Fame!

Imagine a life bereft of things, and fingers pointed at it, and eyebrows raised; tossed and bandied hither and yon; crushed, beaten, bled, rent asunder, outraged, convulsed with pain; and then, into this life while still young, the red, red line of sky!

- Why did I cry out against Fate, says the line; why did I rebel against my term of anguish! I now rather rejoice at it; now in my Happiness I remember it only with deep pleasure. -

Think of that wonderful, most admirable, matchless man of steel, Napoleon Bonaparte. He threw himself heavily on the world, and the world has never since been the same. He hated himself, and the world, and God, and Fate, and the Devil. His hatred was his term of anguish.

Then the sun threw on the sky for him a red, red line - the red line of triumph, glory, fame!

And afterward there was the blackness of Night, the blackness that is not tender, not gentle.

But black as our Night may be, nothing can take from us the memory of the red, red sky. "Memory is possession," and so the red sky we have with us always.

Oh Devil, Fate, World - Someone, bring me my red sky! For a little, brief time and I will be satisfied. Bring it to me intensely red, intensely full, intensely alive! Short as you will, but red, red, red!

I am weary - weary, and oh, I want my red sky!

Short as it might be, its memory, its fragrance would stay with me always - always. Bring me, Devil, my red line of sky for one hour and take all, *all* - everything I possess. Let me keep my Happiness for one short hour and take away all from me forever. I will be satisfied when Night has come and everything is gone.

Oh, I await you, Devil, in a wild frenzy of impatience!

And as I hurry back through the cool darkness of October, I feel this frenzy in every fiber of my fervid woman's-body.

January 19

I come from a long line of Scotch and Canadian MacLanes. There are a great many MacLanes, but there is usually only one real MacLane in each generation. There is but one who feels again the passionate spirit of the Clans, those barbaric dwellers in the bleak but well-beloved Highlands of Scotland.

I am the real MacLane of my generation. The real MacLane in these later centuries is always a woman. The men of my family never amount to anything worth naming - if one excepts the acme, the zenith, of pure Selfishness, with a large letter S.

Life may be easy enough for the innumerable Canadian MacLanes who are not real. But it is certain to be more or less a Hill of Difficulty for the one who is. She finds herself somewhat alone. I have brothers and a sister and a mother in the same house with me - and I find myself somewhat alone. Between them and me there is no tenderness, no sympathy, no binding ties. Would it affect me in the least - do you suppose - if they should all die tomorrow? If I were not a real MacLane perhaps it would have been different, or perhaps I should not have missed these things.

How much, Devil, have I lost for the privilege of being a real MacLane. But yes. I have also gained much.

January 20

I have said that I am quite alone.

I am not quite, quite alone.

I have one friend - of that Friendship that is real and is inlaid with the beautiful thing Truth. And because it has the beautiful thing Truth in it, this my one Friendship is somehow above and beyond me; there is something in it that I reach after in vain - for I have not that divinely beautiful thing Truth. Have I not said that I am a thief and a liar? But in this Friendship nevertheless there is a rare, ineffably sweet something that is mine. It is the one tender thing in this dull dreariness that wraps me round.

Are there many things in this cool-hearted world so utterly exquisite as the pure love of one woman for another woman?

My one friend is a woman some twelve or thirteen years older than I. She is as different from me as day from night. She believes in God - that God that is shown in the Bible of the Christians. And she carries with her an atmosphere of gentleness and truth. The while I am ready and waiting to dedicate my life to the Devil in exchange for Happiness - or some lesser thing. But I love Fannie Corbin with a peculiar and vivid intensity, and with all the sincerity and passion that is in me. Often I think of her, as I walk over the sand in my Nothingness, all day long. The Friendship of her and me is a fair, dear benediction upon me, but there is something in it - deep within it - that eludes me. In moments when I realize this, when I strain and reach vainly at a thing beyond me, when indeed I see in my mind a vision of the personality of Fannie Corbin, it is then that it comes on me with force that I am not good.

But I can love her with all the ardor of a young and passionate heart.

Yes, I can do that.

For a year I have loved my one friend. During the eighteen years of my life before she came into it I loved no one, for there was no one.

It is an extremely hard thing to go through eighteen years with no one to love, and no one to love you - the first eighteen years.

But now I have my one friend to love and to worship.

I have named my friend the "anemone lady," a name beautifully appropriate.

The anemone lady used to teach me Literature in the Butte High School. She used to read poetry in the class room in a clear sweet voice that made one wish one might sit there forever and listen to it.

But now I have left the High School, and the dear anemone lady has gone from Butte. Before she went she told me she would be my friend.

Think of it - to live and have a friend!

My friend does not fully understand me; she thinks much too well of me. She has not a correct idea of my soul's depths and shallows. But if she did know them she would still be my friend. She knows the heavy weight of my unrest and unhappiness. She is tenderly sympathetic. She is the one in all the world who is dear to me.

Often I think, if only I could have my anemone lady and go and live with her in some little out-of-the-world place high upon the side of a mountain for the rest of my life - what more would I desire? My Friendship would constitute my life. The unrest, the dreariness, the Nothingness of my existence now is so dull and gray by contrast that there would be Happiness for me in that life, Happiness softly radiant, if quiet - redolent of the fresh, thin fragrance of the dear blue anemone that grows in the winds and rains of spring.

But Miss Corbin would doubtless look somewhat askance at the idea of spending the rest of her life with me on a mountain. She is very fond of me, but her feeling for me is not like mine for her, which indeed is natural. And her life is made up mostly of sacrifices - doing for her fellow-creatures, giving of herself. She never would leave this.

And so then the mountainside and the solitude and the friend with me are, like every good thing, but a vision.

"Thy friend is always thy friend; not to have, nor to hold, nor to love, nor to rejoice in: but to remember."

And so do I remember my one friend, the anemone lady - and think often about her with passionate love.

January 21

Happiness, don't you know, is of three kinds - and all are transitory. It never stays, but it comes and goes.

There is that happiness that comes from newly-washed feet, for instance, and a pair of clean stockings on them, particularly after one has been upon a tramp into the country. Always I have identified this kind of happiness with a Maltese cat dipping a hungry, stealthy sensual tongue into a bowl of fresh, thick cream.

There is that still happiness that has come to me at rare times when I have been with my one friend - and which does very well for people whose feelings are moderate. They need wish for nothing beyond it. They could not appreciate anything deeper.

And there is that kind of happiness which is of the red sunset sky. There is something terrible in the thought of this indescribable mad Happiness. What a thing it is for a human being to be *happy* - with the red, red Happiness of the sunset sky!

It's like a terrific storm in summer with rain and wind, beating quiet water into wild waves, bending great trees to the ground, - convulsing the green earth with delicious pain.

It's like something of Schubert's played on the violin that stirs you within to exquisite torture.

It's like the human voice divine singing a Scotch ballad in a manner to drag your soul from your body.

But there are no words to tell it. It is something infinitely above and beyond words. It is the kind of Happiness the Devil will bring to me when he comes, - to me, to *me*! Oh, why does he not come now when I am in the midst of my youth! Why is he so long in coming?

Often you hear a dozen stories of how the Devil was most ready and willing to take all from some one and give him his measure of Happiness. And sometimes the person was innately virtuous and so could not take the Happiness when it was offered. But Happiness is its own justification, and it should be eagerly grasped when it comes.

A world filled with fools will never learn this.

And so here I stand in the midst of Nothingness waiting and longing for the Devil, and he doesn't come. I feel a choking, strangling, frenzied feeling of waiting - oh, why doesn't my Happiness come! I have waited so long - so long! -

There are persons who say to me that I ought not to think of the Devil, that I ought not to think of Happiness - Happiness for me would be sure to mean something wicked (as if Happiness could ever be wicked!); that I ought to think of being good, - I ought to think of God. These are persons who help to fill the world with fools. At any rate their words are unable to affect me. I can not distinguish between right and wrong in this scheme of things. It is one of the lines of reasoning in which I have gotten to the edge, the end. I have gotten to the point to which all logic finally leads. I can only say, What is wrong? What is right? What is good? What is evil? The words are merely words, with word-meanings.

Truth is Love and Love is the only Truth, and Love is the one thing out of all that is Real.

God is less than nothing to me. The Devil is really the only one to whom we may turn, and he exacts payment in full for every favor.

But surely he will come one day with Happiness for me.

Yet, oh, how can I wait!

To be a woman, young and all alone, is hard - *hard!* - is to want things, is to carry a heavy, heavy weight.

Oh, damn! damn! damn! Damn every living thing, the world! - the universe be damned!

Oh, I am weary, weary! Can't you see that I am weary and pity me in my own damnation?

January 22

It is night. I might well be in my bed taking a needed rest. But first I shall write.

To-day I walked far away over the sand in the teeth of a bitter wind. The wind was determined that I should turn and come back, and equally I was determined I would go on. I went on.

There is a certain kind of wind in the autumn to walk in the midst of which causes one's spirits to rise ecstatically. To walk in the midst of a bitter wind in January may have almost any effect.

To-day the bitter wind swept over me and around me and into the remote corners of my brain and swept away the delusions, and buffeted my philosophy with rough insolence.

The world is made up mostly of nothing. You may be convinced of this when a bitter wind has swept away your delusions.

What is the wind?

Nothing.

What is the sky?

Nothing.

What do we know?

Nothing.

What is Fame?

Nothing.

What is my heart?

Nothing.

What is my soul?

Nothing.

What are we?

We are nothing.

We think we progress wonderfully in the arts and sciences as one century follows another. What does it amount to? It does not teach us the All-Why. It does not let us cease to wonder what it is that we are doing, where it is that we are going. It does not teach us why the green comes again to the old, old hills in the spring; why the benign balm-o'-Gilead shines wet and sweet after the rain; why the red never fails to come to the breast of the robin, the black to the crow, the gray to the little wren; why the sand and barrenness lies stretched out around us; why the clouds float high above us; why the moon stands in the sky, night after night; why the mountains and valleys live on as the years pass.

The arts and sciences go on and on - still we wonder. We have not yet ceased to weep. And we suffer still in 1901, even as they suffered in 1801, and in 801.

To-day we eat our good dinners with forks.

A thousand years ago they had no forks.

Yet, though we have forks, we are not happy. We scream and kick and struggle and weep just as they did a thousand years ago - when they had no forks.

We are "no wiser than when Omar fell asleep."

And in the midst of our great Wondering, we wonder why some of us are given faith to trust without question, while the rest of us are left to eat out our life's vitals with asking.

I have walked once in summer by the side of a little marsh filled with mint and white hawthorn. The mint and white hawthorn have with them a vivid, rare delicious perfume. It makes you want to grovel on the ground - it makes you think you might crawl in the dust all your days, and well for you. The perfume lingers with you afterward when years have passed. You may scream and kick and struggle and weep right lustily every day of your life, but in your moments of calmness sometimes there will come back to you the fragrance of a swamp filled with mint and white hawthorn.

It is meltingly beautiful.

What does it mean?

What would it tell?

Why does the marsh, and the mint and white hawthorn, freeze over in the fall? And why do they come again voluptuous, enticing in the damp spring days - and rack the souls of wretches who look and wonder?

- You are superb, Devil! You have done a magnificent piece of work. I kneel at your feet and worship you. You have wrought a perfection, a pinnacle of fine, invisible damnation. -

The world is like a little marsh filled with mint and white hawthorn. It is filled with things likewise damnably beautiful. There are the green, green grass-blades and the Gray Dawns; there are swiftly-flowing rivers and the honking of wild geese, flying low; there are human voices and human eyes; there are stories of women and men who have learned to give up and to wait; there is the poetry of James Whitcomb Riley; there is Charity; there is Truth.

The Devil has made all of these things, and also he has made human beings who can feel.

Who was it that said, long ago, "Life is always a tragedy to those who feel?"

In truth the Devil has constructed a place of infinite torture - the fair green earth, the world.

But he has made that other infinite thing - Happiness. I forgive him for making me wonder since possibly he may bring me Happiness. I cast myself at his feet. I adore him.

The first third of our lives is spent in the expectation of Happiness. Then it comes, perhaps, and stays ten years, or a month, or three days, and the rest of our lives is spent in peace and rest - with the memory of the Happiness.

Happiness - though it is infinite - is a transient emotion.

It is too brilliant, too magnificent, too overwhelming to be a lasting thing. And it is merely an emotion. But, ah - *such* an emotion! Through it the Devil rules his domains. What would one not do to have it!

I can think of no so-called vile deed that I would scruple about if I could be happy. Everything is justified if it gives me Happiness. The Devil has done me some great favors: he has made me without a conscience, and without Virtue.

For which I thank thee, Devil, profoundly.

At least I shall be able to take my Happiness when it comes - even though the piles of nice distinctions between it and me be mountains high.

But meanwhile, the world, I say, and the people are nothing, nothing, nothing. The splendid castles, the strong bridges, that we are building are of small moment. We can only go down the wide roadway wondering and weeping, and without where to lay our heads.

January 23

I have eaten my dinner.

I have had, among other things, a fine, rare-broiled porterhouse steak from Omaha, and some fresh, green young onions from California. And just now I am a philosopher, pure and simple - except that there's nothing very pure about my philosophy, nor yet very simple.

Let the Devil come and go; let the wild waters rush over me; let nations rise and fall; let my favorite theories form themselves in line suddenly and run into the ground; let the little earth be bandied about from one belief to the other; but, I say in the midst of my young peripatetic philosophy, I need not be in complete despair - the world still contains things for me, while I have my fine rare porterhouse steak from Omaha - and my fresh green young onions from California.

Fame may pass over my head; money may escape me; my one friend may fail me; every hope may fold its tent and steal away; Happiness may remain a sealed book; every remnant of human ties may vanish; I may find myself an outcast; good things held out to me may suddenly be withdrawn; the stars may go out, one by one; the sun may go dark; yet still I may hold upright my head, if I have but my steak - and my onions.

I may find myself crowded out from many charmed circles; I may find the ethical world too small to contain me; the social world may also exclude me; the professional world may know me not; likewise the worlds of the arts and the sciences; I may find myself superfluous in literary haunts; I may see myself going gladly back to the vile dust from whence I sprung - to live in a green forest like the melancholy Jacques; but fare they well, I will say with what cheerfulness I can summon, while I have my steak - and my onions.

Possibly I may grow old and decrepit; my hair may turn gray; my bones may become rheumatic; I may grow weak in the knees; my ankle-joints which have withstood many a peripatetic journey may develop dropsical tendencies; my heart may miss a beat now and then; my lungs may begin to fight shy of wintry blasts; my eyes may fail me; my figure that is now in its slim gracefulness may swathe itself in layers of flesh, or worse, it may wither and decay and stoop at the shoulders; my red blood may flow sluggishly; but if I still have teeth left to eat with, why need I lament, while I still have my steak - and my onions?

I am obscure; I am morbid; I am unhappy; my life is made up of Nothingness; I want everything and have nothing; I have been made to feel the "lure of green things growing," and I have been made to feel also that something of them is withheld from me; I have felt the deadly tiredness that is among the birthrights of a human being; but with it all the Devil has given me a philosophy of my own - the Devil has enabled me to count, if need be, the world well lost for a fine rare porterhouse steak - and some green young onions.

For which I thank thee, Devil, profoundly.

Who says the Devil is not your friend? Who says that the Devil does not believe in the all-merciful Law of Compensation?

And so it is, do you see, that all things look different after a satisfying dinner, that the color of the world changes, that life in fact resolves itself into two things: a fine rare-broiled porterhouse steak from Omaha, and some fresh green young onions from California.

January 24

I am charmingly original. I am delightfully refreshing. I am startlingly Bohemian. I am quaintly interesting - the while in my sleeve I may be smiling and smiling - and a villain. I can talk to a roomful of dull people and compel their interest, admiration, and astonishment. I do this sometimes for my own amusement. As I have said, I am a rather plain-featured, insignificant-looking genius, but I have a graceful personality. I have a pretty figure. I am well set up. And when I choose to talk in my charmingly original fashion, embellishing my conversation with many quaint lies, I have a certain very noticeable way with me, an "air."

- It is well, if one has nothing, to acquire an air. -

And an air taken in conjunction with my charming originality, my delightfully refreshing candor, is something powerful and striking in its way.

I do not, however, exert myself often in this way; partly because I can sometimes foresee, from the character of the assembled company, that my performance will not have the desired effect - for I am a genius, and genius at close range at times carries itself unconsciously to the point where it becomes so interesting that it is atrocious, and can not be carried farther without having somewhat mildly disastrous results; and then again, the facial antics of some ten or a dozen persons possessed more or less of the qualities of the genus fool - even they become tiresome after a while.

Always I talk about myself on an occasion of this kind. Indeed, my conversation is on all occasions devoted directly or indirectly to myself.

When I talk on the subject of ethics, I talk of it as it is related to Mary MacLane.

When I give out broad-minded opinions about Ninon de l'Enclos, I demonstrate her relative position to Mary MacLane!

When I discourse liberally on the subject of the married relation, I talk of it only as it will affect Mary MacLane.

An interesting creature, Mary MacLane.

- As a matter of fact, it is so with every one, only every one is far from realizing and acknowledging it. -

And I have not lacked listeners, though these people do not appreciate me. They do not realize that I am a genius.

I am of womankind and of nineteen years. I am able to stand off and gaze critically and dispassionately at myself and my relation to my environment, to the world, to everything the world contains. I am able to judge whether I am good and whether I am bad. I am able indeed to tell what I am and where I stand. I can see far, far inward. I am a genius.

Charlotte Brontë did this in some degree, and she was a genius; and also Marie Bashkirtseff, and Olive Schreiner, and George Eliot. They are all geniuses.

And so then I am a genius - a genius in my own right.

I am fundamentally, organically egotistic. My vanity and self-conceit have attained truly remarkable development as I've walked and walked in the loneliness of the sand and barrenness.

Not the least remarkable part of it is that I know my egotism and vanity thoroughly - thoroughly, and plume myself thereon.

These are the ear-marks of a genius - and of a fool. There is a finely drawn line between a genius and a fool. Often this line is overstepped and your fool becomes a genius, or your genius becomes a fool.

It is but a tiny step.

There's but a tiny step between the great and the little, the tender and the contemptuous, the sublime and the ridiculous, the aggressive and the humble, the Paradise and the perdition.

And so it is between the genius and the fool.

I am a genius.

- I am not prepared to say how many times I may overstep the finely drawn line, or how many times I have already overstepped it. 'Tis a matter of small moment. -

I have entered into certain things marvelously deep. I know things, I know that I know them, and I know that I know that I know them. Which is a fine psychological point.

It is magnificent of me to have gotten so far, at the age of nineteen, with no training other than that of the sand and barrenness. Magnificent - do you hear?

Very often I take this fact in my hand and squeeze it hard like an orange, to get the sweet, sweet juice from it. I squeeze a great deal of juice from it every day, and every day the juice is renewed, like the vitals of Prometheus. And so I squeeze and squeeze, and drink the juice, and try to be satisfied.

Yes, you may gaze long and curiously at the portrait in the front of this book. It is of one who is a genius of egotism and analysis, a genius who is awaiting the Devil's coming, - a genius, with a wondrous liver within.

I shall tell you more about this liver, I think, before I have done.

January 25

I can remember a time long, oh, very long ago. That is the time when I was a child. It is ten or a dozen years ago.

Or is it a thousand years ago?

It is when you have but just parted from your friend that he seems farthest from you. When I have lived several more years the time when I was a child will not seem so far behind me.

Just now it is frightfully far away. It is so far away that I can see it plainly outlined on the horizon.

It is there always for me to look at. And when I look I can feel the tears deep within me - a salt ocean of tears that roll and surge and swell bitterly in a dull, mad anguish, and never come to the surface.

I do not know which is the more weirdly and damnably pathetic: I when I was a child, or I when I am grown to a woman, young and all alone. I weigh the question coldly and logically, but my logic trembles with rage and grief and unhappiness.

When I was a child I lived in Canada and in Minnesota. I was a little wild savage. In Minnesota there were swamps where I used to wet my feet in the spring, and there were fields of tall grass where I would lie flat on my stomach in company with lizards and little garter snakes. And there were poplar-leaves that turned their pale green backs upward on a hot afternoon, and soon there would be terrific thunder and lightning and rain. And there were robins that sang at dawn. - These things stay with one always. - And there were children with whom I used to play and fight.

I was tanned and sunburned and I had an unkempt appearance. My face was very dirty. The original pattern of my frock was invariably lost in layers and vistas of the native soil. My hair was braided or else it flew about, a tangled maze, according as I could be caught by some one and rubbed and straightened before I ran away for the day. My hands were little and strong and brown, and wrought much mischief. I came and went at my own pleasure. I ate what I pleased; I went to bed all in my own good time; I tramped wherever my stubborn little feet chose. I was impudent; I was contrary; I had an extremely bad temper; I was hard-hearted; I was full of infantile malice.

Truly I was a vicious little beast.

I was a little piece of untrained Nature.

And I am unable to judge which is the more savagely forlorn: the starved-hearted child, or the woman, young and all alone.

The little wild stubborn child felt things and wanted things. She did not know that she felt things and wanted things.

Now I feel and I want things and I know it with burning vividness.

The little vicious Mary MacLane suffered, but she did not know that she suffered. Yet that did not make the suffering less.

And she reached out with a little sunburned hand to touch and take something.

But the sunburned little hand remained empty. There was nothing for it. No one had anything to put into it.

The little wild creature wanted to be loved; she wanted something to put in her hungry little heart.

But no one had anything to put into a hungry little heart.

No one said "dear."

The little vicious child was the only MacLane, and she felt somewhat alone. But there, after all, were the lizards and the little garter snakes.

The wretched, hardened little piece of untrained Nature has grown and developed into a woman, young and alone. For the child there was a Nothingness, and for the woman there is a great Nothingness.

Perhaps the Devil will bring me something in my lonely womanhood to put in my wooden heart.

But the time when I was a child will never come again. It is gone - gone. I may live through some long, long years, but nothing like it will ever come. For there is nothing like it.

It is a life by itself. It has naught to do with philosophy, or with genius, or with heights and depths, or with the red sunset sky, or with the Devil.

These come later.

The time of the child is a thing apart. It is the Planting and Seed-time. It is the Beginning of things. It decides whether there shall be brightness or bitterness in the long after-years.

I have left that time far enough behind me. It will never come back. And it had a Nothingness - do you hear, a *Nothingness*! Oh, the pity of it! The pity of it -

Do you know why it is that I look back to the horizon at the figure of an unkempt, rough child, and why I feel a surging torrent of tears and anguish and despair?

I feel more than that indeed, but I have no words to tell it.

I shall have to miss forever some beautiful, wonderful things because of that wretched lonely childhood.

There will always be a lacking, a wanting - some dead branches that never grew leaves.

It is not deaths and murders and plots and wars that make life tragedy.

It is Nothing that makes life tragedy.

It is day after day, and year after year, and Nothing.

It is a sunburned little hand reached out and Nothing put into it.

January 26

I sit at my window and look out upon the housetops and chimneys of Butte. As I look I have a weary, disgusted feeling.

People are abominable creatures.

Under each of the roofs live a man and woman joined together by that very slender thread - the marriage ceremony, - and their children, the result of the marriage ceremony.

How many of them love each other? Not two in a hundred, I warrant. The marriage ceremony is their one miserable petty paltry excuse for living together.

This marriage rite, it appears, is often used as a cloak to cover a world of rather shameful things.

How virtuous these people are, to be sure, under their different roof-trees. So virtuous are they indeed that they are able to draw themselves up in the pride of their own purity, when they happen upon some corner where the marriage ceremony is lacking. So virtuous are they that the men can afford to find amusement and diversion in the woes of the corner that is without the marriage rite; and the women may draw away their skirts in shocked horror and wonder that such things can be, in view of their own spotless virtue.

And so they live on under the roofs, and they eat and work and sleep and die; and the children grow up and seek other roofs, and call upon the marriage ceremony even as their parents before them - and then they likewise eat and work and sleep and die; and so on world without end.

This also is life - the life of the good, virtuous Christians.

I think, therefore, that I should prefer some life that is not virtuous.

I shall never make use of the marriage ceremony. - I hereby register a vow, Devil, to that effect. -

When a man and a woman love one another that is enough. That is marriage. A religious rite is superfluous. And if the man and woman live together without the love, no ceremony in the world can make it marriage. The woman who does this need not feel the tiniest bit better than her lowest sister in the streets. Is she not indeed a step lower since she pretends to be what she is not - plays the virtuous woman? While the other unfortunate pretends nothing. She wears her name on her sleeve.

If I were obliged to be one of these I would rather be she who wears her name on her sleeve. I certainly would. The lesser of two evils, always.

I can think of nothing in the world like the utter littleness, the paltriness, the contemptibleness, the degradation, of the woman who is tied down under a roof with a man who is really nothing to her; who wears the man's name, who bears the man's children - who plays the virtuous woman. There are too many such in the world now.

May I never, I say, become that abnormal merciless animal, that deformed monstrosity - a virtuous woman.

Anything, Devil, but that.

And so, as I look over the roofs and chimneys I have a weary, disgusted feeling.

January 27

This is not a diary. It is a Portrayal. It is my inner life shown in its nakedness. I am trying my utmost to show everything - to reveal every petty vanity and weakness, every phase of feeling, every desire. It is a remarkably hard thing to do, I find, to probe my soul to its depths, to expose its shades and half-lights.

Not that I am troubled with modesty or shame. Why should one be ashamed of anything?

But there are elements in one's mental equipment so vague, so opaque, so undefined - how is one to grasp them? I have analyzed and analyzed, and I have gotten down to some extremely fine points - yet still there are things upon my own horizon that go beyond me.

There are feelings that rise and rush over me overwhelmingly. I am helpless, crushed and defeated, before them. It is as if they were written on the walls of my soul-chamber in an unknown language.

My soul goes blindly seeking, seeking, asking. Nothing answers. I cry out after some unknown Thing with all the strength of my being; every nerve and fiber in my young woman's-body and my young woman's-soul reaches and strains in anguished unrest. At times as I hurry over my sand and barrenness all my life's manifold passions culminate in utter rage and woe. Waves of intense, hopeless longing rush over me and envelop me round and round. My heart, my soul, my mind go wandering - wandering; ploughing their way through darkness with never a ray of light; groping with helpless hands; asking, longing, wanting things: pursued by a Demon of Unrest.

I shall go mad - I shall go mad, I say over and over to myself.

But no. No one goes mad. The Devil does not propose to release any one from a so beautifully wrought, artistic damnation. He looks to it that one's senses are kept fully intact, and he fastens to them with steel chains the demon of Unrest.

It hurts, - oh, it tortures me in the days and days! But when the Devil brings my Happiness I will forgive him all this.

When my Happiness is given me, the Unrest will still be with me, I doubt not, but the Happiness will change the tenor of it, will make it an instrument of joy, will clasp hands with it and mingle itself with it, - the while I, with my wooden heart, my woman's-body, my mind, my soul, shall be in transports. I shall be filled with pleasure so deep and pain so intense that my being's minutest nerve will reel and stagger in intoxication, will go drunk with the fullness of Life.

When my Happiness is given me I shall live centuries in the hours. And we shall all grow old rapidly, - I and my wooden heart, and my woman's-body, and my mind, and my soul. Sorrow may age one in some degree. But Happiness - the real Happiness - rolls countless years off from one's finger-tips in a single moment, and each year leaves its impress.

It is true that life is a tragedy to those who feel. When my Happiness is given me life will be an ineffable, a nameless thing.

It will seethe and roar; it will plunge and whirl; it will leap and shriek in convulsion; it will quiver in delicate fantasy; it will writhe and twist; it will glitter and flash and shine; it will sing gently; it will shout in exquisite excitement; it will vibrate to the roots like a great oak in a storm; it will dance; it will glide; it will gallop; it will rush; it will swell and surge; it will fly; it will soar high - high; it will go down into depths unexplored; it will rage and rave; it will yell in utter joy; it will melt; it will blaze; it will ride triumphant; it will grovel in the dust of entire pleasure; it will sound out like a terrific blare of trumpets; it will chime faintly, faintly like the remote tinkling notes of a harp; it will sob and grieve and weep; it will revel and carouse; it will shrink; it will go in pride; it will lie prone like the dead; it will float buoyantly on air; it will moan, shiver, burst, - oh, it will reek of Love and Light!

The words of the English language are futile. There are no words in it, or in any other, to express an idea of that thing which would be my life in its Happiness.

The words I have written describe it, it is true - but confusedly and inadequately.

But words are for every-day use.

When it comes my turn to meet face to face the unspeakable vision of the Happy Life I shall be rendered dumb.

But the rains of my feeling will come in torrents!

January 28

I am an artist of the most artistic, the highest type. I have uncovered for myself the art that lies in obscure shadows. I have discovered the art of the day of small things.

And that surely is Art with a capital A.

I have acquired the art of Good Eating. Usually it is in the gray and elderly forties and fifties that people cultivate this art - if they ever do; it is indeed a rare art.

But I know it in all its rare exquisiteness at the young slim age of nineteen. Which is one more mark of my genius, do you see?

The art of Good Eating has two essential points: one must eat only when one is hungry, and one must take small bites.

There are persons who eat for the sake of eating. They are gourmands and partake of the natures of the pig and the buzzard. There are persons who take bites that are not small. These also are gourmands and partake of the natures of the pig and the buzzard. There are persons who can enjoy nothing in the way of eating except a luxurious, well-appointed meal. These, it is safe to say, have not acquired the art of anything.

But I - I have acquired the art of eating an olive.

Now listen and I will tell you the art of eating an olive.

I take the olive in my fingers, and I contemplate its green oval richness.

It makes me think at once of the land where the green citron grows - where the cypress and myrtle are emblems; of the land of the Sun where human beings are delightfully, enchantingly wicked, - where the men are eager and passionate, and the women gracefully developed in mind and in body - and their two breasts show round and full and delicately veined beneath fine drapery.

The mere sight of the olive conjures up this charming picture in my mind.

I set my teeth and my tongue upon the olive, and bite it. It is bitter, salt, delicious. The saliva rushes to meet it, and my tongue is a happy tongue. As the morsel of olive rests in my mouth and is crunched and squeezed lusciously among my teeth, a quick temporary change takes place in my character. I think of some adorable lines of the Persian poet:

> Give thyself up to Joy, for thy Grief will be infinite.
> The stars shall again meet together
> At the same point in the firmament,
> But of thy body shall bricks be made
> For a palace wall.

"Oh, dear, sweet, bitter olive," I say to myself.

The bit of olive slips down my red gullet, and so into my Stomach. There it meets with a joyous welcome. Gastric juices leap out from the walls and swathe it in loving embrace. My Stomach is fond of something bitter and salt. It lavishes flattery and endearment galore upon the olive. It laughs in silent delight. It feels that the day it has long waited for has come. The philosophy of my Stomach is wholly Epicurean. Let it receive but a tiny bit of olive and it will reck not of the morrow, nor of the past. It lives, voluptuously, in the present. It is content. It is in Paradise.

I bite the olive again. Again the bitter salt crisp ravishes my tongue. "If this be vanity, - vanity let it be." The golden moments flit by and I heed them not. For am I not comfortably seated and eating an olive? - Go hang yourself, you who have never been comfortably seated and eating an olive! - My character evolves farther in its change. I am now bent on reckless sensuality, let happen what will. The fair earth seems to resolve itself into a thing oval and crisp and good and green and deliciously salt. I experience a feeling of fervent gladness that I am a female thing living, and that I have a tongue and some teeth, and salivary glands.

Also this bit slips down my red gullet, and again the festive Stomach lifts up a silent voice in psalms and rejoicing. It is now an absolute monarchy with the green olive at its head. The kisses of the gastric juice become hot and sensual and convulsive and ecstatic. "Avaunt, pale shadowy ghosts of dyspepsia!" says my Stomach. "I know you not. I am of a brilliant shining world. I dwell in Elysian fields."

Once more I bite the olive. Once more is my tongue electrified. And the third stage in my temporary transformation takes place. I am now a gross but supremely contented sensualist. An exquisite symphony of sensualism and pleasure seems to play somewhere within me. My heart purrs. My brain folds its arms and lounges. - I put my feet up on the seat of another chair. - The entire world is now surely one delicious green olive. My mind is capable of conceiving but one idea: that of a green olive. Therefore the green olive is a perfect thing - absolutely a perfect thing.

Disgust and disapproval are excited only by imperfections. When a thing is perfect, no matter how hard one may look at it, one can only see itself - itself, and nothing beyond.

And so I have made my olive and my art perfect.

Well then, this third bit of olive slides down the willing gullet into my Stomach. "And then my heart with pleasure fills." The play of the gastric secretions is now marvelous. It is the meeting of the waters! It were well, ah, how well if the hearts of the world could mingle in peace, as the gastric juices mingle at the coming of a green olive into my Stomach! "Paradise, Paradise!" says my Stomach.

Every drop of blood in my passionate veins is resting. Through my Stomach - my *Stomach*, do you hear - my soul seems to feel the infinite. The minutes are flying. Shortly it will be over. But just now I am safe. I am entirely satisfied. I want nothing, nothing.

My inner quiet is infinite. I am conscious that it is but momentary, and it matters not. On the contrary the knowledge of this fact renders the present quiet - the repose more limitless, more intense.

Where now, Devil, is your damnation? If this be damnation, damnation let it be! If this be the human fall, then how good it is to be fallen! At this moment I would fain my fall were like yours, Lucifer, "never to hope again."

And so, bite by bite, the olive enters into my body and soul. Each bite brings with it a recurring wave of sensation and charm.

No. We will not dispute with the brilliant mind that declared life a tragedy to those who feel. We will let that stand. However there are parts of the tragedy that are not tragic. There are parts that admit of a turning aside.

As the years pass, one after another, I shall continue to eat. And as I eat I shall have my quiet, my brief period of aberration.

This is the art of Eating.

I have acquired it by means of self-examination, analyzing - analyzing - analyzing. Truly my genius is analytical. And it enables me to endure - if also to feel bitterly - the heavy, heavy weight of life.

What a worm of misery I should be were it not for these bursts of philosophy, these turnings aside!

If it please the Devil, one day I may have Happiness. That will be all-sufficient. I shall then analyze no more. I shall be a different being.

But meanwhile I shall eat.

When the last of the olive vanishes into the Stomach, when it is there reduced to animated chyme, when I play with the olive-seed in my fingers, when I lean back in my chair and straighten out my spinal column, - oh, then do you not envy me, you fine, brave world, who are not a philosopher, who have not discovered the art of the small things, who have not conscious chyme in your stomach, who have not acquired the art of Good Eating!

January 29

As I read over now and then what I have written of my Portrayal I have alternate periods of hope and despair. At times I think I am succeeding admirably, - and again, what I have written compared to what I have felt seems vapid and tame. Who has not felt the futility of words when one would express feelings?

I take this hope and despair as another mark of genius. Genius, apart from natural sensitiveness, is prone equally to unreasoning joy and to bitterest morbidness.

I am more than fond of writing, though I have hours when I can not write any more than I could paint a picture, or play Wagner as it should be played.

I think my style of writing has a wonderful intensity in it, and it is admirably suited to the creature it portrays. What sort of Portrayal of myself would I produce if I wrote with the long elaborate periods of Henry James, or with the pleasant ladylike phrasing of Howells? It would be rather like a little tin phonograph trolling out flowery poetry at breakneck speed, or like a deep-toned church organ pouring forth "Goo-Goo Eyes" with ponderous feeling.

When I read a book I study it carefully to find whether the author *knows things*, and whether I could, with the same subject, write a better one myself.

The latter question I usually decide in the affirmative.

A writer who charms me is Maria Louise Pool with her novels of New England. She is fascinating and she knows things. If she had written seventy years ago she would doubtless now be standard literature. One thing I have noticed about her books is that as I read them I find myself thinking not particularly of the characters therein, but of the author who somehow appears between the lines. And I find this very interesting. I have spent a great many half-hours thinking and conjecturing about Maria Louise Pool. Always

I wonder what she likes to eat, and what she does on a pleasant Saturday afternoon when she has nothing else to do, and what kind of clothes she wears, and if she can possibly be as uninteresting at that stout, gray-haired age as most women are. I hope I may see her some day.

The highest thing one can do in literature is to succeed in saying that thing which one meant to say. There is nothing better than that - to make the world see your thoughts as you see them. Eugene Field and Edgar Allan Poe and R. Louis Stevenson and Charles Dickens, among others, have succeeded in doing this. They impress the world with a sense of their courage and realness.

There are people who have written books which did not impress the world in this way, but which nevertheless came out of the feeling and fullness of zealous hearts. Always I think of that pathetic, artless little old-fashioned thing *Jane Eyre* as a picture shown to a world seeing with distorted vision. Charlotte Brontë meant one thing when she wrote the book and the world after a time suddenly understood a quite different thing, and heaped praise and applause upon her therefor. When I read the book I was not quite able to see just what the message was that the Brontë intended to send out. But I saw that there was a message - of bravery, perhaps, or of that good which may come out of Nazareth. But the world that praised and applauded and gave her money seems totally to have missed it.

It takes centuries of tears and piety and mourning to move this world a tiny bit.

But still, it will give you praise and applause and money if you will prostitute your sensibilities and emotions for the gratification of it.

I have no message to hide in a book and send out. I am writing a Portrayal.

But a Portrayal is also a thing that may be misunderstood.

January 30

An idle brain is the Devil's workshop, they say. It is an absurdly incongruous statement. If the Devil is at work in a brain it certainly is not idle. And when one considers how brilliant a personage the Devil is, and what very fine work he turns out, it becomes an open question whether he would have the slightest use for most of the idle brains that cumber the earth. But, after all, the Devil is so clever that he could produce unexcelled workmanship with even the poorest tools.

My brain is one kind of Devil's-workshop, and it is as incessantly hard-worked and always-busy a one as you could imagine.

It is a Devil's workshop, indeed, only I do the work myself. But there is a mental telegraphy between the Devil and me, which accounts for the fact that many of my ideas are so wonderfully groomed and perfumed and colored. I take no credit to myself for this, though, as I say, I do the work myself.

I try always to give the Devil his due - and particularly in this Portrayal.

There are very few who give the Devil his due in this world of hypocrites.

I never think of the Devil as that atrocious creature in red tights, with cloven hoofs and a tail and a two-tined fork. I think of him rather as an extremely fascinating, strong, steel-willed person in conventional clothes - a man with whom to fall completely, madly in love. I rather think, I believe, that he is incarnate at times. Why not?

Periodically I fall completely, madly in love with the Devil. He is so fascinating, so strong - so strong, exactly the sort of man whom my wooden heart awaits. I would like to throw myself at his head. I would make him a dear little wife. He would love me - he would love me. I would be in raptures. And I would love him, oh, madly, madly!

"What would you have me do, little MacLane?" the Devil would say.

"I would have you conquer me, crush me, know me," I would answer.

"What shall I say to you?" the Devil would ask.

"Say to me, 'I love you, I love you, I love you,' in your strong, steel, fascinating voice. Say it to me often, always - a million times."

"What would you have me do, little MacLane?" he would say again.

I would answer: "Hurt me, burn me, consume me with hot love, shake me violently, embrace me hard, *hard* in your strong steel arms, kiss me with wonderful burning kisses - press your lips to mine with passion, and your soul and mine would meet then in an anguish of joy for me!"

"How shall I treat you, little MacLane?"

"Treat me cruelly, brutally."

"How long shall I stay with you?"

"Through the life everlasting - it will be as one day; or for one day - it will be as the life everlasting."

"And what kind of children will you bear me, little MacLane?" he would say.

"I will bear wonderful, beautiful children - with great pain."

"But you hate pain," the Devil will say, "and when you are in your pain you will hate me."

"But no," I will answer. "Pain that comes of you will be ineffable exaltation."

"And how will you treat me, little MacLane?"

"I will cast myself at your feet; or I will minister to you with divine tenderness; or I will charm you with fantastic deviltry; when you weep, I will melt into tears; when you rejoice, I will go wild with delight; when you go deaf I will stop my ears; when you go blind I will put out my eyes; when you go lame I will cut off my legs. Oh, I will be divinely dear, unutterably sweet!"

"Indeed you are rarely sweet," the Devil will say. And I will be in transports.
Oh, Devil, Devil, Devil!

Oh, misery, *misery* of Nothingness!

The days are long - long and very weary as I await the Devil's coming.

January 31

To-day as I walked out I was impressed deeply with the wonderful beautiful-ness of Nature even in her barrenness. The far-distant mountains had that high pure transparent look, and the nearer ones were transformed completely with a wistful beseeching attitude that reminded me of my life. It was late in the afternoon. As the sun lowered, the pure lavender of the far-away hills was tinted with faint-rose, and the gray of the nearer ones with sun-color. And the sand - my sand and barrenness - almost flushed consciously in its wide, mysterious magnitude. In the sky there was a white cloud. The sky was blue - blue almost as when I was a child. The air was very gentle. The earth seemed softened. There was an indefinite caressing something over all that went into my soul and stirred it, and hurt it. There was that in the air which is there when something is going to happen. - Only nothing ever happens. - It is rare, I thought, that my sand and barrenness looks like this. I crouched on the ground, and the wondrous calm and beauty of the natural things awed and moved me with strange, still emotions.

I felt, and gazed about me, and felt again. And everything was very still.

Presently my eyes filled quietly with tears.

I bent my head into the breast of a great gray rock. Oh, my soul, my soul, I said over and over, not with passion. It is so divine - the earth is so beautiful, so untainted - and I, what am I? It was so beautiful that now as I write, and it comes over me again, I can not restrain the tears.

Tears are not common.

I felt my wooden heart, my soul, quivering and sobbing with their un-known wanting. This is my soul's awakening. Ah, the pain of my soul's awakening! Is there nothing, *nothing* to help this pain? I am so lonely, so lonely - Fannie Corbin, my one friend, my dearly-loved anemone lady, I want you so much - why aren't you here! I want to feel your hand with mine as I felt it sometimes before you went away. You are the only one among a worldful of people to care a little - and I love you with all the strength and worship I can give to the things that are beautiful and true. You are the only one, the only one - and my soul is full of pain, and I am sitting alone on the ground, and my head lies on a rock's breast. -

Strange, sweet passions stirred and waked somewhere deep within me as

I sat shivering on the ground. And I felt them singing far away, as if their faint voices came out of that limitless deep, deep blue above me; and it was like a choir of spirit-voices, and they sang of love and of light and of dear tender dreams, and of my soul's awakening. Why is this - and what is it that is hurting so? Is it because I am young, or is it because I am alone, or because I am a woman?

Oh, it is a hard and bitter thing to be a woman! And why - why? Is woman so foul a creature that she must needs be purged by this infinite pain?

The choir of faint, sweet voices comes to me incessantly out of the blue. My wooden heart and my soul are listening to them intently. The voices are trying hard to tell me, to help me, but I can not understand. I know only that it is about pure, exalted things, and about the all-abiding love that is somewhere; and it is about the earth-love, and about Truth, - but I can not understand. And the voices sing of me the child - a song of the unloved, starved little being; and a song of the unloved, half-grown creature; and a song of me, a woman and all alone - awaiting the Devil's coming.

Oh, my soul - my soul!

A female snake is born out of its mother's white egg, and lives a while in contentment among weeds and grass, and dies.

A female dog lives some years, and has bones thrown at her, and sometimes she receives a kick or a blow, and a dog-house to sleep in, and dies.

A female bird has a nest, and worms to eat, and goes south in the winter, and presently she dies.

A female toad has a swamp or a garden, some bugs and flies, contentment - and then she dies.

And each of these has a male thing with her for a time, and shortly there are little snakes or little dogs for her to love as much as it is given her to love - she can do no more.

And they are fortunate with their little snakes and little dogs.

A female human being is born out of her mother's fair body, branded with a strange, plague-tainted name, and let go; and lives awhile, and dies. But before she dies she awakes. There is a pain that goes with it.

And the male thing that is with her for a time is unlike a snake or a dog. It is more like a man, and there is another pain for this.

And when a little human being comes with a soul of its own there must be another awakening, for she has then reached the best and highest state that any human being can reach, though she is a female human being, and plague-tainted. And here also there is heavy soul-pain.

The name - the plague-tainted name branded upon her - means woman.

I lifted my head from the breast of the gray rock. The tears had been falling, falling. Tears are so strange! Tears from the dried-up fountain of nineteen years are like drops of water wrung out of stone. Suddenly I got up from the ground and ran quickly over the sand for several minutes. I did not dare look again at the hilltops and the deep blue, nor listen again to the voices.

Oh, with it all, I am a coward! I shrink and cringe before the pain of the dazzling lights. Yet I am waiting - longing for the most dazzling light of all: the coming of the Devil.

February 1

Oh, the wretched bitter loneliness of me!

In all the deep darkness, and the silence, there is never a faint human light, never a voice!

How can I bear it - how can I bear it!

February 2

I have been looking over the confessions of the Bashkirtseff. They are indeed rather like my Portrayal, but they are not so interesting, nor so intense. I have a stronger individuality than Marie Bashkirtseff, though her mind was probably in a higher state of development than mine, even when she was younger than I.

Most of her emotions are vacillating and inconsistent. She worships a God one day and blasphemes him the next. She never loves her God. And why, then, does she have a God? Why does she not abandon him altogether? He seems to be of no use to her - except as a convenient thing on which to fasten the blame for her misfortunes. - And, after all, that is something very useful indeed. - And she loves the people about her one day, and the next day she hates them.

But in her great passion - her ambition - Marie Bashkirtseff was beautifully consistent. And what terrific storms of woe and despair must have enveloped her when she knew that within a certain period she would be dead - removed from the world, and her work left undone! The time kept creeping nearer - she must have tasted the bitterness of death indeed. She was sure of success, sure that her high-strained ambition would be gratified to its last vestige - and then, to die! It was certainly hard lines for the little Bashkirtseff.

My own despair is of an opposite nature.

There is one thing in the world that is more bitter than death - and that is life.

Suppose that I learned I was to die on the twenty-seventh of June, 1903, for instance. It would give me a soft warm wave of pleasure, I think. I might be in the depths of woe at the time; my despair might be the despair of despair; my misery utterly unceasing, - and I could say, "Never mind, on the twenty-seventh of June, 1903, all will be over - dull misery, rage, Nothingness, obscurity, the unknown longing, every desire of my soul, all the pain - ended inevitably, completely on the twenty-seventh of June, 1903." I might come upon a new pain, but this, my long old torture, would cease.

You may say that I might end my life on that day, that I might do so now. I certainly shall if the pain becomes greater than I can bear - for what else is there to do? But I shall be far from satisfied in doing so. What if I were to end everything now - when perhaps the Devil may be coming to me in two years' time with Happiness?

Upon dying it might be that I should go to some wondrous fair country where there would be trees and running water, and a resting-place. Well - oh, well! But I want the earthly Happiness. I am not high-minded and spiritual. I am earthly, human - sensitive, sensuous, sensual, and, ah, dear, my soul wants its earthly Happiness!

I can not bring myself to the point of suicide while there is a possibility of Happiness remaining. But if I knew that irrevocable, inevitable death awaited me on June twenty-seventh, 1903, I should be satisfied. My Happiness might come before that time, or it might not. I should be satisfied. I should know that my life was out of my hands. I should know, above all, that my long, long, old, old pain of loneliness would stop, June twenty-seventh, 1903.

I shall die naturally some day - probably after I have grown old and sour. If I have had my Happiness for a year or a day, well and good. I shall be content to grow as old and as sour as the Devil wills. But having had no Happiness - if I find myself growing old and still no Happiness - oh, then I vow I will not live another hour, even if dying were rushing headlong to damnation!

I am, do you see, a philosopher and a coward - with the philosophy of cowardice. I squeeze juice also from this fact sometimes - but the juice is not sweet juice.

The Devil - the fascinating man-Devil - it may be, is coming, coming, coming.

And meanwhile I go on and on, in the midst of sand and barrenness.

February 3

The town of Butte presents a wonderful field to a student of humanity and human nature. There are not a great many people - seventy thousand perhaps - but those seventy thousand are in their way unparalleled. For mixture, for miscellany - variedness, Bohemianism - where is Butte's rival?

The population is not only of all nationalities and stations, but the nationalities and stations mix and mingle promiscuously with each other, and are partly concealed and partly revealed in the mazes of a veneer that belongs neither to nation nor to station, but to Butte.

The nationalities are many, it is true, but Irish and Cornish predominate. My acquaintance extends widely among the inhabitants of Butte. Sometimes when I feel in the mood for it I spend an afternoon in visiting about among divers curious people.

At some Fourth of July demonstration, or on a Miners' Union day, the heterogeneous herd turns out - and I turn out, with the herd and of it, and meditate and look on. There are Irishmen - Kelleys, Caseys, Calahans, staggering under the weight of much whiskey, shouting out their green-isle maxims; there is the festive Cornishman, ogling and leering, greeting his fellow-countrymen with alcoholic heartiness, and gazing after every feminine creature with lustful eyes; there are Irish women swearing genially at each other in shrill pleasantry, and five or six loudly-vociferous children for each; there are round-faced Cornish women likewise, each with her train of children; there are suave sleek sporting men just out of the bath-tub; insignificant lawyers, dentists, messenger-boys; "plungers" without number; greasy Italians from Meaderville; greasier French people from the Boulevarde Addition; ancient miners - each of whom was the first to stake a claim in Butte; starved-looking Chinamen here and there; a contingent of Finns and Swedes and Germans; musty, stuffy old Jewish pawn-brokers who have crawled out of their holes for a brief recreation; dirt-encrusted Indians and squaws in dirty-gay blankets, from their flea-haunted camp below the town; "box rustlers" - who are as common in Butte as bar-maids in Ireland; swell, flashy-looking Africans; respectable women with white aprons tied around their waists and sailor-hats on their heads, who have left the children at home and stepped out to see what was going on; innumerable stray youngsters from the dark haunts of Dublin Gulch; heavy restaurant-keepers with tooth-picks in their mouths; a vast army of dry-goods clerks - the "paper-collared" gentry; miners of every description; representatives from Dog Town, Chicken Flats, Busterville, Butchertown, and Seldom Seen - suburbs of Butte; pale thin individuals who sing and dance in beer-halls; smart society people in high traps and tally-hos; impossible women - so-called (though in Butte no one is more possible), in vast hats and extremely plaid stockings; persons who take things seriously and play the races for a living; "beer-jerkers"; "biscuit-shooters"; soft-voiced Mexicans and Arabians; - the dregs, the élite, the humbly respectable, the off-scouring - all thrown together, and shaken up, and mixed well.

One may notice many odd bits of irony as one walks among these. One may notice that the Irish men are singularly carefree and strong and comfortable - and so jolly! While the Irish women are frumpish and careworn and borne earthward with children. The Cornishman who has consumed the greatest amount of whiskey is the most agreeable, and less and less inclined to leer and ogle. The Cornish woman whose profanity is the shrillest and most genial and voluble, is she whose life seems the most weighted and downtrodden. The young women whose bodies are encased in the tightest and stiffest corsets are in the most wildly hilarious spirits of all. The filthy little Irish youngsters from Dublin Gulch are much brighter and more clever in every way than the ordinary American children who are less filthy. A delicate aroma of cocktails and whiskey-and-soda hangs over even the four-in-hands and automobiles of the upper crust. Gamblers, news-boys, and Chinamen are the most chivalrously courteous among them. And the modest-looking "plunger" who has drunk the greatest number of high-balls is the most gravely, quietly polite of all. The rolling, rollicking, musical profanity of the "ould sod" - Bantry Bay, Donegal, Tyrone, Tipperary - falls much less limpidly from the cigaretted lips of the ten-year-old lad than from those of his mother, who taught it to him. One may notice that the husband and wife who smile the sweetest at each other in the sight of the multitudes are they whose countenances bear various scars and scratches commemorating late evening orgies at home; that the peculiar solid, block-shaped appearance of some of the miners' wives is due quite as much to the quantity of beer they drink as to their annual maternity; that the one grand ruling passion of some men's lives is curiosity; - that the entire herd is warped, distorted, barren, having lived its life in smoke-cured Butte.

A single street in Butte contains people in nearly every walk of life - living side by side resignedly, if not in peace.

In a row of five or six houses there will be living miners and their families, the children of which prevent life from stagnating in the street while their mothers talk to each other - with the inevitable profanity - over the back-fences. On the corner above there will be a mysterious widow with one child, who has suddenly alighted upon the neighborhood, stealthily in the night, and is to be seen at rare intervals emerging from her door - the target for dozens of pairs of eager eyes and half as many eager tongues. And when the mysterious widow, with her one child, disappears some night as suddenly and as stealthily as she appeared, an outburst of highly-colored rumors is tossed with astonishing glibness over the various back-fences - all relating to the mysterious widow's shady antecedents and past history, to those of her child, and to the cause of her sudden departure, - no two of which rumors agree in any particular. Across on the opposite corner there will be a company of strange people who also descended suddenly, and upon whom the eyes of the entire block are turned with absorbing interest. They consist of half-a-dozen men and women seemingly bound together only by ties of conviviality. The house is kept closely-blinded and quiet all day, only to burst forth in a blaze of revel in the evening, which revel lasts all night. This goes on until some momentous night, at the request of certain proper ones, a police officer glides quietly into the midst of a scene of unusual gaiety - and the festive company melts quietly into oblivion, never to return. They also are then discussed with rapturous relish and in tones properly lowered, over the back-fences. Farther down the street there will live an interesting being of feminine persuasion who has had five divorces and is in the course of obtaining another. These divorces, the causes therefor, the justice thereof, and the future prospects of the multi-grass widow, are gone over, in all their bearings, by the indefatigable tongues. Every incident in the history of the street is put through a course of sprouts by these same tireless members. The Jewish family that lives in the poorest house in the neighborhood, and that is said to count its money by the hundred thousand; the aristocratic family with the Irish-point curtains in the windows - that lives on the county; the family whose husband and father gains for it a comfortable livelihood - forging checks; the miner's family whose wife and mother wastes its substance in diamonds and seal-skin coats and other riotous living; the family in extremely straitened circumstances into which new babies arrive in great and distressing numbers; the strange lady with an apoplectic complexion and a wonderfully foul and violent flow of invective - all are discussed over and over and over again. No one is omitted.

And so this is Butte, the promiscuous - the Bohemian. And all these are the Devil's playthings. They amuse him, doubtless.

Butte is a place of sand and barrenness.

The souls of these people are dumb.

February 4

Always I wonder, when I die will there be any one to remember me with love?

I know I am not lovable.

That I want it so much only makes me less lovable, it seems. But - who knows? - it may be there will be some one.

My anemone lady does not love me. How can she - since she does not understand me? But she allows me to love her - and that carries me a long way. There are many - oh, a great many - who will not allow you to love them if you would.

There is no one to love me now.

Always I wonder how it will be after some long years when I find myself about to die.

In this house where I drag out my accursed, devilishly weary existence, upstairs in the bath-room, on the little ledge at the top of the wainscoting, there are six tooth-brushes: an ordinary white bone-handled one that is my younger brother's; a white twisted-handled one that is my sister's; a flat-handled one that is my older brother's; a celluloid-handled one that is my stepfather's; a silver-handled one that is mine; and another ordinary one that is my mother's. The sight of these tooth-brushes day after day, week after week, and always, is one of the most crushingly maddening circumstances in my fool's life.

Every Friday I wash up the bath-room. Usually I like to do this. I like the feeling of the water squeezing through my fingers, and always it leaves my nails beautifully neat. But the obviousness of those six tooth-brushes signifying me and the five other members of this family and the aimless emptiness of my existence here - Friday after Friday - makes my soul weary and my heart sick.

Never does the pitiable barren contemptible damnable narrow Nothingness of my life in this house come upon me with a so intense force as when my eyes happen upon those six tooth-brushes.

Among the horrors of the Inquisition, a minute refinement of cruelty was reached when the victim's head was placed beneath a never-ceasing falling of water, drop by drop.

A convict sentenced to solitary confinement, spending his endless days staring at four blank walls, feels that had he committed every known crime he could not possibly deserve his punishment.

I am not undergoing an Inquisition, nor am I a convict in solitary confinement. But I live in a house with people who affect me mostly through their tooth-brushes - and those I should like, above all things, to gather up and pitch out the bath-room window - and oh, damn them, *damn* them!

You who read this, can you understand the depth of bitterness and hatred that is contained in this for me? Perhaps you can a little if you are a woman and have felt yourself alone.

When I look at the six tooth-brushes a fierce, lurid storm of rage and passion comes over me. Two heavy leaden hands lay hold of my life and press, press, press. They strike the sick, sick weariness to my inmost soul.

Oh, to leave this house and these people, and this intense Nothingness - oh, to pass out from them, forever! But where can I go, what can I do? I feel with mad fury that I am helpless. The grasp of the stepfather and the mother is contemptible and absurd - but with the persistence and tenacity of narrow minds. It is like the two heavy leaden hands. It is not seen - it is not tangible. It is felt.

Once I took away my own silver-handled tooth-brush from the bathroom ledge, and kept it in my bed-room for a day or two. I thought to lessen the effect of the six.

I put it back in the bath-room.

The absence of one accentuated the significant damnation of the others. There was something more forcibly maddening in the five than in the six tooth-brushes. The damnation was not worse, but it developed my feeling about them more vividly.

And so I put my tooth-brush back in the bath-room.

This house is comfortably furnished. My mother spends her life in the adornment of it. The small square rooms are distinctly pretty.

But when I look at them seeingly I think of the proverb about the dinner of stalled ox.

Yet there is no hatred here, except mine and my bitterness. I am the only one of them whose bitter spirit cries out against things.

But there is that which is subtler and strikes deeper. There is the lack of sympathy - the lack of everything that counts: there is the great deep Nothing.

How much better were there hatred here than Nothing!

I long hopelessly for will-power, resolution to take my life into my own hands, to walk away from this house some day and never return. I have nowhere to go - no money, and I know the world quite too well to put the slightest faith in its voluntary kindness of heart. But how much better and wider, less damned, less maddening, to go out into it and be beaten and cheated and fooled with, than *this*! - this thing that gathers itself easily into a circle made of six tooth-brushes with a sufficiency of surplus damnation.

I have read about a woman who went down from Jerusalem to Jericho and fell among thieves. Perhaps she had a house at Jerusalem with six tooth-brushes and Nothingness. In that case she might have rushed gladly into the arms of thieves.

I think of crimes that would strike horror and revulsion to my maid-senses. And I think of my Nothingness, and I ask myself were it not better to walk the earth an outcast, a solitary woman, and meet and face even these, than that each and every one of my woman-senses should wear slowly, painfully to shreds, and strain and break - in this unnameable Nothing?

Oh, the dreariness - the hopelessness of Nothing!

There are no words to tell it. And things are always hardest to bear when there are no words for them.

However great one's gift for language may be there is always something that one can not tell.

I am weary of self - always self. But it must be so.

My life is filled with *self.*

If my soul could awaken fully perhaps I might be lifted out of myself - surely I should be. But my soul is not awake. It is awakening, trying to open its eyes; and it is crying out blindly after something, but it can not *know.* I have a dreadful feeling that it will stay always like this.

Oh, I feel everything - everything! I feel what might be. And there is Nothing. There are six tooth-brushes.

Would I stop for a few fine distinctions, a theory, a natural law even, to escape from this into Happiness - or into something greatly less?

Misery - misery! If only I could feel it less!

Oh, the weariness, the weariness - as I await the Devil's coming.

February 8

Often I walk out to a place on the flat valley below the town, to flirt with Death. There is within me a latent spirit of coquetry, it appears.

Down on the flat there is a certain deep dark hole with several feet of water at the bottom.

This hole completely fascinates me. Sometimes when I start out to walk in a quite different direction, I feel impelled almost irresistibly to turn and go down on the flat in the direction of the fascinating, deep black hole.

And here I flirt with Death. The hole is so narrow - only about four feet across - and so dark, and so deep! I don't know whether it was intended to be a well, or whether it is an abandoned shaft of some miner. At any rate it is isolated and deserted, and it has a rare loving charm for me.

I go there sometimes in the early evening and kneel on the edge of it, and lean over the dark pit, with my hand grasping a wooden stake that is driven into the ground near by. And I drop little stones down and hear them splash hollowly, and it sounds a long way off.

There is something wonderfully soothing, wonderfully comforting to my unrestful, aching wooden heart in the dark mystery of this fascinating hole. Here is the End for me, if I want it - here is the Ceasing, when I want it. And I lean over and smile quietly.

"No flowers," I say to myself, "no weeping idiots, no senseless funeral, no oily undertaker fussing over my woman's-body, no useless Christian prayers. Nothing but this deep dark restful grave."

No one would ever find it. It is a mile and a half from any house.

The water - the dark still water at the bottom - would gurgle over me and make an end quickly. Or if I feared there was not enough water, I would bring with me a syringe and some morphine and inject an immense quantity into one white arm, and kneel over the tender darkness until my youth-weary, waiting-worn senses should be overcome, and my slim light body should fall. It would splash into the water at bottom - it would follow the little stones at last. And the black muddy water would soak in and begin the destroying of my body, and murky bubbles would rise so long as my lungs continued to breathe. Or perhaps my body would fall against the side of the hole, and the head would lie against it out of the water. Or perhaps only the face would be out of the water, turned upward to the light above - or turned half-down, and the hair would be darkly wet and heavy, and the face would be blue-white below it, and the eyes would sink inward.

"The End, the End -" I say softly and ecstatically. Yet I do not lean farther out. My hand does not loosen its tight grasp on the wooden stake. I am only flirting with Death now.

Death is fascinating - almost like the Devil. Death makes use of all his arts and wiles, powerful and alluring, and flirts with deadly temptation for me. And I make use of my arts and wiles - and tempt him.

Death would like dearly to have me, and I would like dearly to have him. It is a flirtation that has its source in mutual desire. We do not love each other, Death and I, - we are not friends. But we desire each other sensually, lustfully.

Sometime I suppose I shall yield to the desire. I merely play at it now - but in an unmistakable manner. Death knows it is only a question of time.

But first the Devil must come. First the Devil, then Death: a deep dark soothing grave - and the early evening, "and a little folding of the hands to sleep."

February 12

I am in no small degree, I find, a sham - a player to the gallery. Possibly this may be felt as you read these analyses.

While all of these emotions are written in the utmost seriousness and sincerity, and are exactly as I feel them, day after day - so far as I have the power to express what I feel - still I aim to convey through them all the idea that I am lacking in the grand element of Truth - that there is in the warp and woof of my life a thread that is false - false.

I don't know how to say this without the fear of being misunderstood. When I say I am in a way a sham, I have no reference to the truths as I have given them in this Portrayal, but to a very light and subtle thing that runs through them.

Oh, do not think for an instant that this analysis of my emotions is not perfectly sincere and real, and that I have not felt all of them more than I can put into words. They are my tears - my life-blood!

But in my life, in my personality, there is an essence of falseness and insincerity. A thin, fine vapor of fraud hangs always over me and dampens and injures some things in me that I value.

I have not succeeded thoroughly in analyzing this - it is so thin, so elusive, so faint - and yet not little. It is a natural thing enough viewed in the light of my other traits.

I have lived my nineteen years buried in an environment at utter variance with my natural instincts, where my inner life is never touched, and my sympathies very rarely, if ever, appealed to. I never disclose my real desires or the texture of my soul. - Never, that is to say, to any one except my one friend, the anemone lady. - And so every day of my life I am playing a part; I am keeping an immense bundle of things hidden under my cloak. When one has played a part - a false part - all one's life, for I was a sly, artful little liar even in the days of five and six, then one is marked. One may never rid oneself of the mantle of falseness, charlatanry - particularly if one is innately a liar.

A year ago when the friendship of my anemone lady was given me, and she would sometimes hear sympathetically some long-silent bit of pain, I felt a snapping of tense-drawn cords, a breaking away of flood-gates - and a strange new pain. I felt as if I must clasp her gentle hand tightly and give way to the pent-up surging tears of eighteen years. I had wanted this tender thing more than anything else all my life, and it was given me suddenly.

I felt a convulsion and a melting, within.

But I could not tell my one friend exactly what I felt. There was no doubt in my own mind as to my own perfect sincerity of feeling, but there was with it and around it this vapor of fraud, a spirit of falseness that rose and confronted me and said "hypocrite," "fool."

It may be that the spirit of falseness is itself a false thing - yet true or false, it is with me always. I have tried, in writing out my emotions, to convey an idea of this sham element while still telling everything faithfully true. Sometimes I think I have succeeded, and at other times I seem to have signally failed. This element of falseness is absolutely the very thinnest, the very finest, the rarest of all the things in my many-sided character.

It is not the most unimportant.

I have seen visions of myself walking in various pathways. I have seen myself trying one pathway and another. And always it is the same: I see before me in the path, darkening the way and filling me with dread and discouragement, a great black shadow - the shadow of my own element of falseness.

I can not rid myself of it.

I am an innate liar.

This is a hard thing to write about. Of all things it is the most liable to be misunderstood. You will probably misunderstand it, for I have not succeeded in giving the right idea of it. I aimed at it and missed it. It eluded me completely.

You must take the idea as I have just now presented it for what it may be worth. This is as near as I can come to it. But it is something infinitely finer and rarer.

It is a difficult task to show to others a thing which, though I feel and recognize it thoroughly, I have not yet analyzed for myself.

But this is a complete Portrayal of me - as I await the Devil's coming - and I must tell everything - everything.

February 13

So then yes. As I have said, I find that I am quite, quite odd. My various acquaintances say that I am *funny*. They say, "Oh, it's that May MacLane, Dolly's younger sister. She's funny." But I call it oddity. I bear the hall-mark of oddity.

There was a time, a year or two since, when I was an exceedingly sensitive little fool. Sensitive in that it used to strike very deep when my young acquaintances would call me funny and find in me a vent for their distinctly unfriendly ridicule. My years in the High School were not years of joy. Two years ago I had not yet risen above these things. I was a sensitive little fool.

But that sensitiveness, I rejoice to say, has gone from me. The opinion of these young people, or of these old people, is now a thing that is quite unable to affect me.

The more I see of conventionality, it seems, the more I am odd.

Though I am young and feminine - very feminine - yet I am not that quaint conceit, a *girl*: the sort of person that Laura E. Richards writes about, and Nora Perry, and Louisa M. Alcott, - girls with bright eyes, and with charming faces - (they always have charming faces), - standing with reluctant feet where the brook and river meet, - and all that sort of thing.

I missed all that.

I have read some girl-books, a few years ago - *Hildegarde Graham*, and *What Katy Did*, and all, - but I read them from afar. I looked at those creatures from behind a high board fence. I felt as if I had more tastes in common with the Jews wandering through the Wilderness, or with a band of fighting Amazons. I am not a girl. I am a woman, of a kind. I began to be a woman at twelve, or more properly, a genius.

And then, usually, if one is not a girl one is a heroine - of the kind you read about. But I am not a heroine, either. A heroine is beautiful - eyes like the sea, shoots opaque glances from under drooping lids, walks with undulating movements, her bright smile haunts one still, falls methodically in love with a man - always with a man, - eats things (they are always called "viands") with a delicate appetite, and on special occasions her voice is full of tears. I do none of these things. I am not beautiful. I do not walk with undulating movements - indeed, I have never seen any one walk so, except, perhaps, a cow that has been overfed. My bright smile haunts no one. I shoot no opaque glances from my eyes, which are not like the sea by any means. I have never eaten any viands, and my appetite for what I do eat is most excellent. And my voice has never yet, to my knowledge, been full of tears.

No. I am not a heroine.

There never seem to be any plain heroines, except Jane Eyre, and she was very unsatisfactory. She should have entered into marriage with her beloved Rochester in the first place. I should have, let there be a dozen mad wives up-stairs. But I suppose the author thought she must give her heroine some desirable thing - high moral principles, since she was not beautiful. Some people say that beauty is a curse. It may be true, but I'm sure I should not have minded being cursed a little. And I know several persons who might well say the same. But anyway, I wish some one would write a book about a plain, bad heroine so that I might feel in real sympathy with her.

So far from being a girl or a heroine, I am a thief - as I have before suggested.

I mind me of how, not long since, I stole three dollars. A woman whom I know rather well, and lives near, called me into her house as I was passing and asked me to do an errand for her. She was having an ornate gown made, and she needed some more applique with which to festoon it. The applique cost nine dollars a yard. My trusting neighbor gave me a bit of the braid for a sample and two twenty-dollar bills. I was to get four yards. I did so, and came back and gave her the braid and a single dollar. The other three dollars I kept myself. I wanted three dollars very much, to put with a few that I already had in my purse. My trusting neighbor is of the kind that throws money about carelessly. I knew she would not pay any attention to a little detail like that - she was deeply interested in her new frock; or perhaps she would think I had got thirty-nine dollars' worth of applique. At any rate, she did not need the money, and I wanted three dollars, and so I stole it.

I am a thief.

It has been suggested to me that I am a kleptomaniac. But I am sure my mind is perfectly sane. I have no such excuse. I am a plain, down-right thief.

This is only one of my peculations. I steal money, or anything that I want, whenever I can, nearly always. It amuses me - and one must be amused.

I have only two stipulations: that the person to whom it belongs does not need it pressingly, and that there is not the slightest chance of being found out. (And of course I could not think of stealing from my one friend.)

It would be extremely inconvenient to be known as a thief, merely.

When the world knows you are a thief it blinds itself completely to your other attributes. It calls you a thief, and there's an end. I am a genius as well as a thief - but the world would quite overlook that fact. "A thief's a thief," says the world. That is very true. But the mere fact of being a thief should not exclude the consideration of one's other traits. When the world knows you are a Methodist minister, for instance, it will admit that you may also be a violinist, or a chemist, or a poet, and will credit you therefor. And so if it condemns you for being a thief, it should at the same time admire you for being a genius. If it does not admire you for being a genius, then it has no right to condemn you for being a thief.

- And why the world should condemn any one for being a thief - when there is not within its confines any one who is not a thief in some way - is a bit of irony upon which I have wasted much futile logic. -

I am not trying to justify myself for stealing. I do not consider it a thing that needs to be justified, any more than walking or eating or going to bed. But, as I say, if the world knew that I am a thief without being first made aware with emphasis that I am some other things also, then the world would be a shade cooler for me than it already is - which would be very cool indeed.

And so in writing my Portrayal I have dwelt upon some other things at some length before touching on my thieving propensities.

None of my acquaintances would suspect that I am a thief. I look so respectable, so refined, so "nice," so inoffensive, so sweet, even!

But, for that matter, I am a great many things that I do not appear to be.

The woman from whom I stole the three dollars, if she reads this, will recognize it. This will be inconvenient. I fervently hope she may not read it. It is true she is not of the kind that reads.

But after all, it's of no consequence. This Portrayal is Mary MacLane: her wooden heart, her young woman's-body, her mind, her soul.

- The world may run and read. -

I will tell you what I did with the three dollars. In Dublin Gulch, which is a rough quarter of Butte inhabited by extremely Irish people, there lives an old world-soured, wrinkle-faced woman. She lives alone in a small untidy house. She swears frightfully like a parrot, and her reputation is bad - so bad indeed that even the old woman's compatriots in Dublin Gulch do not visit her lest they damage their own. It is true that the profane old woman's morals are not good - have never been good - judged by the world's standards. She bears various marks of cold, rough handling on her mind and body. Her life has all but run its course. She is worn out.

Once in a while I go to visit this old woman. - My reputation must be sadly damaged now. -

I sit with her for an hour or two and listen to her. She is extremely glad to have me here. Except me she has no one to talk to but the milk man, the grocery man, and the butcher. So always she is glad to see me. There is a certain bond of sympathy between her and me. We are fond of each other. When she sees me picking my way toward her house, her hard sour face softens wonderfully and a light of distinct friendliness comes into her green eyes.

Don't you know, there are few people enough in the world whose hard sour faces will soften at the sight of you and a distinctly friendly light come into their green eyes. For myself I find such people few indeed.

So the profane old woman and I are fond of each other. No question of morals, or of immorals, comes between us. We are equals.

I talk to her a little - but mostly she talks. She tells me of the time when she lived in County Galway, when she was young - and of her several husbands, and of some who were not husbands, and of her children scattered over the earth. And she shows me old tin-types of these people. She has told me the varied tale of her life a great many times. I like to hear her tell it. It is like nothing else I have heard. The story in its unblushing simplicity, the sour-faced old woman sitting telling it, and the tin-types, - contain a thing that is absurdly, grotesquely, tearlessly sad.

Once when I went to her house I brought with me six immense heavy fragrant chrysanthemums.

They had been bought with the three dollars I had stolen.

It pleased me to buy them for the profane old woman. They pleased her also - not because she cares much for flowers, but because I brought them to her. I knew they would please her, but that was not the reason I gave her them.

I did it purely and simply to please myself.

I knew the profane old woman would not be at all concerned as to whether they had been bought with stolen money or not, and my only regret was that I had not had an opportunity to steal a larger sum so that I might have bought more chrysanthemums without inconveniencing my purse.

But as it was they filled her dirty little dwelling with perfume and color.

Long ago when I was six I was a thief - only I was not then, as now, a graceful, light-fingered thief - I had not the philosophy of stealing.

When I would steal a copper cent out of my mother's pocket-book I would feel a dreadful suffocating sinking in my bad heart, and for days and nights afterwards - long after I had eaten the chocolate mouse - the copper cent would haunt me and haunt me, and oh, how I wished it back in that pocket-book with the clasp shut tight and the bureau-drawer locked!

And so is it not fine to be nineteen and a thief, with the philosophy of stealing - than to be six and haunted day and night by a copper cent?

For now always my only regret is, when I have stolen five dollars, that I did not steal ten while I was about it.

It is a long time ago since I was six.

February 17

To-day I walked over the hill where the sun vanishes down in the afternoon.

I followed the sun so far as I could, but two even very good legs can do no more than carry one into the midst of the sunshine - and then one may stand and take leave, lovingly, of it.

I stood in the valley below the hill and looked away at the gold-yellow mountains that rise into the cloudy blue, and at the long gray stretches of rolling sand. It all reminded me of the Devil and the Happiness he will bring me.

Some day the Devil will come to me and say: "Come with me."

And I will answer: "Yes."

And he will take me away with him to a place where it is wet and green - where the yellow, yellow sunshine falls on heaven-kissing hills, and misty, cloudy masses float over the valleys.

And for days I shall be happy - happy - happy!

For *days*! The Devil and I will love each other intensely, perfectly - for days! He will be incarnate but he will not be a man. He will be the man-Devil, and his soul will take mine to itself and they will be one - for days.

Imagine me raised out of my misery and obscurity, dullness and Nothingness, into the full, brilliant life of the Devil - for days!

The love of the man-Devil will enter into my barren, barren life and melt all the cold, hard things, and water the barrenness, and a million little green growing plants will start out of it; and a clear, sparkling spring will flow over it - through the dreary, sandy stretches of my bitterness, among the false stony roadways of my pain and hatred. And a great rushing, flashing cataract of melting love will flow over my weariness and unrest and wash it away forever. My soul will be fully awakened and there will be a million little sweet new souls in the green growing things. And they will fill my life with everything that is beautiful - tenderness, and divineness, and compassion, and exaltation, and uplifting grace, and light, and rest, and gentleness, and triumph, and truth, and peace. My life will be borne far out of self, and self will sink quietly out of sight - and I shall see it farther and farther away, until it disappears.

"It is the last - the *last* - of that Mary MacLane," I will say, and I will feel a long, sighing, quivering farewell.

A thousand years of misery - and now a million years of Happiness.

When the sun is setting in the valley and the crests of those heaven-kissing hills are painted violet and purple, and the valley itself is reeking and swimming in yellow-gold light, the man-Devil - whom I love more than all - and I will go out into it.

We will be saturated in the yellow light of the sun and the gold light of Love.

The man-Devil will say to me: "Look, you little creature, at this beautiful picture of Joy and Happiness. It is the picture of your life as it will be while I stay with you - and I will stay with you for days."

Ah, yes, I will take a last long farewell of this Mary MacLane. Not one faint shadow of her weary wretched Nothingness will remain.

There will be instead a brilliant, buoyant, joyous creature - transformed, adorned, garlanded by the love of the Devil.

My mind will be a treasure-house of Art, swept and garnished and strong and at its best.

My barren hungry heart will come at last to its own. The red flames of the man-Devil's love will burn out forever its pitiable distorted wooden quality, and he will take it and cherish it - and give me his.

My young woman's-body likewise will be metamorphosed, and I shall feel it developing and filled with myriads of little contentments and pleasures. Always my young woman's-body is a great and important part of me, and when I am married to the Devil its finely-organized nerve-power and intricate sensibility will be culminated to marvelous completeness.

My soul - upon my soul will descend consciously the light that never was on land or sea.

This will be for days - for days.

No matter what came before, I will say; no matter what comes afterward. Just now it is the man-Devil, my best-beloved, and I, living in the yellow light.

Think of living with the Devil in a bare little house, in the midst of green wetness and sweetness and yellow light - for days!

In the gray dawn it will be ineffably sweet and beautiful, with shining leaves and the gray unfathomable air, and the wet grass, and all.

"Be happy now, my weary little wife," the Devil will say.

And the long, long yellow-gold day will be filled with the music of Real Life.

My grandest possibility will be realized. The world contains a great many things - and this is my grandest possibility realized!

And in the soft black night I will lie by the side of the man-Devil - and my head will rest in the hollow of his shoulder, and my hand will be clasped in his hand.

I will weep rapturous tears. -

When I think of all this and write it there is in me a feeling that is more than pain.

Perhaps the very sweetest, the tenderest, the most pitiful and benign human voice in the world could sing these things and this feeling set to their own wondrous music, - and it would echo far - far, - and you would understand.

February 19

- Am I not intolerably conceited? -

February 20

At times when I walk among the natural things - the barren natural things - I know that I believe in Something. Why can I not call it God and pray to it?

There is Something - I do not know it intellectually, but I feel it - I *feel* it - with my soul. It does not seem to reach down to me. It does not pity me. It does not look at me tenderly in my unhappiness.

My soul feels only that it is there.

No. It is not all-loving, all-gracious, all-pitying. It hurts me - it hurts me always as I walk over the sand. But even while it hurts me it seems to promise - ah, those beautiful things that it promises me!

And then the hurting is anguish - for I know that the promises will never be fulfilled.

There is within me a thing that is aching, aching, aching always as the days pass.

It is not my pain of wanting, nor my pain of unrest, nor my pain of bitterness, nor of hatred. I know those in all their own anguish.

This aching is another pain. It is a pain that I do not know - that I feel ignorantly but sharply, and oh, it is torture, torture!

My soul is worn and weary with pain. There is no compassion - no mercy upon me. There is no one to help me bear it. It is just I alone out on the sand and barrenness. It is cruel anguish to be always alone - and so long - oh, so long!

Nineteen years are as ages to you when you are nineteen.

When you are nineteen there is no experience to tell you that all things have an end.

This aching pain has no end.

- I feel no tears now, but I feel heavy sobs that shake my life to its center. -

My soul is wandering in a wilderness.

There is a great Light sometimes that draws my soul toward it. When my soul turns toward it, it shines out brilliant and dazzling and awful - and the worn sensitive thing shrinks away, and shivers, and is faint.

Shall my soul have to know this Light, inevitably? Must it, some day, plunge into this?

Oh, it may be - it may be. But I know that I shall die with the pain.

There are times when the great Light is dim and beautiful as the star-light - the utter agony of it - the cruel ineffable loveliness!

- Do you understand this? That I am telling you my young passionate life-agony? Do you listen to it indifferently? Has it no meaning for any one? For me it means everything. For me it makes life old long weariness.

It may be that you know. And perhaps you would even weep a little with me if you had time. -

It is as if this Light were the light of the Christian religion - and the Christian religion is full of hatred. It says, Come unto me - you that are heavy laden, and I will give you rest. But when you would go, when you reach up with your weary hands, it sends you a too-brilliant Light - it makes you fair, wondrous promises - it puts you off. You beseech it in your suffering -

While the waters near me roll,
While the tempest still is high -

but it does not listen - it does not care. Worship me, worship me, it says, but after that let me alone. There is a bookful of promises. Take it and thank me and worship me.

It does not care.

If I obey it, it looks on indifferently. If I disobey it, it looks on indifferently. If I am in woe, it looks on indifferently. If I am in a brief joy, it looks on indifferently.

I am left all alone - all alone.

The Light is shown me and I reach after it, but it is placed high out of my reach.

I see the promises in the Light. Oh, why - *why* does it promise these things! Is not the burden of life already greater than I can bear? And there is the story of the Christ. It is beautiful. It is damningly beautiful. It draws the tears of pain and soft anguish from me at the sense of beauty. And when every nerve in me is melted and overflowing, then suddenly I am conscious that it is a lie - a *lie*.

Everywhere I turn there is Nothing - Nothing.

My soul wails out its grief in loneliness.

My soul wanders hither and thither in the dark wilderness and asks, asks always in blind, dull agony: How long? - how long?

February 22

Life is a pitiable thing.

February 23

I stand in the midst of my sand and barrenness and gaze hard at everything that is within my range of vision - and ruin my eyes trying to see into the darkness beyond.

And nearly always I feel a vague contempt for you, fine brave world, - for you and all the things that I see from my barrenness. But, I promise you, if some one comes from among you over the sunset hill one day with love for me, I will fall at your feet.

I am a selfish, conceited, impudent little animal it is true, but, after all, I am only one grand conglomeration of Wanting - and when some one comes over the barren hill to satisfy the Wanting, I will be humble, humble in my triumph.

It is a difficult thing - a most difficult thing - to live on as one year follows another, from childhood slowly to womanhood, without one single sharer of your life - to be alone, always alone, when your one friend is gone. Oh, yes, it is hard! Particularly when one is not high-minded and spiritual, when one's near longing is not a God and a religion, when one wants above all things the love of a human being - when one is a woman, young and all alone. Doubtless you know this. After all, fine brave world, there are some things that you know very well. Whether or not you care is a quite different matter.

You have the power to take this wooden heart in a tight, suffocating grasp. You have the power to do this with pain for me, and you have the power to do it with ravishing gentleness. But whether or not you will is another matter.

You may think evil of me before you have finished reading this. You will be very right to think so - according to your standards. But sometimes you see evil where there is no evil, and think evil when the only evil is in your own brains.

My life is a dry and barren life. You can change it.

> *Oh, the little more, and how much it is!*
> *And the little less, and what worlds away.*

Yes, you can change it. Stranger things have happened. Again, whether you will - that is a quite different thing.

No doubt you are the people and wisdom will die with you. I do not question that. I will admit and believe anything you may assert about yourselves. I do not want your wisdom, your judgment. I want some one to come up over the barren sunset hill. My thoughts are the thoughts of youth, which are said to be long, long thoughts.

Your life is multi-colored and filled with people. My life is the gray of sand and barrenness, and consists of Mary MacLane, the longing for Happiness, and the memory of the anemone lady.

This Portrayal is my deepest sincerity, my tears, my drops of red blood. Some of it is wrung from me - wrung by my ambition to tell *everything*. It is not altogether good that I should give you all this, since I do not give it for love of you. I am giving it in exchange for a few gaily-colored things. I want you to know all these passions and emotions. I give them with the utmost freedom. I shall be furious indeed if you do not take them. At the same time, the fact that I am exchanging my tears and my drops of red blood for your gaily-colored trifles is not a thing that thrills me with delight.

But it's of little moment. When the Devil comes over the hill with Happiness I will rush at him frantically headlong - and nothing else will matter.

Mary MacLane - what are you, you forlorn, desolate little creature? Why are you not of and in the galloping herd? Why is it that you stand out separate against the background of a gloomy sky? Why can you not enter into the lives and sympathies of other young creatures? There have been times when you have strained every despairing nerve to do so - before you realized that these things were not for you, that the only sympathy for you was that of Mary MacLane, and the only things for you were those you could take yourself - not which were given you. And your things are few, few, you starved, lean little mud-cat - you worn, youth-weary, obscure little genius!

Oh, it is a wearisome waiting - for the Devil.

To-day when I walked over my sand and barrenness I felt Infinite Grief.

Everything is beyond me.

Nothing is mine.

My single friendship shines brightly before me, and is fascinating - and always just out of my reach.

I want the love and sympathy of human beings and I repel human beings.

Yes, I repel human beings.

There is something about me that faintly and finely and unmistakably repels.

When my Happiness comes, shall I be able to have it? Shall I ever have anything?

This repellant power is not an outward quality. It is something that comes from deeply, deeply within. It is something that was there in the Beginning. It is a thing from the Original.

There is no ridding myself of it. There is no ridding myself of it. There is no ridding myself of it.

Oh, I am damned - damned!

There is not one soul in the world to feel for me and with me - not one out of all the millions. No one can understand me - *no one.*

You are saying to yourself that I imagine this.

What right have you to say so? You don't know anything about me. I know all about me. I have studied all the elements and phases in my life for years and years. I do not imagine anything. I am even fool enough to shut my eyes to some things until, inevitably, I know I must meet them. I am racked with the passions of youth, and I am young in years. Beyond that I am mature - old. I am not a child in anything but my passions and my years. I feel and recognize everything thoroughly. I have not to imagine anything. My inner life is before my eyes.

There is something about me that no one can understand. Can there ever be any one to understand? Shall I not always walk my barren road alone?

This follows me incessantly. It is burning like a smouldering fire every hour of my life.

Oh, deep black Despair!

How I suffer, how I suffer - just in being alive.

I feel Infinite Grief.

Oh, Infinite Grief -

Often in the early morning I leave my bed and get me dressed and go out into the Gray Dawn. There is something about the Gray Dawn that makes me wish the world would stop, that the sun would never come up over the edge, that my life would go on and on and rest in the Gray Dawn.

In the Gray Dawn every hard thing is hidden by a gray mantle of charity, and only the light, vague, caressing fancies are left.

Sometimes I think I am a strange, strange creature - something not of earth, nor yet of heaven, nor of hell. I think at times I am a little thing fallen on the earth by mistake: a thing thrown among foreign, unfitting elements, where there is nothing in touch with it, where life is a continual struggle, where every little door is closed - every Why unanswered, and itself knows not where to lay its head. I feel a deadly certainty in some moments that the wide world contains not one moment of rest for me, that there will never be any rest, that my woman's-soul will go on asking long, long centuries after my woman's-body is laid in its grave.

I felt this in the Gray Dawn this morning, but the gray charitable mantle softened it. Always I feel most acutely in the Gray Dawn, but always there is the thing to soften it.

The gray atmosphere was charged. There was a tense electrical thrill in the cold soft air. My nerves were keenly alive. But the gray curtain was mercifully there. I did not feel too much.

How I wished the yellow beautiful sun would never come up over the edge to show me my nearer anguish!

"Stay with me, stay with me, soft Gray Dawn," implored every one of my tiny lives. "Let me forget. Let the vanity, the pain, the longing sink deep and vanish - all of it, all of it! And let me rest in the midst of the Gray Dawn."

I heard music - the silent music of myriad voices that you hear when all is still. One of them came and whispered to me softly: "Don't suffer any more just now, little Mary MacLane. You suffer enough in the brightness of the sun and the blackness of the night. This is the Gray Dawn. Take a little rest."

"Yes," I said, "I will take a little rest."

And then a wild swelling chorus of voices whispered in the stillness: "Rest, rest, rest little Mary MacLane. Suffer in the brightness, suffer in the blackness - your soul, your wooden heart, your woman's-body. But now a little rest - a little rest."

"A little rest," I said again.

And straightway I began resting lest the sun should come too quickly over the edge.

When I have heard in summer the wind in a forest of pines, blowing a wondrous symphony of purity and truth, my varied nature felt itself abashed and there was a sinking in my wooden heart. The beauty of it ravished my senses, but it savored crushingly of the virtue that is far above and beyond me and I felt a certain sore despairing grief.

But the Gray Dawn is in perfect sympathy. It is quite as beautiful as the wind in the pines and its truth and purity are extremely gentle, and partly hidden under the gray curtain.

Almost I can be a different Mary MacLane out in the Gray Dawn. Let me forget all the mingled agonies of my life. Let me walk in the midst of this gray softness and drink of the waters of Lethe.

The Gray Dawn is not Paradise; it is not a Happy Valley; it is not a Garden of Eden; it is not a Vale of Cashmere. It is the Gray Dawn - soft, charitable, tender. "The brilliant, celestial yellow will come shortly," it says. "You will suffer then to your greatest extent. But now I am here - and so, rest."

And so in the Gray Dawn I was forgetting for a brief period. I was submerged for a little in Lethe, river of oblivion. If I had seen some one coming over the near horizon with Happiness I should have protested, Wait, wait until the Gray Dawn has passed.

The deep, deep blue of the summer sky stirs me to a half-painful joy. The cool green of a swiftly-flowing river fills my heart with unquiet longings. The red, red of the sunset sky convulses my entire being with passion. But the dear Gray Dawn brings me Rest.

Oh, the Gray Dawn is sweet - sweet!

Could I not die for very love of it!

The Gray Dawn can do no wrong. If those myriad voices suddenly had begun to sing a voluptuous evil song of the so great evil that I could not understand, but that I could feel instantly, still the Gray Dawn would have been fine and sweet and beautiful.

Always I admire Mary MacLane greatly - though sometimes in my admiration I feel a complete contempt for her. But in the Gray Dawn I love Mary MacLane tenderly and passionately.

I seem to take on a strange calm indifference to everything in the world but just Mary MacLane and the gray dawn. We two are identified with each other and joined together in shadowy vagueness from the rest of the world.

As I walked over my sand and barrenness in the Gray Dawn a poem ran continuously through my mind. It expressed to me in my gray condition an ideal life and death and ending. Every desire of my life melted away in the Gray Dawn except one good wish that my own life and death might be short and obscure and complete like them. The poem was this beautiful one of Charles Kingsley's:

"Oh, Mary, go and call the cattle home,
And call the cattle home,
And call the cattle home,
Across the sands of Dee!"
The western wind was wild and dank with foam,
And all alone went she.

The creeping tide came up along the sand,
And o'er and o'er the sand,
And round and round the sand,
As far as eye could see;
The blinding mist came up and hid the land -
And never home came she.

Oh, is it weed, or fish, or floating hair? -
A tress of golden hair,
Of drowned maiden's hair,
Above the nets at sea.
Was never salmon yet that shone so fair
Among the stakes on Dee.

They rowed her in across the rolling foam,
The cruel, crawling foam,
The cruel, hungry foam,
To her grave beside the sea;
But still the boatmen hear her call the cattle home
Across the sands of Dee.

This is a poem perfect. And in the Gray Dawn it expresses to me a most desirable thing - a short eventless life, a sudden ceasing, and a forgotten voice sometimes calling. This Mary, in the Gray Dawn, would wish nothing else. If the waters rolled over me now - over my short eventless life - there would be the sudden ceasing, - and the anemone lady would hear my voice sometimes, and remember me - the anemone lady and one or two others. And after a short time even my pathetic, passionate voice would sound faint and be forgotten, and my world of sand and barrenness would know me and my weary little life-tragedy no more.

And well for me, I say, - in the Gray Dawn.

It is different - oh, very different - when the yellow bursts through the gray. And the yellow is with me all day long, and at sunset - the red, red line!

Yet - oh, sweet Gray Dawn -

Sometimes I am seized with nearer, vivider sensations of love for my one friend, the anemone lady.

She is so dear - so beautiful!

My love for her is a peculiar thing. It is not the ordinary woman-love. It is something that burns with a vivid fire of its own. The anemone lady is enshrined in a temple on the inside of my heart that shall always only be hers.

She is my first love - my only dear one.

The thought of her fills me with a multitude of feelings, passionate yet wonderfully tender, - with delight, with rare, undefined emotions, with a suggestion of tears.

- Oh, dearest anemone lady, shall I ever be able to forget your beautiful face! There may be some long crowded years before me; it may be there will be people and people entering and departing - but oh, no - no, I shall never forget! There will be in my life always - always the faint sweet perfume of the blue anemone: the memory of my one friend.

Before she went away, to see her, to be near her, was an event in my life - a coloring of the dullness. Always when I used to look at her there would rush a train of things over my mind, a vaguely glittering pageant that came only with her, and that held an always-vivid interest for me.

There were manifold and varied treasures in this train. There were skies of spangled sapphire, and there were lilies, and violets wet with dew. There was the music of violins, and wonderful weeds from the deep sea, and songs of troubadours, and gleaming white statues. There were ancient forests of oak and clematis vines; there were lemon-trees, and fretted palaces, and moss-covered old castles with moats and draw-bridges and tiny mullioned windows with diamond panes. There was a cold glittering cataract of white foam, and a little green boat far off down the river, drifting along under drooping willows. There was a tree of golden apples, and a banquet in a beautiful house with the melting music of lutes and harps, and mulled orange-wine in tall thin glasses. There was a field of long fine grass, soft as bat's-wool, and there were birds of brilliant plumage - scarlet and indigo with gold-tipped wings.

All these and a thousand fancies alike vaguely glittering would rush over me when I was with the anemone lady. Always my brain was in a gentle delirium. My nerves were unquiet.

- It was because I love her. -

Oh, there is not - there can never be - another anemone lady!

My life is a desert - a desert, but the thin, clinging perfume of the blue anemone reaches to its utter confines. And nothing in the desert is the same because of that perfume. Years will not fade the blue of the anemone, nor a thousand bitter winds blow away the rare fragrance.

I feel in the anemone lady a strange attraction of sex. There is in me a masculine element that, when I am thinking of her, arises and overshadows all the others.

"Why am I not a man," I say to the sand and barrenness with a certain strained, tense passion, "that I might give this wonderful, dear, delicious woman an absolutely perfect love!"

And this is my predominating feeling for her.

So then it is not the woman-love, but the man-love, set in the mysterious sensibilities of my woman-nature. It brings me pain and pleasure mingled in that old, old fashion.

Do you think a man is the only creature with whom one may fall in love?

- Often I see coming across the desert a long line of light. My soul turns toward it and shrinks away from it as it does from all the lights. - Some day, perhaps, all the lights will roll into one terrible white effervescence and rush over my soul and kill it. - But this light does not bring so much of pain, for it is soft and silvery, and always with it is the Soul of Anemone.

March 8

There are several things in the world for which I, of womankind and nineteen years, have conceived a forcible repugnance - or rather, the feeling was born in me; I did not have to conceive it.

Often my mind chants a fervent litany of its own that runs somewhat like this:

From good Catholics and virtuous Christians: kind Devil deliver me.

From women and men who dispense odors of musk; from little boys with long curls; from the kind of people who call a woman's figure her "shape": kind Devil deliver me.

From all sweet girls; from "gentlemen"; from feminine men: kind Devil deliver me.

From black under-clothing - and any color but white; from hips that wobble as one walks; from persons with fishy eyes; from the books of Archibald C. Gunter and Albert Ross: kind Devil deliver me.

From the soft, persistent, maddening glances of water-cart drivers: kind Devil deliver me.

From lisle-thread stockings; from round tight garters; from brilliant brass belts: kind Devil deliver me.

From insipid sweet wine; from men who wear moustaches; from the sort of people that call legs "limbs"; from bedraggled white petticoats: kind

Devil deliver me.

From unripe bananas; from bathless people; from a waist-line that slopes up in the front: kind Devil deliver me.

From an ordinary man; from a bad stomach, bad eyes, and bad feet: kind Devil deliver me.

From red note-paper; from a rhinestone-studded comb in my hair; from weddings: kind Devil deliver me.

From cod-fish balls; from fried-eggplant, fried beef-steak, fried pork-chops, and fried French toast: kind Devil deliver me.

From wax-flowers off a wedding-cake, under glass; from thin-soled shoes; from tape-worms; from photographs perched up all over my house: kind Devil deliver me.

From soft old bachelors and soft old widowers; from any masculine thing that wears a pale blue neck-tie; from agonizing elocutionists who recite "Curfew Shall Not Ring To-night," and "The Lips that Touch Liquor Shall Never Touch Mine"; from a Salvation Army singing hymns in slang: kind Devil deliver me.

From people who persist in calling my good body "mere vile clay"; from idiots who appear to know all about me and enjoin me not to bathe my eyes in hot water since it hurts their own; from fools who tell me what I "want" to do: kind Devil deliver me.

From a nice young man; from tin spoons; from popular songs: kind Devil deliver me.

From pleasant old ladies who tell a great many uninteresting, obvious lies; from men with watch-chains draped across their middles; from some paintings of the old masters which I am unable to appreciate; from side-saddles: kind Devil deliver me.

From the kind of man who sings "Oh, Promise Me!" - who sings *at* it; from constipated dressmakers; from people who don't wash their hair often enough: kind Devil deliver me.

From a servant girl with false teeth; from persons who make a regular practice of rubbing oily mixtures into their faces; from a bed that sinks in the middle: kind Devil deliver me.

And so on and on and on. And in each petition I am deeply sincere. But, kind Devil, only bring me Happiness and I will more than willingly be annoyed by all these things. Happiness for two days, kind Devil, and then, if you will, languishing widowers, lisle-thread stockings - anything, for the rest of my life.

And hurry, kind Devil, pray - for I am weary.

It is astonishing to me how very many contemptible, petty vanities are lodged in the crevices of my genius. My genius itself is one grand good vanity - but it is not contemptible. And even those little vanities - though they are contemptible I do not hold them in contempt by any means. I smile involuntarily at their absurdness sometimes, but I know well that they have their function.

They are peculiarly of my mind, my humanness, and they are useful therein. When this mind stretches out its hand for things and finds only wilderness and Nothingness all about it, and draws the hand back empty, then it can only turn back - like my soul - to itself. And it finds these innumerable little vanities to quiet it and help it. - My soul has no vanity, and it has nothing, nothing to quiet it. My soul is wearing itself out, eating itself away. - These vanities are a miserable substitute for the rose-colored treasures that it sees a great way off and even imagines in its folly that it may have, if it continues to reach after them. Yet the vanities are something. They prevent my erratic, analytical mind from finding a great Nothing when it turns back upon itself.

If I were not so unceasingly engrossed with my sense of misery and loneliness my mind would produce beautiful, wonderful logic. I am a genius - a genius - a genius. Even after all this you may not realize that I am a genius. It is a hard thing to show. But, for myself, I feel it. It is enough for me that I feel it.

I am not a genius because I am foreign to everything in the world, nor because I am intense, nor because I suffer. One may be all of these and yet not have this marvelous perceptive sense. My genius is because of nothing. It was born in me as germs of evil were born in me. And mine is a genius that has been given to no one else. The genius itself enables me to be thoroughly convinced of this.

It is hopeless, never-ending loneliness!

My ancestors in their Highlands - some of them - were endowed with second sight. My genius is not in the least like second sight. That savors of the supernatural, the mysterious. My genius is a sound sure earthly sense, with no suggestion of mystery or occultism. It is an inner sense that enables me to feel and know things that I could not possibly put into thought, much less into words. It makes me know and analyze with deadly minuteness every keen tiny damnation in my terrible lonely life. It is a mirror that shows me myself and something in myself in a merciless brilliant light, and the sight at once sickens and maddens me and fills me with an unnamed woe. It is something unspeakably dreadful. The sight for the time deadens all thought in my mind. It freezes my reason and intellect. Logic can not come to my aid. I can only feel and know the thing as it analyzes itself before my eyes.

I am alone with this - alone, alone, alone! There is no pitiful hand extended from the heights - there is no human being - ah, there is Nothing.

How can I bear it! Oh, I ask you - how can I bear it!

My genius is an element by itself and it is not a thing that I can tell in so many words. But it makes itself felt in every point of my life. This book would be a very different thing if I were not a genius - though I am not a literary genius. Often people who come in contact with me and hear me utter a few commonplace remarks feel at once that I am extraordinary.

I am extraordinary.

I have tried longingly, passionately, to think that even this sand and barrenness is mine. But I can not. I know beyond the shadow of a doubt that it, like all good things, is beyond me. It has something that I also have. In that is our bond of sympathy.

But the sand and barrenness itself is not mine.

Always I think there is but one picture in the world more perfect in its art than the picture of me in my sand and barrenness. It is the picture of the Christ crucified with two thieves. Nothing could be more divinely appropriate. The art in it is ravishingly perfect. It is one of the few perfect pictures set before the world for all time. As I see it before my mind I can think only of its utter perfectness. I can summon no feeling of grief at the deed. The deed and the art are perfect. Its perfectness ravishes my senses.

And within me I feel that the picture of me in my sand and barrenness - knowing that even the sand and barrenness is not mine - is only second to it.

Sometimes when I go out in the barrenness my mind wanders afar.

To-day it went to Greece.

Oh, it was very beautiful in Greece!

There was a wide long sky that was vividly, wonderfully blue. And there was a limitless sea that was gray and green. And it went far to the south. The sky and the sea spread out into the vast world - two beautiful elements, and they fell in love with each other. And the farther away they were the nearer they moved together until at last they met and clasped each other in the far distance. There were tall dark-green trees of kinds that are seen only in Greece. They murmured and whispered in the stillness. The wind came off from the sea and went over them and around them. They quivered and trembled in shy, ecstatic joy - for the wind was their best-beloved. There were banks of moss of a deep emerald color, and golden flowers that drooped their heavy sensual heads over to the damp black earth. And they also loved each other, and were with each other, and were glad. Clouds hung low over the sea and were dark-gray and heavy with rain. But the sun shone from behind them at intervals with beams of bronze-and-copper. Three white rocks rose up out of the sea, and the bronze-and-copper beams fell upon them, and straightway they were of gold.

Oh, how beautiful were those three gold rocks that came up out of the sea!

Aphrodite once came up out of this same sea. She came gleaming, with golden hair and beautiful eyes. Her skin glowed with hints of carmine and wild rose. Her white feet touched the smooth, yellow sand on the shore. - The white feet of Aphrodite on the yellow sand made a picture of marvelous beauty. - She was flushed in the joy of new life.

But the bronze-and-copper sunshine on the three white rocks was more beautiful than Aphrodite.

I stood on the shore and looked at the rocks. My heart contracted with the pain that beautiful things bring.

The bronze-and-copper in the wide gray and green sea!

"This is the gateway of Heaven," I said to myself. "Behind those three gold rocks there is music and the high notes of happy voices." My soul grew faint. "And there is no sand and barrenness there, and no Nothingness, and no bitterness, and no hot, blinding tears. And there are no little heart-weary children, and no lonely young women - oh, there is no loneliness at all!" My soul grew more and more faint with thinking of it. "And there is no heart there but that is pure and joyous and in Peace - in long, still, eternal Peace. And every life comes there to its own; and every earth-cry is answered, and every earth-pain is ended; and the dark spirit of Sorrow that hangs always over the earth is gone - gone, - beyond the gateway of heaven. And more than all, Love is there and walks among the dwellers. Love is a shining figure with radiant hands, and it touches them all with its hands so that never-dying love enters into their hearts. And the love of each for another is like the love of each for self. And here at last is Truth. There is searching and searching over the earth after Truth - and who has found it? But here is it beyond the gateway of heaven. Those who enter in know that it is Truth at last."

And so Peace and Love and Truth are there behind the three gold rocks.

And then my soul could no longer endure the thought of it.

Suddenly the sun passed behind a heavy, dark-gray cloud and the bronze-and-copper faded from the three rocks and left them white - very white in the wide water.

The yellow flowers laid their heads drowsily down on the emerald moss. The wind from off the sea played very gently among the motionless branches of the tall trees. The blue, blue sky and the wide, gray-green sea clasped each other more closely and mingled with each other and became one vague, shadowy element - and from it all I brought my eyes back thousands of leagues to my sand and barrenness.

The sand and barrenness is itself an element, and I have known it a long, long time.

March 12

Everything is so dreary - so dreary.

I feel as if I should like to die to-day. I should not be the tiniest bit less unhappy afterward - but this life is unutterably weary. I am not strong. I can not bear things. I do not want to bear things. I do not long for strength. I want to be happy.

When I was very little, it was cold and dreary also, but I was certain it would be different when I should grow and be ten years old. It must be very nice to be ten, I thought, - and one would not be nearly so lonesome. But when the years passed and I was ten it was just exactly as lonesome. And when I was ten everything was very hard to understand.

But it will surely be different when I am seventeen, I said, - I will know so much when I am seventeen. But when I was seventeen it was even more lonely, and everything was still harder to understand.

And again I said - faintly - everything will become clearer in a few years more, and I will wonder to think how stupid I have always been. But now the few years more have gone and here I am in loneliness that is more hope-less and harder to bear than when I was very little. Still, I wonder indeed to think how stupid I have been - and now I am not so stupid. I do not tell myself that it will be different when I am five-and-twenty.

For I know that it will not be different.

I know that it will be the same dreariness, the same Nothingness, the same loneliness.

It is very, very lonely.

It is hope deferred and maketh the heart sick.

It is more than I can bear.

Why - *why* was I ever born!

I can not live, and I can not die - for what is there after I am dead? I can see myself wandering in dark and lonely places.

Yet I feel as if I would like to die to-day.

March 13

If it were pain alone that one must bear, one could bear it. One could lose one's sense of everything but pain.

But it is pain with other things. It is the sense of pain with the sense of beauty and the sense of the anemone. And there is that mysterious pain.

Who knows the name of that mysterious pain?

It is these mingled senses that torture me.

March 14

I have been placed in this world with eyes to see and ears to hear, and I ask for Life. Is it to be wondered at? Is it so strange? Should I be content merely to see and to hear? There are other things for other people. Is it atrocious that I should ask for some other things also?

Is thy servant a dog?

March 15

In these days of approaching emotional Nature even the sand and barrenness begins to stir and rub its eyes.

My sand and barrenness is clothed in the awful majesty of countless ages. It stands always through the never-ending march of the living and the dead. It may have been green once - green and fertile, and birds and snakes and everything that loves green growing things may have lived in it. It may have sometime been rolling prairie. It may have been submerged in floods. It changed and changed in the centuries. Now it is sand and barrenness and there are no birds and no snakes; only me. But whatever change came to it, whatever its transfiguration, the spirit of it never moved. Flood, or fertility, or rolling prairie, or barrenness - it is only itself. It has a great self, a wonderful self.

I shall never forget you, my sand and barrenness.

Some day, shall my thirsty life be watered, my starved heart fed, my asking voice answered, my tired soul taken into the warmth of another with the intoxicating sweetness of love?

It may be.

But I shall remember the sand and barrenness that is with me in my Nothingness. The sand and barrenness and the memory of the anemone lady are all that are in any degree mine.

And so then I shall remember it.

As I stand among the barren gulches in these days and look away at the slow-awakening hills of Montana, I hear the high, swelling, half-tired, half-hopeful song of the world. As I listen I know that there are things, other than the Virtue and the Truth and the Love, that are not for me. There is beyond me, like these, the unbreaking, undying bond of human fellowship - a thing that is earth-old.

It is beyond me and it is nothing to me.

In my intensest desires - in my widest longings - I never go beyond *self.* The ego is the all.

Limitless legions of women and men in weariness and in joy are one. They are killing each other and torturing each other, and going down in sorrow to the dust. But they are one. Their right hands are joined in unseen sympathy and kinship.

But my two hands are apart, and clasped together in an agony of loneliness.

I have read of women who have been strongly, grandly brave. Sometimes I have dreamed that I might be brave. The possibilities of this life are magnificent.

To be saturated with this agony, I say at times, and to bear with it all; not to sink beneath it but to vanquish it, and to make it the grace and comeliness of my entire life from the Beginning to the End!

Perhaps a woman - a real woman - could do this.

But I? - No. I am not real - I do not seem *real* to myself. In such things as these my life is a blank.

There was Charlotte Corday - a heroine whom I admire above all the heroines. And more than she was a heroine she was a woman. And she had her agony. It was for love of her fair country.

To suffer and do and die for love of something! It is glorious! What must be the exalted ecstasy of Charlotte Corday's soul now!

And I - with all my manifold passions - I am a coward.

I have had moments when, vaguely and from far off, it seemed as if there might be bravery and exaltation for me, - when I could rise far over myself. I have felt unspeakable possibilities. While they lasted - what wonderful emotion was it that I felt?

But they are not real.

They fade away - they fade away.

And again come the varied phenomena of my life to bewilder and terrify me.

Confusion! Chaos! Damnation! They are not moments of exaltation now. Poor little Mary MacLane!

> *If to do were as easy as to know what were good to do,*
> *Chapels had been churches, and poor men's cottages*
> *Princes' palaces.*

I do not know what to do.

I do not know what were good to do.

I would do nothing if I knew.

I might add to my litany this: Most kind Devil deliver me - from myself.

To-day I walked over the sand and it was almost beautiful. The sun was sinking and the sky was filled with roses and gold.

Then came my soul and confronted me. My soul is wondrous fair. It is like a young woman. The beauty of it is too great for human eyes to look upon. It is too great for mine. Yet I look.

My soul said to me: "I am sick."

I answered: "And I am sick."

"We may be well," said my soul. "Why are we not well?"

"How may we be well?" I asked.

"We may throw away all our vanity and false pride," said my soul. "We may take on a new life. We may learn to wait and possess ourselves in patience. We may labor and overcome -"

"We can do none of these things," I cried. "Have I not tried all of them sometime in my short life? And have I not waited and waited until you have become faint with pain? Have I not looked and longed? Dear soul, why do you not resign yourself? Why can you not stay quiet and trouble yourself and me no more? Why are you always straining and reaching? There isn't anything for you. You are wearing yourself out."

My soul made answer: "I may strain and reach until only one worn nerve of me is left. And that one nerve may be scourged with whips and burned with fire. But I will keep one atom of faith. I may go bad, but I will keep one atom of faith in Love and in the Truth that is Love. You are a genius, but I am no genius. The years - a million of years - may do their utmost to destroy the single nerve. They may lash and beat it. I will keep my one atom of faith."

"You are not wise," I said. "You have been wandering and longing for a time that seems a thousand years - through my cold dark childhood to my cold dark womanhood. Is that not enough to quiet you? Is that not enough to teach you the lesson of Nothing? You are not a genius, but you are not a fool."

"I will keep my one atom of faith," said my soul.

"But lie and sleep now," I said. "Don't reach after that Light any more. Let us both sleep a few years."

"No," said my soul.

"Oh, my soul," I wailed, "look away at that glowing copper horizon - and beyond it. Let us go there now and take an infinite rest. Now! We can bear this no longer."

"No," said my soul. "We will stay here and bear more. There would be no rest yet beyond the copper horizon. And there is no need of going anywhere. I have my one atom of faith."

I gazed at my soul as it stood plainly before me, weak and worn and faint, in the fading light. It had one atom of faith, it said, and tried to hold its head high and to look strong and triumphant. Oh, the irony - the pathos of it!

My soul, with its one pitiful atom of faith, looked only what it was - a weeping, hunted thing.

March 17

In some rare between-whiles it is as if nothing mattered. My heart aches, I say; my soul wanders; this person or that person was repelled to-day; but nothing matters.

A great inner languor comes like a giant and lays hold of me. I lie fallow beneath it.

Someone forgot me in the giving of things. But it does not matter. I feel nothing.

Persons say to me, don't analyze any more and you will not be unhappy.

When Something throws heavy clubs at you and you are hit by them, don't be hurt. When Something stronger than you holds your hands in the fire, don't let it burn you. When Something pushes you into a river of ice, don't be cold. When Something draws a cutting lash across your naked shoulders, don't let it concern you - don't be conscious that it is there.

This is great wisdom and fine clear logic.

It is a pity that no one has ever yet been able to live by it.

But after all it's no matter. Nothing is any one's affair. It is all of no consequence.

And have I not had all my anguish for nothing? I am a fool - a fool.

A handful of rich black mud in a pig's yard - does it wonder why it is there? Does it torture itself about the other mud around it, and about the earth and water of which it is made, and about the pig? Only fool's-mud would do so. And so then I am fool's-mud.

Nothing counts. Nothing can possibly count.

Regret, passion, cowardice, hope, bravery, unrest, pain, the love-sense, the soul-sense, the beauty-sense - all for nothing! What can a handful of rich black mud in a pig's yard have to do with these? I am a handful of rich black mud - a fool-woman, fool's-mud.

All on earth that I need to do is to lie still in the hot sun and feel the pig rolling and floundering and slushing about. It were folly to waste my mud-nerves on wondering. - Be quiet, fool-woman, let things be. Your soul is a fool's-mud soul and is governed by the pig; your heart is a fool's-mud heart, and wants nothing beyond the pig; your life is a fool's-mud life and is the pig's life.

Something within me shrieks now, but I do not know what it is - nor why it shrieks.

It groans and moans.

There is no satisfaction in being a fool - no satisfaction at all.

March 18

But yes. It all matters, whether or no. Nature is one long battle and the never-ending perishing of the weak. I must grind and grind away. I have no choice. And I must know that I grind.

Fool, genius, young lonely woman - I must go round and round in the life within, for how many years the Devil knows. After that my soul must go round and round, for how many centuries the Devil knows.

What a master-mind is that of the Devil! The world is a wondrous scheme. For me it is a scheme that is black with woe. But there may be in the world some one who finds it beautiful Real Life.

I wonder as I write this Portrayal if there will be one person to read it and see a thing that is mingled with every word. It is something that you must feel, that must fascinate you, the like of which you have never before met with.

It is the unparalleled individuality of me.

I wish I might write it in so many words of English. But that is not possible. If I have put it in every word and if you feel it and are fascinated, then I have done very well.

I am marvelously clever if I have done so.

I know that I am marvelously clever. But I have need of all my peculiar genius to show you my individuality - my aloneness.

I am alone out on my sand and barrenness. I should be alone if my sand and barrenness were crowded with a thousand people each filled with melting sympathy for me - though it would be unspeakably sweet.

People say of me, "She's peculiar." They do not understand me. If they did, they would say so oftener and with emphasis.

And so I try to put my individuality in the quality of my diction, in my method of handling words.

My conversation plainly shows this individuality - more than shows it indeed. My conversation hurls it violently at people's heads. My conversation - when I choose - makes people turn around in their chairs and stare and give me all of their attention. They admire me, though their admiration is mixed decidedly with other feelings.

I like to be admired.

It soothes my vanity.

When you read this Portrayal you will admire me. You will surely have to admire me.

And so this is life and everything matters.

But just now I will stop writing and go down-stairs to my dinner. There is a porterhouse steak, broiled rare, and some green onions. Oh, they are good! And when one is to have a porterhouse steak for one's dinner - and some green young onions - one doesn't give a tuppenny damn whether anything else matters or not.

March 19

On a day when the sky is like lead and a dull, tempestuous wilderness of gray clouds adds a dreariness to the sand, there is added to the loneliness of my life a deep bitterness of gall and wormwood.

Out of my bitterness it is easy for bad to come.

Surely Badness is a deep black pool wherein one may drown dullness and Nothingness.

I do not know Badness well. It is something material that seems a great way off now but that might creep nearer and nearer as I became less and less young.

But now when the day is of the leaden dullness I look at Badness and long for it. I am young and all alone, and everything that is good is beyond my reach. But all that is bad - surely that is within the reach of every one.

I wish for a long pageant of bad things to come and whirl and rage through this strange leaden life of mine and break the spell.

Why should it not be Badness instead of Death? Death, it seems, will bring me but a change of agony. Badness would perhaps so crowd my life with its vivid phenomena that they would act as a narcotic to the racked nerves of my Nothingness. It would be an outlet - and possibly I could forget some things.

I think just now of a woman who lived long ago and in whom the world at large seems not to have found anything admirable. I mean Messalina Valeria, the wife of the stupid emperor Claudius. I have conceived a profound admiration for this historic wanton. She may not indeed have had anything to forget; she may not have suffered. But she had the strength of will to take what she wanted, to do as she liked, to live as she chose to live.

It is admirable and beautiful beyond expression to sacrifice and give up and wait for love of that good that gives in itself a just reward. And only next to this is the throwing to the winds of all restraint when the good holds itself aloof and gives nothing. We are weak, contemptible fools who do not grasp the resources within our reach when there is no just reward for our restraint. Why do we not take what we want of the various temptations? It is not that we are virtuous. It is that we are cowards.

And is it worth while to remain true to an ideal that offers only the vaguest hopes of realization? It is not philosophy. When one has made up one's mind that one wants a dish of hot stewed mushrooms, and set one's heart on it, should one scorn a handful of raw evaporated apples, if one were starving, for the sake of the phantom dish of hot stewed mushrooms? Should one say, "Let me starve, but I will never descend to evaporated apples; I will have nothing but a dish of hot stewed mushrooms"? If one is sure one will have stewed mushrooms finally, before one dies of starvation, then very well. One should wait for them and take nothing else.

But it is not in my good peripatetic philosophy to pass by the Badness that the gods provide for the sake of a far-away, always-unrealized ideal, however brilliant, however beautiful, however golden.

When the lead is in the sky and in my life, a vision of Badness looms up on the horizon and looks at me and beckons with a fascinating finger. Then I say to myself: What is the use of this unsullied, struggling soul; this unbesmirched, empty heart; this treasureless, innocent mind; this insipid maid's-body? There are no good things for them. But here, to be sure, are fascinating, glittering bad things - the goods that the gods provide, the compensation of the Devil.

Comes Death, some day, I said - but to die, in the sight of glittering bad things - and I only nineteen! These glittering things appear fair.

There is really nothing evil in the world. Some things appear distorted and unnatural because they have been badly done. Had they been perfect in compensation and execution they would strike one only with admiration at their fine, iridescent lights. You remember Don Juan and Haidee. That to be sure was not evil in any event - they loved each other. But if they had had only a passing, if intense, fancy for one another, who would call it evil? Who would call it anything but wonderful, charming, enchanting? The Devil's bad things - like the Devil's good things - may gleam and glisten, oh, how they may gleam and glisten! I have seen them do so, not only in a poem of Byron's - but in the life that is.

Always when the lead is in the sky I would like to cultivate thoroughly this branch of the vineyard. Now doesn't it make you shiver to think of this dear little Mary MacLane wandering unloved through dark by-ways and deadly labyrinths? It makes me shiver. But it needn't. If I am to wander unloved, why not as well wander there as through Nothingness?

I fancy it must be wonderfully easy to become used to the many-sided Badness. I have lived my nineteen years in the midst of Nothingness, and I have not yet become used to it. It has sharp knives in it, has Nothingness. Badness may have some sharp knives also - but there are other things. Yes, there are other things.

Kind Devil, if you are not to fetch me Happiness, then slip from off your great steel key-ring a bright little key to the door of the glittering, gleaming bad things, and give it me, and show me the way, and wish me joy.

I would like to live about seven years of judicious Badness, and then Death, if you will. Nineteen years of damnable Nothingness, seven years of judicious Badness - and then Death. A noble ambition! But might it not be worse? If not that, then nineteen years of damnable Nothingness, and then Death. No. When the lead is in the sky that does not appeal to me. My versatile mind turns to the seven years of judicious Badness.

There is nothing in the world without its element of Badness. It is in Literature; it is in every art - in pictures - sculpture - even in music. There are certain fine, deep, minute passages in Beethoven and in Chopin that tell of things wonderfully, sublimely bad. Chopin one can not understand. - Is there any one in the world who can understand him? - But we know at once that there is the Badness - and it is music!

There is the element of Badness in me.

I long to cultivate my element of Badness.

Badness compared to Nothingness is beautiful.

And so, then, I wait also for some one to come over the hill with things other than Happiness.

But whatever I wait for, nothing comes.

March 20

There were pictures in the red sunset sky to-day. I looked at them and was racked with passions of desire. I fancied to myself that I could have any of the good things in the pictures for the asking and the waiting. The while I knew that when the sunset should fade from the sky I would be overwhelmed by my heaviest woe.

There was a picture of intense peace. There were stretches of flat, green country, and oak-trees and aspens, and a still, still lake. In the dim distance you could see fields of wheat and timothy-grass that moved a little as if in the wind. You could fancy the cows feeding just below the brow of the near hills, and a hawk floating and wheeling among the clouds. A rainbow arched over the lake. There is nothing lacking here, I thought. "Life and health and peace possessing." Give me this, kind Devil.

There was a picture of endless, limitless strength. There were the oak-trees again but bereft now of every leaf, and the bristling, jagged rocks back of them were not more coldly staunch. The sun poured brilliantly bright upon them. A river flowed unmoved and quiet between yellow clay banks. A tornado might sweep over this and not one twig would be disturbed, not one ripple would come to the river. "Is it not fine!" I said to myself. No feeling, no self-analysis, no aching, no pain - and the strength of the Philistines. Oh, kind Devil, I entreat you, let me have that!

There was a picture of untrammeled revel and forgetfulness. There were fields of swaying daffodils and red lilies. The young shrubs tossed their heads and were joyous. Lambs gamboled and the happy meadow-lark knew whereof she sang.

> *The winds with wonder whist*
> *Smoothly the waters kissed.*

Be carefree, be light-hearted, be wicked, - above all, forget. The deeds are what you will; the time is now; the aftermath is nothing; the day of reckoning is never. Love things lightly, take all that you see, and to the winds with regret! Gracious Devil, I whispered intensely, give me this and no other!

There was a picture of raging elements. "The winds blew, and the rains descended and the floods came." The sky was overcast with rolling clouds. The air was heavy with unrest. There was a gray stone house set upon a rocky point, and I had momentary glimpses of an unquiet sea below it. Back on the surface of the land slender trees were waving wildly in the gale. The wind and the rain were saying, "Damn you, little earth, I have you now, - I will rend and ruin you." They whipped and raged in frenzied joy. The little earth liked it. The elements whirled and whistled round the gray stone house. A lurid light came from a ghastly moon between clouds. The entire scene was desolately savage and forlorn, but attractive. As I listened in fancy to that shrieking wailing wind, and saw green branches jerked and twisted asunder in the storm, my barren, defrauded heart leaped and exulted. If I could live in the midst of this and be beaten and shaken roughly, would not that deep sense forget to ache? Kind Devil, pray send me some storms. It is Nothingness that bears down heavy.

There was a picture of an exalted spiritual life. There was that strange bright Light. And the things in the picture were those things alone in this world that are real, and the only things that count. The old soft green of the old, old rolling hills was the green of love - the earth-love and the love that comes from beyond the earth. The air and the blue water and the sunshine were so beautifully real and true that except for their deep-reaching, passionate tenderness human strength could not endure them. There were lanes of climbing vines and white violets. Was it my fancy that brought their thin fragrance to me over piles of billowy clouds? There was something there that was old - old as the race. Those green valleys were the same as when the mists first lifted from the earth. As I looked my life stood still. My soul shivered faintly. As I looked I felt nearer my God to thee - though I have no God and everything is away from me, nothing tender comes to me.

Still it was nearer my God to thee.

A voice came out of the far, far distant ages and said very gently: "All these shadows are falling in vain. You are blinded and bewildered in the darkness - the darkness is deep - deep. There is not one dim ray of light. Your feet falter and stumble. You can not see. But the shadows are falling in vain."

I ask you, why is this life not mine?

I implore and wring my hands in agonized entreaty, and almost it seems sometimes my fingers can grasp these things - but there is something cold and strong between them and me. Oh, what is it!

There was a picture of various castles in Spain. They were most beautiful, were those castles. The lights that shone on the battlements were soft bright lights. For one thing, I fancied I saw myself and Fame with me. Fame is very fine. The sun and moon and stars may go dark in the heavens. Bitter rain may fall out of the clouds. But never mind. Fame has a sun and moon and gently brilliant stars of her own, and these, shining once, shine always. The green river may run dry in the land. But Fame has a green river that never runs dry. One may wander over the face of the earth. But Fame is herself a refuge. One may be a target for stones and mud. Yes - but Fame stands near with her arm laid across one's shoulders - as no other arm can be laid across one's shoulders. Fame would fill several empty places. Fame would continue to fill them for some years.

Fame, if you please, Devil.

There was a picture of Death. I saw a figure lying in the midst of a desert that was rather like my sand and barrenness. Not far off a wolf sat on his haunches and waited for the end. A buzzard perched near and waited also. They both appeared hungry. It seemed as though the end might come quickly.

Let it come, kind Devil.

And a wolf and a buzzard are better than an undertaker and some worms. Although that doesn't much matter.

And oh, there again was the dearest picture of all - the red, red picture of Happiness for me, Happiness with the sunshine falling on the Heaven-kissing hills! There was I, and I loved and was loved. I - out of loneliness into perfect Happiness! The yellow-gold of the glorious hot sun melted and poured over the earth and over everything that was there. The river ran and rippled and sang the most sweetly glad song that ever river sang. Winged things sparkled in the gold light and flew down the sky.

The wonderful air was over me;
The wonderful wind was shaking the tree.

The silent voices in the air rang out like flutes and clarionets. And the love of the man-Devil for me was everywhere - above me, around me, within me. It would last for a number of beautiful yellow-gold days. I - out of the anguish of loneliness into this!

My heart is filled with desire.

My soul is filled with passion.

My life is a life of longing.

All pictures fade before this picture. They fade completely. When the sun itself faded I gazed over my sand and barrenness with blurred, unseeing eyes and wished only with a heavy, desolate spirit for the coming of the Devil.

March 21

Some people think, absurdly enough, that to be Scotch or descended from the Scottish clans is to be rather strong, rather conservative, firm in faith, and all that. The idea is one that should be completely exploded by this time. I think that the Scotch as a nation are the most difficult of all to characterize. Their traits and tendencies cover a wider field than those of any other. To be Scotch is to be anything. There is no man so narrow as a Scotchman. There is no man so broad as a Scotchman. There is no mind so versatile as a Scotch mind. At the same time only a Scotch mind is capable of clinging with bull-dog tenacity to one idea. A Scotch heart, out of all, and through all, can be as true as death. A Scotch heart - the same one - can be as cunning and treacherous as false human hearts are made. To be English is to have limits; the Germans, the French, the Russians - they have all some inevitable attributes to modify their genius.

But one may be anything - anything, if one is Scotch.

Always I think of the cruel, hardened, ferocious, weather-beaten, kilted Clan MacLean wandering over the bleak winter hills, fighting the powerful MacDonalds and MacGregors - and generally wiping them from the earth, - marching away with merrily shrieking pipes from fields of withered, blood-soaked heather - and all this merely to gather intensified life for me. I feel that the causes of my tragedy began long, long ago from remote germs.

My Scotch blood added to my genius sense has made me into a dangerous chemical compound.

By analyzing I have brought an almost clear portrait of myself up before my mind's eyes.

When I was a child I did not analyze knowingly, but the child was this same genius, though I am one of the kind that changes widely and decidedly in the years. This weary unhappiness is not a matter of development.

When I was a child I felt dumbly what I feel now less dumbly. At the age of five I used sometimes to weep silently in the night - I did not know why. It was that I felt my aloneness, my foreignness to all things. I felt the heavy, heavy weight of life - and I was only five.

I was only five, and it seems a thousand years ago. But sometimes back through the long, winding unused passages of my mind I hear that silent sobbing of the child and the unnamed wailing of a tiny, tired soul.

It mingles with the bitter Nothingness of the grown young woman, and oh, with it all - with it all I am so unhappy!

There is something subtly *Scotch* in all this.

But Scotch or Indian or Japanese, there is no stopping of the pain.

March 22

I fear, do you know, fine world, that you do not yet know me really well - particularly me of the flesh. Me of the peculiar philosophy and the unhappy spirit you know rather well by now, unless you are stupider than I think you are. But you might pass me in the street - you might spend the day with me and never suspect that I am I. Though for the matter of that, even if I had set before you a most graphic and minutely drawn portrait of myself, I am certainly clever enough to act a quite different role if I chose - when you came to spend the day. Still, if the world at large is to know me as I desire it to know me without ever seeing me, I shall have to bring myself into closer personal range with it - and you may rise in your seats and focus your opera glasses, stare with open mouths, stand on your hind-legs and gape - I will myself turn on glaring green and orange lights from the wings.

I believe that it's the trivial little facts about anything that describe it the most effectively. In *Vanity Fair*, when Becky Sharpe was describing young Crawley in a letter to her friend Amelia, she stated that he had hay-colored whiskers and straw-colored hair. And knowing this you feel that you know much more about the Crawley than you would if Miss Sharpe had not mentioned these things. And yet it is but a mere matter of color!

When you think that Dickens was extremely fond of cats you feel at once that nothing could be more fitting. Somehow that marvelously mingled humor and pathos and gentle irony seem to go exceeding well with a fondness for soft, green-eyed purring things. If you had not read the pathetic humor but knew about Dickens and his warm feline friends you might easily expect such things from him.

When you read somewhere that Dr. Johnson is said never to have washed his neck and his ears, and then go and read some of his powerful, original philosophy, you say to yourself, "Yes, I can readily believe that this man never troubled himself to wash his neck and his ears." I, for my part, having read some of the things he has written, can not reconcile myself to the fact that he ever washed any part of his anatomy. I admire Dr. Johnson - though I wash my own neck occasionally.

When you think of Napoleon amusing himself by taking a child on his knee and pinching it to hear it cry, you feel an ecstatic little wave of pleasure at the perfect fitness of things. You think of his hard, brilliant, continuous victories, and you suspect that Napoleon Bonaparte lived but to gratify Napoleon Bonaparte. When you think of the heavy, muscular man smilingly pinching the child, you are quite sure of it. Such a method of amusement for that king among men is so exquisitely appropriate that you wonder why you had not thought of it yourself.

So then yes. I believe strenuously in the efficacy of seemingly trivial facts as portrayers of one's character - one's individual humanness.

Now I will set down for your benefit divers and varied observations relative to me - an interesting one of womankind and nineteen years, and curious and fascinating withal.

Well then.

Nearly every day I make me a plate of hot rich fudge, with brown sugar, - (I should be an entirely different person if I made it with white sugar - and the fudge would not be nearly so good) - and take it up-stairs to my room, with a book or a newspaper. My mind then takes in a part of what is contained in the book or the newspaper, and the stomach of the MacLane takes in all of what is on the plate. I sit by my window in a miserable uncomfortable stiff-backed chair, but I relieve the strain by resting my feet on the edge of the low bureau. Usually the book that I read is an old dilapidated bound volume of that erstwhile periodical *Our Young Folks*. It is a thing that possesses a charm for me. I never grow tired of it. As I eat my nice brown little squares of fudge I read about a boy whose name is Jack Hazard and who, J.T. Trowbridge informs the reader, is doing his best, and who seems to find it somewhat difficult. I believe I could repeat pages of J.T. Trowbridge from memory, and that ancient bound volume has become a part of my life. I stop reading after a few minutes but I continue to eat - and gaze at the toes of my shoes which need polishing badly, or at the conglomeration of brilliant pictures on my bed-room wall, or out of the window at the children playing in the street. But mostly I gaze without seeing, and my versatile mind is engaged either in nothing or in repeating something over and over, such as, "But the sweet face of Lucy Gray will never more be seen." Only I am not aware that I have been repeating it until I happen to remember it afterward. Always the fudge is very good, and I eat and eat with unabated relish until all the little squares are gone. A very little of my fudge has been known to give some people a most terrific stomach-ache - but my own digestive organs seem to like nothing better. It's so brown - so rich!

I amuse myself with this for an hour or two in the afternoon. Then I go down-stairs and work a while. -

There are few things that annoy me so much as to be called a young lady. I am no lady - as any one could see by close inspection, and the phrase has an odious sound. I would rather be called a sweet little thing, or a fallen woman, or a sensible girl - though they would each be equally a lie. -

Always I am glad when night comes and I can sleep. My mind works busily repeating things while I divest myself of my various dusty garments. As I remove a dozen or two of hair-pins from my head I say within me:

> You are old, father William, one would hardly suppose
> That your eye is as steady as ever;
> Yet you balanced an eel on the end of your nose -
> What made you so awfully clever?

Always I take a little clock to bed with me and hang it by a cord at the head of my bed, for company. I have named the clock Little Fido because it is so constant and ticks always. It is beginning to stand in the same relation to me as J.T. Trowbridge's magazine. If I were to go away from here I should take Little Fido and the magazine with me. -

Every morning, being beautifully hungry after my walk, I eat three boiled eggs out of the shell for my breakfast. The while I mentally thank the kind Providence that invented hens. Also I eat bits of toast. I have my breakfast alone - because the rest of the family are still sleeping, - sitting at a corner of the kitchen table. I enjoy those three eggs and those bits of toast. Usually when I am eating my breakfast I am thinking of three things: the varying prices of any eggs that are fit to eat; of what to do after I've finished my house-work and before lunch; and of my one friend. And I meditatively and gently kick the leg of the table with the heel of my right foot. -

I have beautiful hair. -

In the front of my shirt-waist there are nine cambric handkerchiefs cunningly distributed. My figure is very pretty, to be sure, but not so well developed as it will be in five years - if I live so long. And so I help it out materially with nine cambric handkerchiefs. You can see by my picture that my waist curves gracefully out. Only it is not all flesh - some of it is handkerchief. It amuses me to do this. It is one of my petty vanities. -

Likewise by an ingenious arrangement of my striped moreen petticoat I contrive to display a more evident pair of hips than Nature seems to have intended for me at this stage. Doubtless they also will take on fuller proportions when some years have passed. Still I am not dissatisfied with them as they are. It is not as if they were too well developed - in which case I should have need of all my skill in arranging my moreen petticoat so as to lessen their effect. It is easy enough to add on to these things, but one would experience serious difficulty in attempting to take from them. I hate that heavy, aggressive kind of hips. Moreover small graceful ones are desirable when one is nineteen. The world at large judges you more leniently on that account - usually. Narrow shapely hips may give one an effect of youth and harmlessness which is a distinct advantage, when, for instance, one is writing a Portrayal and so will be at the world's mercy. I believe I should not think of attempting to write a Portrayal if I had hips like a pair of saddle-bags. Certainly it would avail me nothing. -

Sometimes I look at my face in a mirror and find it not plain but ugly. And there are other times when I look and find it not pretty but beautiful with a Madonna-like sweetness. -

I told you I might say more about the liver that is within me before I have done. Well then, I will say this: that the world, if it had a liver like mine, would be very different from what it is. The world would be many-colored and mobile and passionate and nervous and high-strung and intensely alive and poetic and romantic and philosophical and egotistic and pathetic, and oh, racked to the verge of madness with the spirit of unrest - if the world had a liver like mine. It is not all of these now. It is rather stupid. Gods and little fishes! would not the world be wonderful if all in it were like me? And it would be if it had a liver like mine. For it is my liver mostly that makes me what I am - apart from my genius. My liver is fine and perfect, but sensitive, and, well - it's a dangerous thing to have within you.

It is the liver of the MacLanes.

It is the foundation of the curious castle of my existence.

And after all, fine brave stupid world, you may be grateful to the Devil that yours is not like it. -

I have seventeen little engraved portraits of Napoleon that I keep in one of my bureau-drawers. Often late in the evening, between nine and ten o'clock, when I come in from a walk over the sand and barrenness, I take these pictures from the drawer and gaze at them carefully a long time and think of that man until I am stirred to the depths.

And then easily and naturally I fall in love with Napoleon.

If only he were living now, I think to myself, I would make my way to him by whatever means and cast myself at his feet. I would entreat him with the most passionate humbleness of spirit to take me into his life for three days. To be the wife of Napoleon for three days - that would be enough for a life-time! I would be much more than satisfied if I could get three such days out of life.

I suppose a man is either a villain or a fool, though some of them seem to be a judicious mingling of both. The type of the distinct villain is preferable to a mixture of the two, and to a plain fool. I like a villain anyway - a villain that can be rather tender at times. And so then as I look at the pictures I fall in love with the incomparable Napoleon. The seventeen pictures are all different and all alike. I fall in love with each picture separately.

In one he is ugly and unattractive - and strong. I fall in love with him.

In another he is cruel and heartless and utterly selfish - and strong. I fall in love with him.

In a third he has a fat, pudgy look, and is quite insignificant - and strong. I fall in love with him.

In a fourth he is grandly sad and full of despair - and strong. I fall in love with him.

In the fifth he is greasy and greedy and common-looking - and strong. I fall in love with him.

In the sixth he is masterly and superior and exalted - and strong. I fall in love with him.

In the seventh he is romantic and beautiful - and strong. I fall in love with him.

In the eighth he is obviously sensual and reeking with uncleanness - and strong. I fall in love with him.

In the ninth he is unearthly and mysterious and unreal - and strong. I fall in love with him.

In the tenth he is black and sullen-browed and ill-humored - and strong. I fall in love with him.

In the eleventh he is inferior and trifling and inane - and strong! I fall in love with him.

In the twelfth he is rough and ruffianly and uncouth - and strong. I fall in love with him.

In the thirteenth he is little and wolfish and vile - and strong. I fall in love with him.

In the fourteenth he is calm and confident and intellectual - and strong. I fall in love with him.

In the fifteenth he is vacillating and fretful and his mouth is like a woman's - and still he is strong. I fall in love with him.

In the sixteenth he is slow and heavy and brutal - and strong. I fall in love with him.

In the seventeenth he is rather tender - and strong. I fall vividly in love with him.

Napoleon was rather like the Devil, I think as I sit in the straight-backed chair with my feet on the bureau and gaze long and intently at the seventeen pictures, late in the evening.

Then I wearily put them away, maddened with the sense of Nothingness, and take Little Fido and go to bed. -

Sometimes early in the evening just before dinner I sit in the stiff-backed chair with my elbows on the window-sill and my head resting on one hand, and I look out of the window at a Pile of Stones and a Barrel of Lime. These are in the vacant lot next to this house.

I fix my eyes intently on the Pile of Stones and the Barrel of Lime. And I fix my thoughts on them also. And some of my widest thoughts come to me then.

I feel an overwhelming wave of a kind of pantheism which, at the moment I feel it, begins to grow less and less and continues in this until finally it dwindles to a Pile of Stones and a Barrel of Lime.

I feel at the moment that the universe is a Pile of Stones and a Barrel of Lime. They alone are the Real Things.

Take anything at any point and deceive yourself into thinking that you are happy with it. But look at it heavily; dig down underneath the layers and layers of rose-colored mists and you will find that your Thing is a Pile of Stones and a Barrel of Lime.

A struggle or two, a fight, an agony, a passing - and then the only Real Things: a Pile of Stones and a Barrel of Lime.

Damn everything, beginning with that fool-God that you have set up for yourself and ending with the Devil. Afterward you will find that you have done all your damning for naught. For there is nothing worthy of damnation except a Pile of Stones and a Barrel of Lime - and they are not damnable. They have never harmed you, and moreover they alone are the Real Things.

Julius Caesar made many wars. Sir Frances Drake went sailing over the seas. It was all child's play and counts for nothing. Here are a Pile of Stones and a Barrel of Lime.

And so this is how it is early in the evening just before dinner, when I sit in the uncomfortable chair with my elbows on the window-sill and my head resting on one hand. -

I have two pictures of Marie Bashkirtseff high upon my wall. Often I lean my head on the back of the chair with my feet on the bureau - always with my feet on the bureau - and look at these pictures.

In one of them she is eighteen years old and wears a green frock which is extremely becoming - of which fact the person inside seems fully aware. The other picture is taken from her last photograph, when she was twenty-four.

Marie Bashkirtseff is a very beautiful creature. And evidently *she* is not obliged to arrange a moreen petticoat over her plumpness. She has a wonderfully voluptuous look for a woman of eighteen years. In the later picture vanity is written in every line of her graceful form and in every feature of that charming face. The picture fairly yells: "I am Marie Bashkirtseff - and, oh, I am splendid!"

And as I look at the pictures I am glad. For though she was admirable and splendid, and all, she was no such genius as I. She had a genius of her own it is true. But the Bashkirtseff, with her voluptuous body and her attractive personality, is after all a bit ordinary. My genius though not powerful is rare and deep and no one has ever had or ever will have a genius like it.

- Mary MacLane, if you live - if you live, my darling, the world will one day recognize your genius. And when once the world has recognized such genius as this - oh, then no one will ever think of profaning it by comparing it with any Bashkirtseff! -

But I would give up this genius eagerly, gladly - at once and forever - for one dear, bright day free from loneliness.

The portraits of the Bashkirtseff are certainly beautiful but there is something about them that is - well, not common, but bourgeois at least, as if she were a German waitress of unusual appearance, or an aristocratic shop-girl, or a nurse with good taste who would walk out on pleasant forenoons wheeling a go-cart - something of that sort. Perhaps it is because her neck is too short, or because her wrists are too muscular-looking. I thank a gracious Devil as I look at the pictures that I have not these particular points and that particular bourgeois air. I am bound to confess that I have one of my own, but mine is Highland Scotch - and anyway, I am Mary MacLane.

Marie Bashkirtseff is beautiful enough, however, that she can easily afford to look rather second-rate.

I like to look at my two pictures of her. -

I value money literally for its own sake. I like the feeling of dollars and quarters rubbing softly together in my hand. Always it reminds me of those lovely chestfuls of gold that Captain Kidd buried - no one seems to know just where. Usually I keep some fairly-clean dollars and quarters to handle. "Money is so nice!" I say to myself. -

If you think, fine world, that I am always interesting and striking and admirable, always original, showing up to good advantage in a company of persons, and all - why then you are beautifully mistaken. There are times to be sure when I can rivet the attention of the crowd heavily upon myself. But mostly I am the very least among all the idiots and fools. I show up to the poorest possible advantage.

Of several ways that are mine there is one that gives me a distinct and hopeless air of insignificance. I have seen people, having met me for the first time, glance carelessly at me as if they were quite sure I had not an idea in my brain - if I had a brain; as if they wondered why I had been asked here; as if they were fully aware that they had but to fiddle and It would dance. Sometimes before this highly intellectual gathering breaks up I manage to make them change their minds with astonishing suddenness. But nearly always I don't bother about it at all. I go among people occasionally because it amuses me. It may be a literary club where they talk theosophy, or it may be a Cornish dance where they have pastry and saffron cake and the chief amusement is sending beer-bottles at various heads, or it may be a lady-like circle of married women with cerise silk drop-skirts and white kid gloves, drinking chocolate in the afternoon and talking about something "shocking!"

And often, as I say, I am the least of them.

Genius is an odd thing. -

When certain of my skirts need sewing, they don't get sewed. I simply pin the rents in them together and it lasts as long or longer than if I had seated myself in my stiff-backed chair with a needle and thread and mended them - like a sensible girl. (I hate a sensible girl.)

Though I have never yet hurriedly pinned up a torn flounce or several inches of skirt-binding without saying softly to myself, using a trite, expressive phrase, "Certainly it's a hell of a way to do." Still I never take a needle and mend my garments. I couldn't anyway. I never learned to sew, and I don't intend ever to learn. It reminds me too much of a constipated dress-maker.

And so I pin up the torn places - though, as I say, I never fail to make use of the quaint, expressive phrase.

All of which a reasonably astute reader will recognize as an important point in the portraying of any character - whether mine or the queen of Spain's. -

I had for my dinner to-day some whole-wheat bread, some liver-and-bacon, and some green, green early asparagus. While I was eating these the world seemed a very nice place indeed. -

I never see people walking along on the opposite side of the street, as I sit by my window, without wondering who they are, and how they live, and how ugly they would look if their bodies were not adorned with clothes. Always I feel certain that some of them are bow-legged. -

And sometimes I see a woman in a fearful state of deshabille walk across the vacant lot next to this: "A plague on me," I say then to myself, "if I ever become middle-aged and if my entire being seems to tip up in the front, and if I go about with no stays so that when I tie an apron around my waist my upper fatness hangs over the band like a natural blouse." -

And so - I could go on writing all night these seemingly trivial but really significant details relating to the outer genius. But these will answer. These to any one who knows things will be a revelation.

Sometimes you know things, fine brave world.

You must know likewise that though I do ordinary things, when *I* do them they cease to be ordinary. I make fudge - and a sweet girl makes fudge, but there are ways and ways of doing things. This entire affair of the fudge is one of my uniquest points.

No sweet girl makes fudge and eats it, as I make fudge and eat it.

So it is.

But oh - who is to understand all this? Who will understand any of this Portrayal? My unhappy soul has delved in shadows far, far beyond and below.

March 23

My philosophy, I find after very little analysis, approaches precariously near to sensualism.

It is wonderful how many sides there can be to just one character.

Nature with all those suns, and all those hill-tops, and all those rivers, and all those stars, is inscrutable - intangible - maddening. It affects one with unutterable joy and anguish, but no one can ever begin to understand what it means.

Human nature is yet more inscrutable - and nothing appears on the surface. One can have no idea of the things buried in the minds of one's acquaintances. And mostly they are fools and have no idea themselves of what germs are in themselves - of what they are capable. And in most minds it is true the dormant devils never awaken and never are known.

It is another sign of my analytical genius, that I, aged nineteen, recognize the devils in my character. I have not the slightest wish, since things are as they are with me, to rid myself of them. There is in me much more of evil than of good. Genius like mine must needs have with it manifold bad. "I have in me the germ of every crime." I have no desire to destroy these germs. I should be glad indeed to have them develop into a ravaging disease. Something in this dreadful confusion would then give way. My wooden heart and my soul would cry out in the darkness less heavily, less bitterly.

They want something - they know not what.

I give them poison.

They snatch it and eat it hungrily.

Then they are not so hungry. They become quieter.

The ravaging disease soothes them to sleep - it descends on them like rain in the autumn. And so.

When I hurry over my sand and barrenness my vivid passions come to me - or when I sit and look at the horizon. When I walk slowly I consider calmly the question of how much evil I should need to kill off my finer feelings, to poison thoroughly this soul of unrest and this wooden heart so that they would never more be conscious of too-brilliant Lights, and to make myself over into a quite different creature.

A little evil would do - a little of a fine, good quality.

I should like a man to come (it is always a man, have you ever noticed? - whatever one contemplates when one is of womankind and young). I should like a man to come, I said calmly to myself to-day as I walked slowly over my barrenness - a perfect villain to come and fascinate me and lead me with strong gentle allurements to what would be technically termed my ruin. And as the world views such things it would be my ruin. But as I view such things it would not be ruin. It would be a new lease on life.

Yes. I should like a man to come - any man so that he is strong and thoroughly a villain, and so that he fascinates me. Particularly he must fascinate me. There must be no falling in love about it. I doubt if I could fascinate him but I should ask him quite humbly to lead me to my ruin.

I have never yet seen the man who would not readily respond to such an appeal.

This villain would be no exception.

I would then jerk my life out of this Nothingness by the roots. Farewell, a long farewell, I would say. Then I would go forth with the man to my ruin. The man would be bad to his heart's core. And after living but a short time with him my shy, sensitive soul would be irretrievably poisoned and polluted. The defilement of so sacred and beautiful a thing as marriage is surely the darkest evil that can come to a life. And so everything within me that had turned toward that too-bright Light would then drink deep of the lees of death.

The thirst of this incessant unrest and longing, this weariness of *self*, would be quenched completely.

My life would be like fertile soil planted thickly with rank wild mustard. On every square inch of soil there would be a dozen sprouts of wild mustard. There would be no room - no room at all - for an anemone to grow. If one should start up, instantly it would be choked and overrun with wild mustard.

- But no anemone would start up. -

My life now is a life of pain and revolt.

My life darkened and partly killed would be more than content to drift along with the current.

Oh, it would be a rest!

The Christians sing, there is rest for the weary, on the other side of Jordan, where the tree of life is blooming. But that rest of course is for the Christians. My rest will have to come on this side of Jordan. Let the impress of a thoroughly evil and strong man be stamped upon my inner life and I am convinced there would come a wonderful settled quiet over it. Its spirit would be broken. It would rest. Why not? I have no virtue-sense. Nothing to me is of any consequence except to be rid of this unrest and pain. Yes, surely I might rest.

The coming of the man-Devil would bring rest. But am I fool enough to think that marriage - the real marriage - is possible for me?

This other thing is within the reach of every one - of fools and geniuses alike - and of all that come between.

And so I want a fascinating wicked man to come and make me positively, rather than negatively, wicked. I feel a terrific wave of utter weariness. My life lies fallow. I am tired of sitting here. The sand and barrenness is gray with age. And I am gray with age.

Happiness - the red of the sunset sky - is the intensest desire of my life.

But I will grasp eagerly anything else that is offered me - *anything*.

The poisoning of my soul - the passing of my unrest - would rouse my mental power. My genius would receive a wonderful impetus from it. You would marvel, good world, at the things I should write. Not that they would be exalted - not that they would surge upward. Do men gather grapes of thorns or figs of thistles? But they would be marvels of fire and intensity. I should no longer exhaust much of my energy in grinding, grinding within. The things that would come of the thorns and thistles would excite your astonishment and admiration, though they be not grapes and figs.

And as for me - the real me - the creature imbued with a spirit of intense femininity, with a spirit of an intense sense of Love - with a spirit like that of the Magdalene who loved too much, with the very soul of unrest and Nothingness - this thing would vanish swiftly into oblivion, and I, a despoiled animal, should go down a dark world and feel not.

March 25

One of the remarkable points about my life is that it is so completely, hopelessly alone - a lonely, lonely life. This book of mine contains but one character - myself.

There is also the Devil - as a possibility.

And there is also the anemone lady - my dearest beloved - as a memory.

I have read books that were written to portray but one character and there were various people brought in to help in the portraying. But my one friend is gone, and there is no person who enters into my inner life in the very least. I am always alone. I might mingle with people intimately every hour of my life - still I should be alone.

Always alone - alone.

Not even a God to worship.

How do I bear this! How do I get through the days and days!

And oh, when it all comes over me, what frightful rage - what long agony of my breaking heart - what utter woe!

When the stars shine down upon me with cold hatred; when miles and miles of barrenness stretch out around me and envelop me in its weary, weary Nothingness; when the wind blows over me like the breath of a vicious giant; when the ugly, ugly sun radiates centuries of hard, heavy bitterness around me from its stinging rays; when the sky maddens me with its cold careless blue; when the rivers that are flowing over the earth send echoes to me of their hateful voices; when I hear wild geese honking in bitter wailing melody; when bristling edges of jagged rocks cut sharply into my tired life; when drops of rain fall on me and pierce me like steel points; when the voices in the air shriek little-minded malice in my ears; when the green of Nature is the green of spitefulness and cruelty; when the red, red of the setting sun burns and consumes me with its horrid feverish effervescence; when I feel the all-hatred of the Universe for its poor little earth-bugs: then it is that I approach nearest to Rest.

The softnesses are my Unrest.

I do not want those bitter things.

But I must have them if I would rest.

I want the softnesses and I want Rest!

Oh, dear faint soul, it is hard - hard for us.

We are sick with loneliness.

Now and again I have torturing glimpses of a Paradise. And I feel my soul in its pain every moment of my life. Otherwise, how gladly would I deny the existence of a soul and a life to come!

For my soul is beset with Nothingness, and the Paradise that shows itself is not for me.

Hatred, after all, is the easiest thing of all to bear.

If you have been forgotten by the one who must have made you, and if you have been left alone of human beings all your life - all your nine-teen years, - then, when at last you see some one looking toward you with beautiful eyes, and extending to you a beautiful hand, and showing you a beautiful heart wherein is just a little of beautiful sympathy for you - for you - oh, that is harder than anything to bear. Harder than the loneliness and the bitterness - and the tears are nearer and nearer.

But one would be hurt often, often for the sake of the beautiful things. Yes, one would gladly be hurt long and often.

I shall never forget how it was with me when I first saw the beautiful eyes of the dearest anemone lady when they were looking gently - at me, - and the beautiful hand, and the beautiful heart. The awakening of my racked soul is hardly more heavily laden with passion and pain. I shall never forget.

Though I feel away from her also, she is the only one out of all to look gently at me.

- Let me writhe and falter with pain; let me go mad - but oh, worldful of people - for the love of your God - give me out of this seething darkness only one beautiful human hand to touch mine with *love*, one beautiful human heart to know the aching sad loneliness of mine, one beautiful human soul to mingle with mine in long, long Rest. -

Oh, for a human being, my soul wails - a human being to love me!

Oh, to know - just once - what it is to be loved!

Nineteen years without one faint shadow of love is mouldy, crumbling age - is gray with the dust of centuries.

How long have I lived!

How long must I live!

I am shrieking at you, cold stupid world.

Oh, the long, long waiting -

The millions of human beings -

I am a human being and there is no one - no one - no one.

Who can know this that has not felt it? You do not know - you can not know.

Surely I do not ask too much. But whether or not it is too much I can not go through the years without it - oh, I can not!

You have lived your nineteen years, fine world, and you have lived through some after years.

But in your nineteen years there was some one to love you.

It is that that counts.

Since you have had that some one, in your nineteen years, can you understand what life is to me - me - in my loneliness?

My wailing, waiting soul burns with but one desire: *to be loved - oh, to be loved*.

March 29

I am making the world my confessor in this Portrayal. My mind is fairly bursting with egotism and pain and in writing this I find a merciful outlet. I have become fond of my Portrayal. Often I lay my forehead and my lips caressingly upon the pages.

And I wish to let you know that there is in existence a genius - an unhappy genius, a genius starving in Montana in the barrenness - but still a genius. I am a creature the like of which you have never before happened upon. You have never suspected that there is such a person. I know that there is not such another. As I said in the beginning, the world contains not my parallel.

I am a fantasy - an absurdity - a genius!

Had I been one of the beasts that perish I had been likewise a fantasy. I think I should have been a small animal composite of a pig, a leopard, and a skunk: an animal that I fancy would be uncanny to look upon but admirable for a pet.

However I am not one of the beasts that perish.

I am human.

That is another remarkable point.

I have heard persons say they can hardly believe I am quite human.

I am the most human creature that ever was placed on the earth. The geniuses are always more human than the herd. Almost a perfection of humanness is reached in me. This by itself makes me extraordinary. The rarest thing in the world, I find, is the quality of humanness.

Humanity and humaneness are much less rare.

"It is a brave thing to understand something of what we see." Indeed it is. An exceeding brave thing. The one who said that had surely gone out on the highways and byways and found how little he could understand.

To understand oneself is not so brave a thing. To go in among the hidden gray shadows of the deep things is a fool's errand. It is not from choice that I do it. No one carries a mill-stone around her neck from choice. When I see what is among the hidden gray shadows - when I see a vision of *Myself* - I am seized with a strange sick terror.

A fool's errand - but one on which I must need go.

- And for that matter I myself am a fool. -

Yet to know oneself well is a rare fine art.

I analyze myself now. I analyzed myself when I was three years old.

The only difference is that at the age of three I was not aware that I analyzed. - It is true, that is a great difference. - Now I know that I am analyzing at nineteen, and now I know that I analyzed at three.

And at the age of nineteen I know that I am a genius.

A genius who does not know that he is a genius is no genius. A drunken man might stagger up to a piano and accidentally play music that vibrates to the soul - that touches upon the mysteries. But he does not know his power and he is no genius though men awaken and go mad therefrom.

I know I am a genius more than any genius that has lived.

I have a feeling that the world will never know this.

And as I think of it I wonder if angels are not weeping somewhere because of it.

March 31

> *She only said: "My life is dreary,*
> *He cometh not," she said;*
> *She said, "I am weary, aweary.*
> *I would that I were dead."*

All day long this heart-sickening song of Mariana has been reeling and swimming in my brain. I awoke with it early in the morning and it is still with me now in the lateness. I wondered at times during the day why that very gentle and devilishly persistent refrain did not drive me insane or send me into convulsions. I tried vainly to fix my mind on a book. I began reading *The Mill on the Floss*, but that weird poem was not to be foiled. It bewitched my brain. Now as I write I hear twenty voices chanting it in a sad minor key - twenty voices that fill my brain with sound to the bursting point. "He cometh not - he cometh not - he cometh not." "That I were dead" - "I am aweary, aweary," - "that I were dead - that I were dead." "He cometh not - that I were dead."

It is maddening in that it is set sublimely to the music of my own life.

Now that I have written it I can hope that it may leave me. If it follows me through the night and if I awake to another day of it the cords of my overworked mind will surely break.

But let me thank the kind Devil.

It is leaving me now!

It is as if tons were lifted from my brain.

How can any one bring a child into the world and not wrap it round with a certain wondrous tenderness that will stay with it always!

- There are persons whose souls have never entered into them. -

My mother has some fondness for me - for my body because it came of hers. That is nothing - nothing.

A hen loves its egg.

A hen!

This evening in the slow-deepening dusk I sat by my window and spent an hour in passionate conversation with the Devil. I fancied I sat, with my hands folded and my feet crossed, on an ugly but comfortable red velvet sofa in some nondescript room.

And the fascinating man-Devil was seated near in a frail willow chair.

He had willingly come to pass the time of day with me. He was in a good-humored mood and I amused and interested him. And for myself, I was extremely glad to see the Devil sitting there and felt vividly as always. But I sat quietly enough.

The fascinating man-Devil has fascinating steel-gray eyes, and they looked at me with every variety of glance - from quizzical to tender.

- It were easy - oh, how easy - to follow those eyes to the earth's ends. -

The Devil leaned back in the frail willow chair and looked at me.

"And now that I am here, Mary MacLane," he said, "what would you?"

"I want you to marry me," I replied at once. "And I want it more than ever anything was wanted since the world began."

"So? I am flattered," said the Devil, and smiled gently, enchantingly.

At that smile I was ravished and transported and a spasm of some rare emotion thrilled all the little nerves in me from my heels to my forehead. And yet the smile was not for me but rather somewhat at my expense.

"But," he went on, "you must know it is not my custom to marry the women."

"I am sure it is not," I agreed, "and I do not ask to be peculiarly favored. Anything that you may give me, however little, will constitute marriage for me."

"And would marriage itself be so small a thing?" asked the Devil.

"Marriage," I said, "would be a great, oh, a wonderful thing, the most beautiful of all. I want what is good according to my lights, and because I am a genius my lights are many and far-reaching."

"What do your lights tell you?" the man-Devil inquired.

"They tell me this: that nothing in the world matters unless love is with it, and if love is with it and it seems to the virtuous a barren and infamous thing, still - because of the love - it partakes of the very highest."

"And have you the courage of your convictions?" he said.

"If you offered me," I replied, "that which to the blindly virtuous seems the worst possible thing, it would yet be for me the red, red line on the sky, my heart's desire, my life, my rest. You are the Devil. I have fallen in love with you."

"I believe you have," said the Devil. "And how does it feel to be in love?"

Sitting composedly on the ugly red velvet sofa, with my hands folded and my feet crossed, I attempted to define that wonderful feeling.

"It feels," I said, "as if sparks of fire and ice crystals ran riot in my veins with my blood; as if a thousand pin-points pierced my flesh, and every other point a point of pleasure, and every other point a point of pain; as if my heart were laid to rest in a bed of velvet and cotton-wool but kept awake by sweet violin arias; as if milk and honey and the blossoms of the cherry flowed into my stomach and then vanished utterly; as if strange beautiful worlds lay spread out before my eyes, alternately in dazzling light and complete darkness with chaotic rapidity; as if orris-root were sprinkled in the folds of my brain; as if sprigs of dripping wet sweet-fern were stuck inside my hot linen collar; as if - well, you know," I ended suddenly.

"Very good," said the Devil. "You are in love. And you say you are in love with me."

"Oh, with you!" I exclaimed with suppressed violence. The effort to suppress this violence cost me pounds of nerve-power. But I kept my hands still quietly folded and my feet crossed, and it was a triumph of self-control. "I want you to marry me," I added despairingly.

"And you think," he inquired, "that apart from the opinion of the wise world, it would be a suitable marriage?"

"A suitable marriage!" I exclaimed. "I hate a suitable marriage! No, it would not be suitable. It would be Bohemian, outlandish, adorable!"

The Devil smiled.

This time the smile was for me. And oh, the long, old overpowering enchantment of the smile of steel-gray eyes! - the steel-gray eyes of the Devil!

It is one of those things that one remembers.

"You are a beautifully frank little feminine creature," he said. "Frankness is in these days a lost art."

"Yes, I am beautifully frank," I replied. "Out of countless millions of the Devil's anointed I am one to acknowledge myself."

"But withal you are not true," said the man-Devil.

"I am a liar," I answered.

"You are a liar, surely," he said, "but you stay with your lies. To stay with anything is Truth."

"It is so," I replied. "Nevertheless I am as false as woman can be."

"But you know what you want."

"Oh, yes," I said, "I know what I want. I want you to marry me."

"And why?"

"Because I love you."

"That seems an excellent reason, certainly," said the Devil.

"I want to be happy for once in my life," I said. "I have never been happy. And if I could be happy once for one gold day I should be satisfied, and I should have that to remember in the long years."

"And you are a strangely pathetic little animal," said the Devil.

"I am pathetic," I said. I clasped my hands very tightly. "I know that I am pathetic: and for this reason I am the most terribly pathetic of all in the world."

"Poor little Mary MacLane," said the Devil. He leaned toward me. He looked at me with those strange, wonderfully tender, divine steel-gray eyes. "Poor little Mary MacLane," he said again in a voice that was like the Gray Dawn. And the eyes - the glance of the steel-gray eyes entered into me and thrilled me through and through. It frightened and soothed me. It racked and comforted me. It ravished me with inconceivable gentleness so that I bent my head down and sobbed as I breathed.

"Don't you know, you little thing," said the man-Devil, softly-compassionate, "your life will be very hard for you always - harder when you are happy than when you go in Nothingness?"

"I know - I know. Nevertheless I want to be happy," I sobbed. I felt a rush of an old thick heavy anguish. "It is day after day. It is week after week. It is month after month. It is year after year. It is only time going and going. There is no joy. There is no lightness of heart. It is only the passing of days. I am young and all alone. Always I have been alone: when I was five and lay in the damp grass and tortured myself to keep back tears; and through the long cold lonely years till now - and now all the torture does not keep back the tears. There is no one - nothing - to help me bear it. It is more than pathetic when one is nineteen in all young new feeling and sees Nothing anywhere - except long dark lonely years behind her and before her. - No one that loves me and long, long years. -"

I stopped. The gray eyes were fixed on me. Oh, they were the steel-gray eyes! - and they had a look in them. The long bitter pageant of my Nothingness mingled with this look and the coming together of these was like the joining of two halves.

I do not know which brings me the deeper pain - the loneliness and weariness of my sand and barrenness, or the look in the steel-gray eyes. But as always I would gladly leave all and follow the eyes to the world's ends. They are like the sun's setting. And they are like the pale beautiful stars. And they are like the shadows of earth and sky that come together in the dark.

"Why," asked the Devil, "are you in love with me?"

"You know so much - so much," I answered. "I think it must be that. The wisdom of the spheres is in your brain. And so then you must understand me. Because no one understands all these smouldering feelings my greatest agony is. You must need know the very finest of them. - And your eyes! Oh, it's no matter why I'm in love with you. It's enough that I am. And if you married me I would make you happier than you are."

"I am not happy at all," said the man-Devil. "I am merely contented."

"Contentment," I said, "in place of Happiness, is a horrid feeling. Not one of your countless advocates loves you. They serve you faithfully and well, but with it all they hate you. Always people hate their tyrant. You are my tyrant but I love you absorbingly, madly. Happiness for me would be to live with you and see you made happy by the overwhelming flood of my love."

"It interests me," he said. "You are a most interesting feminine philosopher - and your philosophy is after my own heart, in its lack of *virtue*. It is to be hoped that you are not 'intellectual,' which is an unpardonable trait."

"Indeed I am not," I replied. "Intellectual people are detestable. They have pale faces and bad stomachs and bad livers, and if they are women their corsets are sure to be too tight, and probably black, and if they are men they are *soft*, which is worse. And they never by any chance know what it means to walk all day in the rain, or to roll around on the ground in the dirt. And above all, they never fall in love with the Devil."

"They are tiresome," the Devil agreed. "If I were to marry you how long would you be happy?"

"For three days."

"You are wise," he said. "You are wonderfully wise in some things though you are still very young."

"I am wise," I answered. "Being of womankind and nineteen years I am more than ready to give up absolutely everything that is good in the world's sight, though they are contemptible things enough in my own, for love. All for love. Therefore I am wise. Also I am a fool."

"Why are you a fool?"

"Because I am a genius."

"Your logic is good logic," said the Devil.

"My logic - oh, I don't care anything about logic," I said with sudden complete weariness. I felt buried and wrapped round and round in weariness. Everything lost its color. Everything turned cold.

"At this moment," said the Devil, "you feel as if you cared for nothing at all. But if I chose I could bring about a transfiguration. I could kiss your soul into Paradise."

I answered "Yes," without emotion.

"An hour," said the Devil, "is not very long. But we know it is long enough to suffer in, and go mad in, and live in, and be happy in. And the world contains a great many hours. Now I am leaving you. It is likely that I may never come again, and it is likely that I may come again."

It all vanished. I still sat by my window in the gloom. "It is dreary," I said.

But yes. The world contains a great many hours.

April 4

I have asked for bread, sometimes, and I have been given a stone.

Oh, it is a bitter thing - oh, it is piteous, piteous!

I find that I am not far apart from human beings. I can still be crushed, wounded, stunned - by the attitude of human beings.

To-day I looked for human-kindness, and I was given coldness. I repelled human beings.

I asked for bread and I was given a stone.

Oh, it is bitter - bitter.

Oh, is there a thing in the wide world more bitter?

God, where are you! I am crushed, wounded, stunned - and oh, - I am alone!

April 10

I have a sense of humor that partakes of the divine in life - for there are things even in this chaotic irony that are divine. My genius is not divine. My pathet-icness is not divine. My philosophy is not divine, nor my originality, nor my audacity of thought. These are peculiarly of the earth. But my sense of humor -

It is humor that is far too deep to admit of laughter. It is humor that makes my heart melt with a high, unequaled sense of pleasure and ripple down through my body like old yellow wine.

A rare tone in a person's voice, a densely wrathful expression in a pair of slate-colored eyes, a fine, fine shade of comparison and contrast between a word in a conversation and an angle-worm pattern in a calico dressing-jacket - these are the things that make me conscious of divine emotion.

One day last summer an Italian peddler-woman stopped at the back door and rested herself. I stood in the doorway and the peddler-woman and I talked. She had a dirty white handkerchief tied over her head - as all Italian peddler-women do - and she had a telescope valise filled with garters, and hair-pins, and soap, and combs, and pencils, and china buttons on blue cards, and bean-shooters, and tacks, and dream-books, and mouth-organs, and green glass beads, and jew's-harps. - There is something fascinating about a peddler-woman's telescope valise. - This peddler-woman wore a black satine wrapper and an ancient cape. She said that she would like to stop and rest a while, and I told her she might. I had always wanted to talk to a peddler-woman, and my mother never would allow one in the house.

"Is it nice to be a peddler?" I asked her.

"It ain't bad," replied the peddler-woman.

"Do you make a great deal of money?" I next inquired.

"Sometime I do, and sometime I don't," said the woman. She spoke with an accent that, while it sounded Italian, still showed unmistakably that she had lived in Butte.

"Well, do you make just enough to live on, or have you saved some money?" I asked.

"I got four hundred dollar in the bank," she replied. "I been peddlin' eight year."

"Eight years of tramping around in all kinds of weather," I said. "Your philosophy must be peripatetic, too. Haven't you ever had rheumatism in your knees?"

"I got rheumatism in every joint in my body," said the woman. "I have to lay off, sometime."

"Have you a husband?" I wished to know.

"I had a man - oh, yes," said the peddler-woman.

"And where is he?"

"Back home - in Italy."

"Why doesn't he come out here and work for you?" I asked.

"Yes, w'y don't he?" said the woman. "Dat-a man, he's dem lucky w'en he can git enough to eat - he is."

"Why don't you send him some money to pay his way out, since you've saved so much?" I inquired.

"Holy God!" said the peddler-woman. "I work hard for dat-a money. I save ev'ry cent. I ain't go'n now to t'row it away - I ain't. Dat-a man, he's all right w'ere he is - he is."

"What did you marry him for?" I asked.

The peddler-woman looked at me with that look which seems to convey the information that curiosity once killed a cat.

"What for?" I persisted - "for love?"

"I marry him w'en I was young girl. And he was young, too."

"Yes - but what did you do it for? Was he awfully nice, and did he say awfully sweet things to you?"

"He was dem sweet - oh, yes," said the peddler-woman. She grinned. "And I was young."

"And you liked it when you were young and he was sweet, didn't you?"

"Yes, I guess so. I was young," she answered.

The fact that one is young seems to imply - in the Italian peddler mind - a lacking in some essential points.

"And don't you like your man now?" I asked.

"Dat-a man, he's all right, in Italy - he is," replied the woman.

"Well," I observed, "if I had a man who had been dem sweet once, when I had been young, but who was not sweet any more, I think I should leave him in Italy, too."

"You'll git a man some day soon," said the peddler-woman.

I was interested to know that.

"They all do - oh, yes," she said. "But you likely to be better off peddlin', I tell you."

"Yes, I think it would be amusing to be a peddler for a while," I said. "But I should want the man, too, as long as he was dem sweet."

The peddler-woman picked up the telescope valise.

"Yes," she remarked, "a man, he's sweet two days, t'ree days, then - holy God! he never work, he git-a drunk, he make-a rough house, he raise hell."

The peddler-woman nodded at me and limped out of the yard. The telescope valise was heavy. When she walked every muscle in her body seemed pressed into the service. She had a heavy solid look. She seemed as though she might weigh three hundred pounds though she was not large. The afternoon sun shone down brightly on her dirty white handkerchief, on her brown comely face, on her brown brass-ringed hands, on her black satine wrapper, on her ancient cape.

As I watched her walk out of sight I thought to myself: "Two days, t'ree days, then - holy God! he never work, he git-a drunk, he make-a rough house, he raise hell."

I was conscious of an intense humor that was so far beyond laughter that it was too deep even for tears. But I felt tears vaguely as I watched the peddler-woman limping up the road.

It was not pathos. It was humor - humor. My emotion was one of vivid pleasure - pleasure at the sight of the woman, and at the telescope valise, and at her conversation supplemented by my own.

This emotion is divine and I can not grasp it.

As I looked after the Italian peddler-woman it came to me with sudden force that the earth is only the earth, but that it is touched here and there brilliantly with divine fingers.

Long and often as I've sat in intense silent passion and gazed at the red, red sunset sky I have never felt this sense of the divine.

It comes only through humor.

It comes only with things like an Italian peddler-woman in a black satine wrapper and an ancient cape.

My soul - how heavily it goes.

Life is a journeying up a spring-time hill. And at the top we wonder why we are there. Have mercy on me, I implore in a dull idea that the journey is so long - so long, and a human being is less than an atom.

The solid heavy figure of an Italian peddler-woman with a telescope valise, limping away in the afternoon sunshine, is more convincing of the Things that Are than would be the sound of the wailing of legions of lost souls, could it be heard.

- For the world must be amused. -

And the world's wind bloweth as it listeth.

April 11

I write a great many letters to the dear anemone lady. I send some of them to her and others I keep to read myself. I like to read letters that I have written - particularly that I have written to her.

This is a letter that I wrote two days ago to my one friend:

To you: -

And don't you know, my dearest, my friendship with you contains other things. It contains infatuation, and worship, and bewitchment, and idolatry, and a tiny altar in my soul-chamber whereon is burning sweet incense in a little dish of blue and gold.

Yes, all of these.

My life is made up of many outpourings. All the outpourings have one point of coming-together. You are the point of coming-together. There is no other.

You are the anemone lady.

You are the one whom I may love.

To think that the world contains one beautiful human being for me to love! It is wonderful.

My life is longing for the sight of you. My senses are aching for lack of an anemone to diffuse itself among them.

A year ago when you were in the High School often I used to go over there when you would be going home, so that my life could be made momentarily replete by the sight of you. You didn't know I was there - only a few times when I spoke to you.

And now it is that I remember you.

Oh, my dearest, - you are the only one in the world!

We are two women. You do not love me, but I love you -

You have been wonderfully-beautifully kind to me.

You are the only one who has ever been kind to me.

There is something delirious in this - something of the nameless quantity.

It is old grief and woe to live nineteen years and to remember no person ever to have been kind. But what is it - do you think? - at the end of nineteen years, to come at last upon one who is wonderfully-beautifully kind!

Those persons who have had some one always to be kind to them can never remotely imagine how this feels.

Sometimes in these spring days when I walk miles down into the country to the little wet gulch of the sweet-flags, I wonder why it is that this thing does not make me happy. "She is wonderfully-beautifully kind," I say to myself - "and she is the anemone lady. She is *wondrously* kind and though she's gone, nothing can ever change that."

But I am not happy.

Oh, my one friend - what is the matter with me? What is this feeling? Why am I not happy?

But how can you know?

You are beautiful.

I am a small vile creature.

Always I awake to this fact when I think of the anemone lady.

I am not good.

But you are kind to me - you are kind to me - you are kind to me.

You have written me two letters.

The anemone lady came down from her high places and wrote me two letters.

It is said that God is somewhere. It may be so.

But God has never come down from his high places to write me two letters. Dear, - do you see, you are the only one in the world.

Mary MacLane

April 12

Oh, the dreariness, the Nothingness!

Day after day - week after week, - it is dull and gray and weary. It is *dull*, DULL, DULL!

No one loves me the least in the world.

"My life is dreary - he cometh not."

I am unhappy - unhappy.

It rains. The blue sky is weeping. But it is not weeping because I am unhappy.

I hate the blue sky, and the rain, and the wet ground, and everything. This morning I walked far away over the sand and these things made me think they loved me - and that I loved them. But they fooled me. Everything fools me. I am a fool.

No one loves me. There are people here. But no one loves me - no one understands - no one cares.

It is I and the barrenness. It is I - young and all alone.

Pitiful Heaven! - but no, heaven is not pitiful.

Heaven also has fooled me, more than once.

There is something for every one that I have ever known - some tender thing. But what is there for me? What have I to remember out of the long years?

The blue sky is weeping, but not for me. The rain is persistent and heavy as damnation. It falls on my mind and maddens my mind. It falls on my soul and hurts my soul. - Everything hurts my soul. - It falls on my heart and it warps the wood in my heart.

Of womankind and nineteen years, a philosopher of the peripatetic school, a thief, a genius, a liar, and a fool - and unhappy, and filled with anguish and hopeless despair. What is my life? Oh, what is there for me!

There has always been Nothing. There will always be Nothing.

There was a miserable, damnable, wretched lonely childhood. Itself has passed, but the pain of it has not passed. The pain of it is with me and is added to the pain of now. It is pain that never lets itself be forgotten. The pain of the childhood was the pain of Nothing. The pain of now is the pain of Nothing. Oh, the pathetic burlesque-tragedy of Nothing!

It is burlesque but it is none the less tragedy. It is tragedy that eats its way inward.

It is only I and the sand and barrenness.

I have never a tender thing in my life. The sand and barrenness has never a grass-blade.

I want a human being to love me. I have need of it. I am starving to death for lack of it.

Bitterest salt tears surge upward - sobs are shaking themselves out from the depths. Oh, the salt is bitter. I might lay me down and weep all day and all night - and the salt would grow more bitter and more bitter.

But life in its Nothingness is more bitter still.

It is burlesque-tragedy that is the most tragic of all.

It is an inward dying that never ends. It is the bitterness of death added to the bitterness of life.

What hell is there like that of one weak little human being placed on the earth - and left *alone*?

There are people who live and enjoy. But my soul and I - we find life too bitter, and too heavy to carry alone. Too bitter, and too heavy.

Oh, that I and my soul might perish at this moment, forever!

April 13

I am sitting writing out on my sand and barrenness. The sky is pale and faded now in the west, but a few minutes ago there was the same old-time always-new miracle of roses and gold, and glints and gleams of silver and green, and a river in vermilions and purples - and lastly the dear, the beautiful: the red, red line.

There also are heavy black shadows.

I have given my heart into the keeping of this.

And still as always I look at it - and feel it all with thrilling passion - and await the Devil's coming.

*

L'Envoi

October 28, 1901

And so there you have my Portrayal. It is the record of three months of Nothingness. Those three months are very like the three months that preceded them, to be sure, and the three that followed them - and like all the months that have come and gone with me, since time was. There is never anything different; nothing ever happens.

Now I will send my Portrayal into the wise wide world. It may stop short at the publisher; or it may fall still-born from the press; or it may go farther indeed and be its own undoing.

That's as may be.

I will send it.

What else is there for me, if not this book?

And, oh, that some one may understand it!

- I am not good. I am not virtuous. I am not sympathetic. I am not generous. I am merely and above all a creature of intense passionate *feeling*. I feel - everything. It is my genius. It burns me like fire. -

My portrayal in its analysis and egotism and bitterness will surely be of interest to some. Whether to that one alone who may understand it; or to some who have themselves been left alone; or to those three whom I, on three dreary days, asked for bread, and who each gave me a stone - and whom I do not forgive (for that is the bitterest thing of all): it may be to all of these.

But none of them, nor any one, can know the feeling made of relief and pain and despair that comes over me at the thought of sending all this to the wise wide world. It is bits of my wooden heart broken off and given away. It is strings of amber beads taken from the fair neck of my soul. It is shining little gold coins from out of my mind's red leather purse. It is my little old life-tragedy.

It means everything to me.

Do you see, it means *everything* to me.

It will amuse you. It will arouse your interest. It will stir your curiosity. Some sorts of persons will find it ridiculous. It will puzzle you.

But am I to suppose that it will also awaken compassion in cool indifferent hearts? And will the sand and barrenness look so unspeakably gray and dreary to coldly critical eyes as mine? And shall my bitter little story fall easily and comfortably upon undisturbed ears, and linger for an hour, and be forgotten?

Will the wise wide world itself give me in my outstretched hand a stone -

*

"THE REAL MARY MACLANE"

FEATURE ARTICLES

"The Real Mary MacLane"

by Zona Gale · *New York World* · 17 August 1902

Mary MacLane, of Butte, Montana, wrote the story of herself and committed it to the "wise, wide world." She told everything she knew about herself, and everything she thought and felt - but not everything she is.

For last week, as I sat with her for three hours at the home of Miss Corbin, her "Anemone Lady," in Cambridge, and as we two lunched together next day, I believe I saw her as she is, and I believe I know the real Mary MacLane. And so this is the story of Mary MacLane, which her book does not tell.

Inasmuch as I did not go to Cambridge to pass judgment on Mary Mac-Lane, or to find out whether she poses or whether she is a genius, or whether she is good, or she loves her mother, or steals - or indeed whether any of her book is really herself - I shall not say what I thought about any of these things.

I will simply tell what she did and said in the time we were together, prefaced by two statements which ought to be taken into consideration at every step.

First: she is exceedingly pretty - far prettier than her pictures.

Second: nobody can repeat what she says verbatim and at the same time be perfectly fair to her. For her manner and her voice and her pretty ripply laugh are extra-illustrations not to be reproduced.

When I heard her steps on the stair at the home of the "Anemone Lady," they came tapping out a little refrain, the burden of her portrayal of herself: "I am not good," they said, singing from her book; "I am not virtuous; I am not generous. I am awaiting the coming of the Devil and I know that he usually comes. I am a genius."

"And, oh dear," I thought, "you are not pretty. For only otherwise unattractive people give out that they are not good."

She came in and took my hand in her own warm and firm and rather large hand. She sat down in a big leather chair and waited for me to begin. The little refrain her tan boots had tapped out died in my head as I looked at her.

*

Mary MacLane, alert for the coming of the Devil, looks like a Madonna, and a pot of sweet lavender and a fall of old lace. Mary MacLane is not little. She is tall - 5 feet and 6 inches, really - and she has a pretty figure and a well-set head.

Her hair, which is her chief glory, is all ripples and brown shadows, and in tendrils about her face.

Her eyes are blue and direct and old and sad. Her chin is round and petulant and faintly dimpled like a child's.

Her mouth is nearly perfect.

Her nose is straight and delicate, and all her features are small.

She looks both child and woman. She has a ready, merry little laugh, like a child's, and a frequent, only partly-suppressed yawn, like a child's, and a quick nod of understanding that is some way childlike, too.

Her eyes alone are old, and "her eyelids are a little weary." Yet, curiously enough, her sudden far-away look, the droop of her mouth sometimes, and even her direct gaze, are more childish tiredness than ennui.

*

When she makes the most *outre* statements you feel a quick impulse to have her learn her lesson better; but the next minute she may be teaching you.

She was wearing a little pale-blue muslin frock, flowery and trailing, with something dainty and tucked and white for a yoke, and little clusters of baby-blue ribbons. She looked like a Dresden shepherdess, or like Phyllis at a spinning-wheel, and far, far less wise than either ingenue or debutante.

Yet for that matter she herself had written: "None of my acquaintances would suspect I am a thief. I look so respectable, so refined, so 'nice,' so inoffensive, so sweet, even!"

And yet she had also written: "The world is like a little marsh filled with mint and white hawthorn."

At all events, I decided she should have the benefit of the mint and white hawthorn side of her. And I straightway tried to forget everything her book had said and to start afresh on the story of Mary MacLane.

*

"Do you wish you hadn't published your book?" I asked. For she so little resembled her book that her answer seemed inevitable, and my question pardonable.

"No," she said, "because when I wrote it I was only nineteen. Now I am twenty-one."

"Is it the true story of yourself as you were then?" I said, "and don't you mind the 'wise, wide world' knowing all about it?"

"It is the true story of myself," she answered. "Why should I have written untruly? The only joy I had was writing what was. That book was. It no longer amuses me to be all the things I was when I wrote that. But it is my story as I was then.

"I am a genius. Then it amused me to keep saying so, but now it does not. I expected to be happy sometime. Now I know I shall never be."

I looked at the dimple in her chin.

"Why not?" I said.

"The only time I could ever be happy," said Mary MacLane, "would be not when I was really happy, but just the instant before that happiness. And that I am sure I shall never have.

"When I wrote my book I wanted to love someone. I wanted to be in love. Now I know that I shall never be in love - and I no longer wish to be.

"I don't like men. I met a man in Chicago with whom I should like to have been in love," she added, "but I couldn't fall in love with him. I was born to be alone, and I always shall be; but now I want to be.

"When I wrote my book," she went on, "I hated Butte. I hated the sand and the barrenness. I hated the people and the life.

"Now I know I should love to go back there and live there. I know that I love Butte. I didn't at nineteen. I do at twenty-one."

*

It began to look as if these two years had made a woman out of the child who laid bare her soul to the "wide, wise world." Here was no self-assertive being breathing invectives at home and the universe. Here was a girl with shadow hair and a blue flowered gown who said she longed for her home.

"And the Devil," I asked her; "you are not waiting for him?"

"Oh, yes, I am," she said, simply.

So there we were back two full years.

"Such a mountain has been made of that," she said, "hasn't there? I don't want the Devil particularly, but I do want experience. So does every one. Every one keeps quite still about it and goes softly along to meet the Devil, quite silently. I said I was going to meet him, and the rest didn't know I spoke for them too. But I knew. Don't let's talk of that."

"There are two things in your book," I said, "that I wish you hadn't written. One was that your mother is nothing to you."

"Of course," she answered, without surprise, "I don't expect you to approve of that. I don't approve of it myself. Only it was true, so I said it. Oh!" she exclaimed, "don't think that I approve of what I say in my book. I don't - of much of it. I don't approve of myself.

"I know I am unworthy, through and through, and I don't approve of that, but it is all true.

"I was writing about myself as I knew myself. And so I put in everything. What was the other thing you didn't like?"

"I wish," I said, "that you had not said that you are a thief."

"Oh!" said Mary MacLane, laughing, "but I'm not now. It doesn't amuse me any longer. It used to then. But I really haven't stolen anything now in some months."

"Now see," I said, "never mind for a minute about the morality of stealing. Suppose that we set that aside. Do you think it is good breeding to steal?"

"Why," she said, "if it amuses you, and the people you steal from are not inconvenienced, I don't see why it is any worse than half the diversions of society, and just as honest too. I did steal eight spoons on the dining-car, but they were to give away. Besides, every one steals dining-car things.

"I do think," she added, "that the point you make about good breeding is an important one. All the Ten Commandments that really need be kept and that are not now outworn, are those that offend good taste only. There is really no right and wrong. I recognize no right and wrong."

"Why did you say a moment ago that you were unworthy, then?" I asked. "Don't you want to speak quite frankly for a minute and let us talk about whichever is not the pose?"

It is curious when you begin to be frank how hopelessly rude you have to be. A perfectly truthful world would be intensely bad-mannered.

"But I pose all the time," said Mary MacLane. "I never give my real self. I have a hundred sides, and I turn first one way and then the other. I am playing a deep game. I have a number of strong cards up my sleeve. I have never been myself, excepting to two friends."

I laughed and took her hand.

"Your real self was in every sentence just then," I said, "don't you see?"

"But," she exclaimed, "why shouldn't everybody pose? Most people are stupid unless they do. I wouldn't be, but it is so amusing to pose. Besides, unless you aren't clever enough to select poses, why ever be yourself to any one? You have a right to yourself for yourself and a few friends. Why should I give myself to you? You are nothing to me."

"That motorman," I said, "looks better in his uniform than in silver armor or doublet and hose. But you and I take it for granted. We don't say it to the motorman, especially when the motorman is our guest."

The blue figure flashed across the room and put out its hand.

"I know," she said, with a pretty gesture. "I beg your pardon."

"See the ink," she observed presently, looking at her finger, "but don't look at my hands. They are large. I don't like my hands, but I do like my feet. Don't you?" she added.

*

She pointed forward a prettily shaped buckled shoe.

"When people say I have pretty hair," she went on, "I always correct them by saying at once, 'I have beautiful hair.' It is so funny. I did that several times in Chicago. Oh," she said, "the people at the teas in Chicago - you should have seen me caper for them.

"I dislike myself far less for capering than those for wanting to see me. 'How do you do, Miss MacLane? I am so interested in you,' they all said. Many of them didn't know how to be interested in me. Oh, but there were a few," she said, "whom I did love."

Her face was very tender for a minute, until she recalled something.

"One woman," she said, "said to me, 'Oh, you haven't found yourself yet. That's all. You will.' How I hated her. Don't they suppose I know I'm not the way I will be? Why can't they see I am the way I am, and I say so; that's all."

"Don't you think you will be different in two years?" I asked her.

"Yes," she said, "I know I shall. I shall write three more books - four in all. I shall do these before I am twenty-five. After that I shall be nothing. We MacLanes all go down after twenty-five.

"My other books will be very different from this. I don't know whether they will be novels or not. But people are going to say, 'Oh, that is her real self now.' They will say that of each book.

"But fifty years after I am dead they will say, 'Her first book was her masterpiece.' Not only that, but it *is* a masterpiece."

"And what will become of you after you are twenty-five?" I asked her.

"I don't care. But I shall not be forgotten."

*

She leaned back in the deep leather chair and let the lace ruffles fall over her hands.

"I am," she said simply, "one of the great ones of earth."

"Tell me," I said, "whom of the other great ones of earth you are most fond of. What do you read?"

"I don't read," she said.

"They say you are a feminine Walt Whitman," I suggested, "who began younger."

"I have never read a line of Walt Whitman," she declared.

"They say," I went on, "that you are, now and then, like Elbert Hubbard."

"I never read him," she said. "I have seen a copy or two of *The Philistine*, that is."

"They say," I concluded, "that you are like Marie Bashkirtseff. Do you think that?"

"I am greater than she," she said. "I have only read two or three entries in her journal, but I know that."

Then she told me what she had read.

"I don't care at all about Browning," she began. "I hold Mrs. Browning far more of a poet than he. No, I haven't read all he wrote, of course. I don't know Christina Rossetti, but I know a few of Dante Rossetti's. And Longfellow I don't care for.

"Of poets I put Virgil first - he was greatest. Poe next, and the greatest thing he wrote was 'Annabel Lee.' And Chaucer third. 'Annabel Lee' is the greatest poem ever written.

"I have read Stevenson - I like him. And some of Dickens, and *Jane Eyre*, and Albert Ross."

"In your book," I said, "you quoted 'The lure of green things growing.' You evidently liked that. Wouldn't you like to read Keats and Pater and Dante and Shakespeare and find more like that?"

"No," she said, "I don't have to do that. I have all those beautiful things in myself."

There was a pause.

"Read me something from my book," she said, finally. "Read me the chapter I like best - the one about the Gray Dawn. That has all my soul in it. I will tell you if I don't like the way you read it."

I read it, and when I misplaced a word she told me just what was wrong.

"Now read the entry about Greece," she said, "and then the one about asking for bread and receiving a stone. The last is the most intense in the book. In the first a Chicago woman emphasized the word 'music' as she read. I could have murdered her."

"When I wrote my book," she said after I finished, "I wrote from nine or ten at night until four in the morning. Then I would be too exhausted to undress and I would throw myself on the bed and sleep. But at six the next morning I was up again and out in the sand to see the Gray Dawn. All of myself is in that book - myself, as I was then."

"'Why should I give myself?'" I quoted from her words. "Why did you give yourself?"

"I wished to, then," she answered. "No," she answered me in a moment, quite simply. "I do not see any beauty in self-restraint. Give something. If not yourself, then a pose. I gave myself."

Then she read to me - the chapter about her sense of humor and the Italian woman-peddler.

"' - an angle-worm pattern in a calico dressing-jacket,'" she read. "Wasn't that clever of me to select just that?" she looked up to say.

"' - and tacks and dream-books and mouth-organs,'" she read. "Mouth-organs, do you fancy?" she broke off again. "Wasn't that a fine streak of mine to say mouth-organs?

"' - on her brown brass-ringed hands, on her black satine wrapper' - wasn't that wonderful detail to say black satine wrapper?" she interrupted herself. "Yes, that is where I am great - in my use of detail."

It was growing dark in the drawing-room of the Anemone Lady. Outside the window a group of curious girls stood, pointing out the house.

Mary MacLane read on, her voice vibrating with real feeling and notable for its complete lack of emphasis. There is a curious levelness in her voice. She reads and talks as one pronounces French words.

Often she turned her face to the window and read on as faultlessly as Cyrano read his letter. She knows every word of her story of herself.

In the half light her blue gown and lace ruffles and her hair looked so newly inconsistent that I could not resist reassuring myself, at the door, that it was she.

"What would you rather do with your life than anything in the world - honestly?" I asked her.

"I would rather be a fairly happy wife and mother," she said simply. "There is nothing better in the world. But I never shall be. I am not worthy to be. You see, all the tastes and instincts with which I was born are not high. I am not good at heart."

So I said good-night to her, standing in the vine-set doorway of the old Cambridge house, looking like a pot of lavender and a fall of old lace.

The next day we lunched together.

I talked with her about Radcliffe, about Boston, about Butte, about frankness, about Chicago people, about a book or two, about those at the other tables. Of all these it was naturally the personal aspect and its relation to her which interested her.

"Indeed," runs one paragraph in Mary MacLane's book, "my conversation is at all times devoted, directly or indirectly, to myself."

Over luncheon she never for a moment ceased to do her part.

"One must always say things that aim to interest," she said, "because in the world one must after all pay for one's keep."

These two things happened -

From the little dish of cracked ice Miss MacLane took half a dozen olives and dropped them deliberately in the blouse of her shirt-waist.

"I love them so!" she explained. "They are wonderful to eat - in very small bites."

And when the waiter was bowing over his tip she addressed him -

"Waiter," said Miss MacLane, "will you match me for the tip?"

"Madam?" said the waiter.

"Will you match me for the tip?" she asked.

"But yes, Madam," he complied. The first quarter he lost; the second time he won them both.

"Do you think I am crazy, waiter?" asked Miss MacLane, as she rose.

"No, madam," said the waiter, "I have seen many others many times."

"And yet," I said to Mary MacLane, "you wrote well indeed about the three gold rocks that came up out of the sea."

She crossed Tremont Street to the Common, and her lithe, athletic figure and erect head were those of any healthy-minded girl, only a bit more attractive than most. As she walked she ate an olive delicately.

"Mary MacLane at Newport"

New York World · 24 August 1902

I am come down out of Butte-Montana into the mysterious East. I go here and there in trains in the mysterious East and gaze at things.

In very truth, the mysterious East is not so greatly different from Butte-Montana, and a person is a person, I find, east or west.

But there are differences.

For instance it's a far and exceeding confounding cry from Butte-Montana to Newport - Newport with a very large N.

Upon occasion I have read in the well-filled Bible about the pomps and vanities of this wicked world. And I have wondered what it meant - it hath indeed a glittering sound. The pomps and vanities must need be of always-vivid interest and this wicked world, as we all know, is fascinating.

And always when I have seen the phrase in the well-filled Bible I have thought within me: "Until I have really come upon the pomps and vanities of this wicked world my life is not complete." There are, to be sure, a great many things in Butte-Montana which relate quite directly to this wicked world - but not just what one might call pomps and vanities. They're a trifle too heavy for that.

In Chicago I happened upon a friendly gaiety, and some fine and good impressions that will last. In Boston, if you please, I happened upon something so still, so cold, so unrelenting - so utterly intolerant of anything that may come down out of Butte-Montana - that my thanks for the strength that must come of it died instantly upon my lips. In New York I came upon a strenuous thing, to be sure, but mostly commercial as yet, and it glittered little. But all upon a fine bright summer morning I anchored my bark at Newport and lo - I, of Butte-Montana, straightaway walked into the midst of the pomps and vanities of this wicked world!

Only think, now. 'Tis a most grotesque conceit.

Newport is a little lovely restful town in itself. There are few things new, and the old things are earth-old. The stars and the dust and the wild weeds are there, as in the beginning. And in the gray morning a pale, pale sky hangs over wonderful wide water - a sky so pale that one half-expects a Raphael virgin's head to emerge slowly, sleepily from it. And the sea - the sea runs on always, in weariness, in joy - the gray, the blue, the gray, the blue - world with no end. Far away in Butte-Montana I had fancied the sea, and here is it. And the sea has a sister in Newport - a fascinating seductive sloe-eyed sister with soft long hair and magic finger-tips. She is the Air, and she is incomparable. After the first look into the sloe-eyes you close your own and lift your face and feel the sweep of the long soft locks of hair upon your chin and forehead. You feel the touch of those finger-tips upon your shoulder-blades, and straightaway you give your quiet heart into her hands to keep for a season.

The perfume of her long hair is of sea-weed and salt and of moss and decayed wood, and of half-sunk islands over the sea. In the plains of heaven is there any more exquisite thing? Round and about Newport there are bits of rude country that, after the shaven lawns of other parts, rest the nerves and senses. There are places where long dry yellow grass grows confusedly, and tiny rocks, and spaces between that are like the sand and barrenness of Butte-Montana, - but a long, long way apart. Here and there is a fresh-water pond and some lilies and wet, wet leaves. The wild grasses grow tall by the pond, and are also wet and very sweet. Back from the sea I looked long at a prospect that was fair and exceeding good. It was of smiling farms and rolling country and dark-colored trees and fields of corn. And all was green, green, green. It is gray in Butte-Montana, and my mind then opened and took in a new color. And all was green. The flowers bloomed in plenty, and the farms - and Jersey cows fed from the land. To my mind there came a bit of very old poetry from that same well-filled Bible, which seemed to tell it all in a serene voice saying: "My well-beloved hath a vineyard in a very fruitful hill." All this is the background. In the foreground there are people, and there is life: in truth, the pomps and vanities of this wicked world.

How glittering, to be sure, is the pageant at Newport, - how the women and men reek with The Money, how unreal - how like phantoms do they seem to one who has thus far been wont to take a few things seriously and has lived a small, narrow life in Butte-Montana. I gazed at this glittering pageant until my senses were strained and a faint sickening influence came to them. As I looked there came a feeling of deadly weariness and sickness of heart. For through this false brilliant procession, the infinite - life itself - shows in poignant bitter intensity. There is a thing in the life of the women and men that one can not grasp. The stars and the dust and the wild weeds give at once of their deepest and the pain that they send is soft. The vision of the pageant at Newport tells of something so false, so distorted, so sharply cruel, that all of life - all of the past and all of the present - becomes useless. The Universe shrinks into a damnable little thing, and the souls - there are no souls.

Well, then.

At Newport I looked at a wedding. I looked very hard at that wedding. I had been told that I must, and so I did. It seemed excessively like every other little extravaganza in B-flat that I have seen, but it did have a few distinctive points. All the women and men were thoroughly sated, thoroughly steeped. Their bodies were the much-indulged, much-groomed kind - some of The Money certainly buys them the flesh-pots. And a few of the feminine bodies were truly exquisite - the few that were not overdone. The heads and hands had been worked at minutely with little ivory implements until Nature was obliterated and art - albeit with a painfully small "a" - reigned supreme. There were hands of alabaster - a very old simile but still good - with nails delicately wrought as miniature paintings. Each nail meant hours of work and more of The Money. The frocks that adorned these persons were equally exquisite - they represented labor and capital. Physically the women were pieces of fine workmanship - excellent products of skill. Except those that were overdone. They were sadly grotesque indeed.

Some of the bodies that were driven to the wedding were groomed to the nearly annihilation point - just a little more, one thought involuntarily, and they were surely mummified. Certainly no more skilful work could ever have been put on the body of a long-since Egyptian king than that on those nervous American persons. And Solomon in all his glory was not arrayed like one of these. A single bright stone on one of those patrician fingers would have purchased sea air for a very great number of the little bare-footed New York populace - which, however, is entirely without the question and an entirely impertinent idea. These are the pomps and vanities of this wicked world. Let them go down as such.

- When one sees a face - even a wrought Newport summer face at a wedding - one looks at once for the soul - well, no, not the soul. Impossible! But the mind. And one finds - what does one find?

One finds a once beautiful and vital thing dead or dying in the faces of women and men. One finds something subtly imbecile - a strange, weird, and tragic thing. There is surely nothing like unto this in Butte-Montana. It has come from generations of indulgence at the flesh-pots, and years of disuse and reckless wasting of nerves; and too much perfume, and too much music, and too much food. And it has come from the mad straining after pleasure, the devising of ways to spend The Money, the petty rivaling of one another, the utter futility. -

And so it was a very pretty wedding indeed. There was something quite distracting in the way those equipages pulled up at the church, and in the way the high-heeled occupants tottered up the walk to the door. And there was something more distracting still in the way the populace - for Newport boasts a very well-assorted populace likewise - lined up on the opposite street and gazed almost as hard as if they had every one of them just come down out of Butte-Montana to contemplate the pomps and vanities of this wicked world. And the most distracting thing of all, I assure you, was when a goodly carriageful of bridesmaids and things rolled neatly down upon a fat little dog in the street and rolled him over and over and over - a bunch of ruined and feebly-yelping hair. Oh, it was very distracting - hard on the dog, doubtless, but the lace on the gowns of those bridesmaids was worth many thousands of good American dollars with Liberty-heads on one side and eagles on the other.

And when every one had finally arrived the bride tottered up to the altar on the arm of somebody and her own high white heels, and met the groom and they were married and lived happily ever after.

A very charming wedding, to be sure.

And another time I went to see the powers at play - the people of The Money soaking their persons in salt water at Bailey's Beach. 'Twas very interesting and these people ran about and disported themselves and skipped like young lambs just exactly as if they hadn't a cent of money in the world.

Only it was here that I had explained to me the names and the Cottages and the numbers of millions and the Divorces - particularly the Divorces.

I beheld a striped lady with quite the best shoulders I have ever seen emerge from a bunch of waves - she had a figure and a laugh and several high spirits of her own. "That, surely, now, is real," I observed. "That?" responded my guide with elevated brows. "That? Only last year her conduct was scandalous, and her husband - that man in the blue pajamas - obtained a Divorce. She lives in the swell little place I pointed out to you, and her Money is - ." I find that I've forgotten the large number. They have larger ones in Butte-Montana.

And I saw a bright red lady with a pair of eyes - a very good looker, she was. She knew things, moreover. "What is that?" I inquired of the guide. "That," the guide replied, "has the prettiest Cottage in Newport. She has no Divorce as yet, but is getting one as fast as ever she can. Her husband - the man with the green tennis-shoes - went somewhere with that heavy purple lady, and so it is all off." "And what will the red lady do after she has procured her Divorce?" I asked. "She will marry that pretty little thing with the freshness of youth still upon him," answered my guide with remarkable promptness and accuracy. "Her Money is estimated at - ." I find that I've forgotten the large number. They have larger ones in Butte-Montana.

And I saw a brilliant small pink lady leap joyously into the wild waves. She was not much of anything to look at, but she had a way with her.

"Whom is that divorced from?" I said. "Oh, that," said the guide. "She is not married. Her mother is working to obtain that simple figure in black. He has good horses, and his Money is - ." I find that I've forgotten the large number. They have larger ones in Butte-Montana.

And I saw a tall man in a fine plain bathing-suit walking by the sad sea waves, with melancholia on his forehead and a tennis-racquet in his hands. "Wherefore?" said I to my guide. "Oh, that is an old, old story," she murmured. "He married somebody, and no one ever speaks to them. They have that big pile on the hill. They are left alone. There's a Scandal with it." "What's a Scandal?" I asked eagerly. "A Scandal's a reason and a back-thought," said the guide, and went on. "His yacht is immense and his Money is - ." I find that I've forgotten the large number. They have larger ones in Butte-Montana.

And I saw two young creatures - a pale-blue-and-white lady and a reddish-grayish man. The pale-blue-and-white lady was attending the reddish-grayish man with the utmost solicitude. "What of them?" I inquired - (I was there to inquire, don't you know). "They are engaged," answered the guide. "And are they quite happy?" I asked, in the innocence of my heart.

"Well, she ought to be," said the guide, cold-bloodedly. "She has worked hard for two years to get it. And now she works harder to keep it. And certainly she's done well for herself. None but the brave deserve the fair. His house is the one with all the gables and his Money is - ." I find that I've forgotten the large number. They have larger ones in Butte-Montana.

So then these, too, are the pomps and vanities - bathing-dresses, salt water, Divorces, and all.

'Tis most awfully interesting.

And another day I looked at a polo game. I have seen polo several times - polo is much the same everywhere. But there were some fine contrasts about the setting of this game. The horses were good to look at - and some of the women who looked at them wore blue or white or black shoes with very red heels! Those red heels taken with polo made a delicate little incongruity that is quite rare and appeals directly to the artistic sense. The horses were so very good, do you see, and the heels were so very red.

Newport teems, bristles, with just such delicate little incongruities. Set down among small quaint ramshackle houses and new staring red brick buildings, and surrounded farther away by the Cottages - some of which resemble one's idea of a Venetian palace more than anything else - is a church which is a really fine thing. It is small and old - it is of the days of the Revolution, and the air in it is true. The architecture is the simplest and plainest, and inside the wood-work and upholstering are plain and poor to ugliness. George Washington sat in this place on Sundays, when time was. And - it rings utterly true. And now, likewise on Sundays, the sated Newport pageant assembles in it - the dear knows what for - to pray, it may be: a delicate little incongruity.

There is one thing in Newport that is absolutely and quite its own, which suits every element and everything there, and fits in as it surely could not elsewhere. This is the hydrangea bloom - a grafted and artificially colored shrub. The tints of the large round flower bunches are indescribably delicate and lovely, and they grow in the utmost lavishness. The color comes from the application of salt water to the roots and is a blending of the pale sea and the paler sky with a brief vivid gleam of sun.

Also the sea's sloe-eyed sister gives of herself to this flower and rests her magic finger-tips on the stems. Straightaway they bloom delicately, gracefully, immensely, with astonishing and delicious recklessness.

They are fascinating and false - like many, many other things in Newport-by-the-sea.

There is here indeed the little rift that sometime, somehow, inevitably must widen, and - as always - ever widening, slowly silence all.

And thus it is that one receives an Impression, having come down out of Butte-Montana in the days of her youth, and having lo! - walked into the midst of the pomps and vanities of this wicked world.

"Mary MacLane on Wall Street"

New York World · 7 September 1902

I have been a day in Wall Street.

To one who is in Wall Street day after day it doubtless is something peculiarly of now. To one who stands without the whirl an age-worn line of life shows plain-written upon those modern brick walls.

There is a soft monotonous ancient choir that sounds low and deep in the midst of the noise.

There is an old dull gray shadow that shows pale yet marked in the midst of glaring tones.

There is the spirit of an old, old fashion that is as old, older far than the avarice of the money-changers in the temple.

There are human beings grasping, straining madly after treasure, each for himself.

A human being changes not from the long ago till now. In a human being there is the one long old undying element of treasure for himself. There is the first drop of blood that never changes and is transmitted from father to son unto the ten-thousandth generation, and again unto the ten-thousandth generation, and still again.

Wall Street is short and dark and irregular, and the buildings are tall and narrow, and the ground is closely crowded and paved with cobble-stones - so there is no ground.

There is something to loathe and something to worship in the buildings. Some of them have stood for many a good year, and still they stand, and will stand. They are of brick and of stone with touches of marble and bronze. They are strong. They say: "We are the seats of the mighty. These dark walls shelter the millions. Many, many go down in the depths - and never rise. But we stand. The dust of countless yesterdays is gathered in our cracks and crannies. Before the end there will be more dust. More than this, our tall grim stone pinnacles stand out against the vast shadowy sky at dusk - and our mysterious strength is more fearsome than the shadowy sky."

Inside the Stock Exchange the stream of money goes its way. Men shout with lungs of leather, and their mouths and eyes are strained. The atmosphere of this building is of a greenish-grayish and copper-colored hue, and if one is standing aside and looking one imagines it plainly enough.

The men who are shouting are surely thinking of nothing but the shouting. My mind stops and marvels at this. My own mind wanders at will to the times of the Crusades, to the Ptolemys in Egypt, to Darius, to the Philistines, and to the far countries. But here are minds that stay all day long, all month long, all year long between four high narrow walls. And they are minds that go wild at times in that tiny space, in agony of suspense and anxiety for paltry reasons enough, that are aching in unrest which is more than pitiful in its utter unconsciousness.

These minds are they that mourn. Whether or not they reach their desire - whether they grow rich or poor - they are among the most unfortunate ones of earth. They mourn, mourn, mourn always and unconsciously for what is not theirs - each over his condition in life, over the money of his fellows, over the real want of anything vital in his life. For there is nothing vital in all this straining.

A sometime promise to those that mourn is that they shall be comforted. Blessed are they that mourn - but these seem most utterly accursed.

Still it may be that in a day of far reckoning they shall be comforted.

These buildings are peculiarly places of men. There are no feminine elements, no feminine colorings, no feminine hands. Everything is abrupt and unyielding and masculine. One can be sure, as one contemplates them, that these men have no thought of women in this mad whirling. There is no far faint echo of that soft tale within the gray high walls. To be sure, there are but few large human ways of living, such as this, in the world where there is no looking of man to woman. It is one of many outside elements lacking in Wall Street. It is well doubtless that it is lacking. All desires are distorted there - and so that also, were it present.

One knows as little as possible about the buying and selling in the Stock Exchange, or the varying conditions of the money market, or the going up or going down of stocks, or the panics, or indeed any of it. But to look at it from afar it seems utterly absurd. It is obviously one-sided and the profits are so surely with the middle-man. And yet men have no greater pleasure in life than to risk their fortunes in this bottomless pit. And the brokers seemingly ask no greater pleasures than to gratify them. It is one of those mills of the gods that are said to grind slow but exceeding fine.

The great mournful spirit of unrest has come and made this her abiding place. She lays her cold hand upon the eyes of these men and brushes their forms with her somber gray garments as she walks. She leaves naught but rage and woe behind her in her path, and the hearts that she touches are heavy. And men thereafter know not one moment's peace. A tragic vision looms before one's eyes as this thought comes - a vision of two things: one of the wondrous fair green earth, of rapid rushings of water, of the bend of weeping willows, of the white necks of swans upon a lake, of a steep hillside, of the green bay-tree that flourisheth, and of the balm-o'-Gilead: and another and present vision of minds that have wandered far from truth, that are passing by the real things, that seem fallen and lost, that are fighting, struggling, raging in a torrid glare of greenish lights in the company of ghoulish phantoms, that have forgotten the first old lessons, and go on and on with deaf ears and blinded eyes, and hearts eternally bowed down. The more so that they are unconscious and even imagine themselves content.

The life of the street, equally mad as it is, is preferable to the inside of the buildings. The street seethes with life. I have never seen so many different kinds of men as I saw during my day in Wall Street. There were men who knew values, and men who didn't know anything. There were men with murder in their eyes, and men with fair good-tempered faces. There were men in white duck, and men in clerical cloth, and men in unquiet plaids, and men in nondescript clothes, and men in rags, and men in shabby-genteel garments - and a fruit-vender on the curb in a dubious red jacket and waistcoat, with brass rings in his ears. And there were as many young boys plying various extremely small trades - mostly selling the newspapers, but there was also the festive boot-black, and the vender of shoe-strings, and the dealer in pies and gum-drops. And there was a morose individual who displayed fascinating little mechanical toys on the pavement - a strange contrast to the mighty tide of Wall Street.

The cobble-stones of Wall Street have also a voice of their own. They say: "We lie under the feet of the men. We are infinitely wiser than they are. We have been here more years than have passed over their heads. Their gigantic choruses of still voices sometimes cry out together in unanalysed misery: 'My god, why hast thou forsaken me!' But we lie here strong and content. We do not cry; we do not rave; we do not moan. Our name is Strength-and-Patience. We are merely waiting for the end."

Ah, yes - a strong, strong voice comes up from the dark-gray cobblestones, a strong and somehow hateful voice. But it sounds most true.

Often, often in this long journeying it is the hateful thing that is true.

At high noon the sun shines heavy and hot upon Wall Street and all that therein is. The faces of the tall buildings appear all threatening in the thick air, and the faces and the voices of the people are heated to the crackling point. The hoarse yelling of the curb-brokers becomes hoarser and louder. The news-boys frantically cry their papers in the harsh voices of their kind. The shoe-string dealers become agonizingly persistent with their line of goods, which certainly at high noon seem somewhat of a drug on the market. The gum-drop vender gazes in heated despair at his melting delicacies but increases his efforts to dispose of them. The morose individual with his gaily-colored little toys winds them up and sets them going with two-fold velocity until they seem to dance before one's eyes like motes and beams in mid-air. The fruit man in the dingy red garments and the brass ear-rings regards his goods with extreme solicitude and raises a pathetic discordant voice in praise of them. The entire boiling mass of humanity surges and sweeps in every direction, and pushes and jostles and becomes profane. It is an inevitable rule that all must hate each other in a crowd on a hot day, and this seemed particularly evident in Wall Street. Torrid as it was, the look in some of the faces expressed, plainly, desires to see some other faces in yet warmer climes - and different kinds of hatred radiated from eyes and finger-tips.

One's brain seems to ferment in that atmosphere. One thinks vaguely to one's self that hell and damnation must be like this. One looks at the buildings and the cobble-stones and the people and wonders if these are things of the moment or things of all time. Then one is sure that they are things only of the moment - that one, with one's own eyes, can see them all passing, passing, passing in one long dead march to their damp black graves. But still as at first one sees that vague vacillating vanishing, but true, shadow of a thing out of the long ago - that human beings are always human beings and have, each of them, a soul.

These things are mingled but they are kept markedly separate also.

The men move and mourn with their minds of unrest.

The high gray walls stand always, passionless, baffling - and the cobble-stones.

The spire of Trinity rises high in the direction of the stars.

Then render unto Caesar that which is Caesar's, and also unto God that which is God's - and so likewise unto Wall Street that which is Wall Street's.

Two Days Later - Post Scriptum

Having written the foregoing I leaned back in my chair and contemplated it with mixed feelings.

One of them was of profound astonishment that I should have written it at all - considering how and with whom I had visited Wall Street. (I was chaperoned by a man, that time.) And it happens that it is my real, genuine, bona-fide impression of the place. But - will you believe it? - when the Atrocious Editor read it he leaned back in his chair and said: "Mary MacLane, what do you mean by all this? This isn't what I want. Look here." And he wrote me out the following questions to answer in as quiet, pleasant, sane, and ladylike a fashion as is customary in Butte-Montana. And so now I'll answer them - out of the kindness of my heart and to earn my salary - particularly to earn my salary.

Well, then.

The Atrocious Editor's First Question: How did the men you saw in Wall Street compare with the men of Butte-Montana?

My Little Answer: They seemed about alike. I couldn't, for my life, see any difference, - except - ah, yes - their manners. On that point the odds were heavily in favor of Butte-Montana.

The Atrocious Editor's Second Question: Do you regard Wall Street as compatible with personal righteousness?

My Little Answer: I have not the least idea what personal righteousness is. But if it is what I - upon second thoughts - think it is, then I should say: Don't on any account take any of it into Wall Street. 'Twould be a drug on that market.

The Atrocious Editor's Third Question: Do you approve of gambling?

My Little Answer: To be sure. Life is one long gamble, don't you know.

The Atrocious Editor's Fourth Question: How would you define gambling?

My Little Answer: A plunge and a holding of one's breath - and a tinge of profanity.

The Atrocious Editor's Fifth Question: What are your views on other people's money?

My Little Answer: Now, did you ever hear anything like that! Other people's money, indeed!

The Atrocious Editor's Sixth Question: What should you do with a million dollars?

My Little Answer: I should spend it - what else, pray? That's not so large a number. They have larger ones in Butte-Montana.

The Atrocious Editor's Seventh Question: If you received such a legacy in the form of stock would you try Wall Street?

My Little Answer: Certainly not. I might as well go out on the highways and byways and make presents of it to the lame, the halt, and the blind. There is no reason in the world why I should make such presents to Wall Street brokers with whom I have not fallen in love.

The Atrocious Editor's Eighth and Last Question: Do you think that views of money have changed since ancient times?

My Little Answer: No, I really don't think so. They all seem to have had two purposes for things - one for ornamental purposes and the other to earn their salaries - particularly to earn their salaries - from Rome in Nero's time to Butte-Montana in Senator Clark's.

"The Second 'Story of Mary MacLane'"

Butte Evening News · 31 December 1909

This is an expurgated review of my later impressions of Butte and a few crudely-drawn contrasts between the me that was and the me that is.

I, of womankind and unpleasingly more than nineteen years, will now take the *Evening News* and the hybrid Butte public some three thousand words deep into my confidence. I am the Mary MacLane of purple memory whom, slam me though it did, Butte will never, never forget. I have proofs of that on me - some in my two hands and some in the top of my stocking.

Seven years ago I left this weird little town. I left it while myself in a blaze of notoriety made of tinsel and brass, and yet in its own way deep and far-reaching. It went half across the world, did the thing of brass and tinsel, and, too, it clings to me yet. I love my notoriety more, oh, much more than if it were pale, solid gold. It has given me such a run for my money - it has brought me close, close to human realities. I have sat all these seven years not in a shadowy literary niche, but have gone down into the seething market-places. I have felt the hot pulse and tasted the red blood of the cruel and adorable world. Seven years ago I left little old Butte far behind me. And now that the seven years have slipped away I'm here again and for the first time. It's to me a situation piquant and picturesque. I lived in Butte, but little more than seven years ago, the obscurest of shy maids. Butte now looks upon me as a returned and limelighted prodigal, a woman with a past, and an insolent young jade withal. It is wondering divers things about me as it sees me in its midst - if I've spent all my money, why I put on so much complexion, where I acquired my taste for cocktails, and whether I'm still single-hearted. Butte takes note of all these changes in me and shows a tendency to give me a gladdening hand. Well, though I know Butte for exactly what it is, I have none but a joyous hand for it. Butte is sordid, beastly, and time-serving - but withal full of romance and poetry and the wideness of the West. It is fascinating and picturesque, which is all I ask of anything. Morals are nothing but boresome trifles, and art is too often like a nightgown on a hot August night by the sea - superfluous. But the fascinating and the picturesque are never lost.

The Mary MacLane who rose to a so-sudden and somewhat terrific notoriety in 1902 was pre-eminently a Butte product - a shy and delicate creature born of this convulsive desolation. And when at nineteen my head broke out in brains and I wrote my wail of adolescence, with damns and devils and little knocks at Butte, Butte promptly gave me a curse, a blow upon the heart, also on the point of the jaw - a few surreptitious curses, and saw me slip away into the glooms and terrors of the many-pitfall'd world. I went away eagerly enough, but in all the seven years something in Butte subtly called me. I have heart-feelings for it. These barren hills saw my mind's awakening. I once walked over them in the loneliness of nine-teen, or sat on some granite boulder with my hands about my knees, and watched the lights of the horizon, and realized the half-sullen, half-brilliant depths in me. I even thought I had a soul in those days (see the red Mary MacLane book) and a heart, of sorts. But the soul I have since passed up as a bore and an uncertainty (it is buried deep in the said red book), and the heart is now - battered and parched from the salt of dried tears. But the mind of black-and-white brilliance remains - and largely I thank Butte for it. A certain deadly thrall hangs over this little place, which impregnates one's mind, if one happens to possess one - they're rare - and brings to it a reckoning and an *accouchement*.

I had an incomparable thrill at my first glimpse of the town, a week or two ago, when I watched it from the windows of the night train sliding slowly in around the mountainside: a million starry gems scintillated on a black hill as if fallen from the spangled blue, and just above them the large deep-gold evening star hung low with down-dropping, glowing-wire rays. Nothing was there but the black hill and the countless diamonds, the silence and the evening star. It was mysterious and enchanting. "And that," I thought to myself, "is the pungent little place which saw the sudden jerking of me from the quietest obscurities into the glaringest limelights - and itself did it." It added depths to the thrill.

The next day I walked into its narrow highways and looked hard at it. It has an exquisite forlornness on it, with the deadly thrall: it is elementally the same little old Butte.

Since then I have done the highways daily and I've become used to the thrall and the forlornness. I am becoming once more a citizen of Butte.

And I've met most of the people with whom I once went to the Butte High School, and most of the people whom I met just after I developed from me into Mary MacLane, and a few more. I do not think the Butte people have changed any since I last knew them. But my attitude has changed toward them as it has toward everything since I wrote my book. So that they all seem different. Seven years ago I took myself and everybody and everything seriously - with nearly always disastrous results. (Do you remember how I "shocked Butte society"?) Now I take nothing seriously. I meet misfortune with an insolent laugh and the malice of my fellows with light-hearted contempt. What I cannot laugh at I pass up. I'll no more of the small tragedies that come from too much faith. They sear and corrode one's heart - they scar one's brain. And so, I've nothing but plaisance for the Butte people; they're all of that for me. In short, we get along fine.

I left Butte crude, innocent, and inexperienced. I return to it in the role of a frazzled old rounder. New York has been my abiding place these many, many moons, and it's been in some ways my undoing. It's a city of a million treacherous delights-and-horrors, and of a thousand grievous slips 'twixt the cup and the lip. It is vast and cruel - it devours youth, feminine youth, with the jaws and the palate of a monstrous insatiate demon. I and my folly - for I'm very much of a fool, among other things - were an easy prey. And so I come back to the scene of my youthful faiths with half my bloom irrevocably rubbed away. Still, even more than I love Butte I love New York.

I was at first bored stiff, after the fresh thrill of getting home had subsided, by the ghastly lack of things to do. There's no Rector's to go to after the play and sit drinking that which bubbles long; no Knickerbocker wherein to browse amid the Broadway chorus people with a swissesse beneath one's chin, no Tom Sharkey's wherein to drink beer in delicate abandonment amid the ribald revelry of hilarious sailors, no Cafe Martin wherein to mingle with the absinthe drinkers at four in the afternoon. There's no Maria's and no Jack's, no White Way and no Bowery. But I find there's a hybrid Indian-village sort of imitation of them all. They are live imitations. Butte is the one Indian village that could do it. Butte has gone off and down since I last knew it, and languishes in the clutch of a deadlock. But the glamor of its golden days still lingers on and there is an alcoholic haze to its nights. Moreover, a kindly law of contrast helps things along in my case. Certain men of Butte have taken me to the "Brewery" and Browne's, and out to Jack Reagan's and Billy Smith's and some others whose names I heard too late in the night to recall. We stayed very late in the night, and they introduced everybody to me - bartenders and Chinese waiters and the drivers of deep-sea-going cabs. Everybody seemed pleased to meet me. I seemed to be the only woman the night contained. The next day I went to an afternoon tea amid West Side ladies galore - they were few but select. I enjoyed both those functions. Butte people are very much Butte people, whether lined up in front of the bar at Jack Reagan's or drinking tea in West Granite street. They didn't happen to be the same people, though. At the time I wrote the book which we all thought was so wicked I considered it quite an awful thing for a young woman to go out to the "roadhouses," and I looked upon Mercury street as the haunt of the damned. But I've changed those opinions, partly because I've found by long experience that you can be as virtuous in a roadhouse as in a morgue, and partly because my attitude toward people-at-large has changed and I take nothing seriously: even if you aren't virtuous you aren't necessarily damned. I suppose there may be a lightness of heart, as well as of morals, in Mercury street, and, taken by and large, I fancy life is rather more human there than in Granite. I prefer Granite street, though, because there seem to be cockroaches in Mercury street, and of all things, kind Devil, deliver me from cockroaches. Rather even a cab driver for a husband or a waiter for a lover. More than I like the roadhouses and the afternoon teas I like the people I once went to school with. I like meeting them, shocking them, and having ardent friendships with them. It's fun to be Mary MacLane, a set-apart individuality in any gathering, as marked a woman as Evelyn Thaw or Carrie Nation. And it's pleasing to my vanity to reflect that I was as marked in New York as in Butte.

As to the things the massed Butte public seems to be wondering about me - I'll tell you some of them with a blending of audacity and chaste aloofness that's all mine. As to whether I've spent all my money: well, most of it. There was quite a lot forthcoming from the wicked book and, as I said, I've had a bully run for it. As to why I'm wearing so much complexion, not unnaturally I prefer to be good-looking than otherwise. As to where I acquired my taste for the dry Martini: that's an easy one - on the Great White Way. As I once loved the pallid olive so I now love the dry Martini - all melted gold in a cup of glass. The poetry that lurks in it can be written but scantily. It transfigures one's body as the colorful religion of the Buddhist transfigures the soul and the mind. I shall write more about it one day. As to whether I'm still single-hearted: it's too leading a question to answer. 'Twere folly to confess it at this stage, if I were or if I weren't. I maintain many a chaste aloofness that would make very interesting reading if done in plain terms. The best policy to pursue, whether in writing or war or love, is to combine limitless audacity with virginal reserves. I have myself tried it countless times and it never failed me. It is a combine that keeps the human equation perennially guessing. I think it's the policy which God pursues with all of us.

Another thing they're all asking me is what I have done with myself these seven years. I rather like to be asked that because it's so obviously and delightfully none of their business. For which reason I will say a few things about it. I have lived - for one thing, and it's a thing I never did here. I have been in love - or fancied myself so, which is exactly the same thing - not with vapid shadows, but with men. I am thinking at this moment of the little London Jew with whom I plighted troth and to whom I was engaged for the space of one week. He is now four years in the past, but himself and the memory of him still rouse deep-red poetry and passion in the black-and-rainbowed personality of me. He was tender-souled, beautiful to look at, and absolutely "on the level," which latter counts heavily. He was far too good for me, for I was never quite on the level with him. To me he was to be but a poetic incident, though I intended being married to him by a civil contract. He was seductive, but not the conquering devil of my dreams. But, to him, I was to be his wife till the grave yawned for one of us - and that sort of thing. Upon that we disagreed, so he went back to London beyond the sea - after a week of delicate and delicious cross-purpose. No other woman has yet got him for her own, which thought gives me a savage pleasure, and at times, as now, he glows warm in my memory. He was but one of several, but incomparably the most alluring and the only one to whom I waft still-born regrets through fast-darkening distance.

The Devil I once wanted never arrived - him of the steel-gray eyes - but so many imitations of him presented themselves, all with the one crude purpose, that he and his sometimes charm grew a bore and a monotony.

But I've not confined myself entirely to efforts to be gaily led adown the primrose path these seven years. I have gone everywhere and seen everything on the island of Manhattan. I have met fascinating people galore, from Ann O'Delia Dis Debar to Elinor Glyn - and back again, and from Mark Twain to Tom Sharkey in his native gin palace, the odds, as an interesting character, being heavily in favor of Tom. More than prize-fighters and literary people, both of whom I do like, I like vaudeville people on and off the stage. I fall the quickest of all for the people from the London music halls. They are artists on the stage, in their own lines of business - people like Cecilia Loftus, Marie Lloyd, Alice Lloyd, and Vesta Victoria - and off the stage, sitting in Rector's, with a pint of 'alf-and-'alf, they prove to be traditional British types of a most delectable brand. They combine a high-colored and high-seasoned domesticity with the thick local-color of the halls. They earn fabulous salaries over here, for they have a charm we cannot duplicate in America, and as they sit in the gilded thick-padded splendor of New York cafes they'll tell you how they started twenty years ago in the Shoreditch hall at "ten-and-six the night." There is nothing introspective about vaudeville people, nothing shadowy and sinister. They have brains of the sanest and simplest. In short, they are so satisfyingly different from myself, of whom, at times, I'm deadly weary, that I find a deep restfulness in their atmosphere.

Which brings me back to me. The thing I took away with me from Butte seven years ago - a restlessness of spirit, a shadowed and turbulent mentality, a lack of inward peace - is the thing I've brought back with me, and which will follow me to what I trust will be a young grave. I am myself like this little town with its subtle deadly thrall upon it, yet fired with certain head-long madnesses of youth. It is so with many, many others in Butte. Their inward fires glow and smoulder, with a dull personal menace, the more for the outward deadlock of this semi-bewitched Butte.

I have written this article, as I wrote the wicked red Mary MacLane book, as personally, as egotistically, as insolently as it's in me to write - because I know that only so could I picture the human equation. I write as many another feels, as many another is - and with the darksome spirit of Butte-Montana hard and fast upon me.

Because the *Evening News* seems to me more vividly Butte-Montana than any other sheet in this place I write it for the *Evening News*.

I am once more a citizen of Butte.

"Mary MacLane Meets the Vampire on the Isle of Treacherous Delights"

Butte Evening News · 27 March 1910

It is close upon the witching hour of midnight. I, of womankind and some-thing-and-twenty years, sit alone in my little blue and white room, fallow and eke somewhat forlorn. I am surrounded by the silence of West Park street, than which the vast stillnesses of the everlasting hills to the southwest are not more profound. It sets somberly upon me for I, who imagined myself built for si-lences, solitudes, sunsets, still gray dawns - I am longing for little old New York.

New York - oh, New York - the mere thought of it fills me with a subtle restlessness, a half-insane emotion of far desire. Its name calls up a throng of turbulent memories, of mingled mournfulness and the utter reckless joy of living such as nothing but a dweller in New York can know.

All - all that is in the soul, the body, the mind, the heart of a human being, New York, the vampire, the cruel and much-loved, drags out. It demands the last fluttering gasp of breath, the last drop of blood, the last thrill of the worn nerves. While there's left one glimmer of light in one's mind, or one conscious nerve in one's body, the lips of the vampire are pressed close upon one's human lips, passionate, insatiate, mad until all is over and one lies abandoned, cold and dead.

There's nothing, nothing, nothing that New York gathers in and holds as it does youth. The mind and the body in the fullness of their youth are the food of the vampire. It devours, but, oh, it gives in exchange - life!

All the life, the youth; all the brain, such as it is, and all the restless heart; all the wild, nameless vitalities that make me human, every treasured thing I have to give, I waft at this moment, over frozen river and snow-clad hill - a thousand leagues - to New York, the exquisite vampire, merciless, bewitching.

I know New York as I know Butte-Montana, for exactly what it is. I have no roseate illusions about it. It has lodged me not as a transient bird of passage, but as one of the four million who call it home. I well know that it is no place to go to gather lilies. Its paving stones are the paving stones of hell. But on them walk people who are more wonderful than lilies. And the lesson it teaches is the adamant truth itself.

I first went to New York in the summer of 1902, at the age of 19, when I was a crude but successful child, guarded and looked-after and chaperoned to the point of atrophy. New York seemed to me then a vast, tiresome Babel, with a mingled atmosphere of skyscrapers and of alcoholic beverages, which latter continually were being offered me and which I did not like. I last went to New York at the age of five-and-twenty, when I was cast into it as into a seething whirlpool, "broke," at the time, heavy-hearted, and alone. My little body, like Juliet's, was already aweary of this great world. But what it and the heart in it had to suffer before they caught the meaning and the pace of the seething whirlpool only the silent gods know. I may one day write it or I may keep it, a black memory, locked fast within me. But this much let me say for myself, that I bore misfortune in solitude and with cold disdain for its slings and arrows, and New York, though it has got everything else out of me that I could give it, wrung not one salt tear from my tired eyes. It gives me infinite satisfaction to be able to say it now and before I left New York, but a little time ago - yet, I remembered even that crucial time as a precious and informing experience. Also before I left I could gauge New York - I could grasp it, as I now grasp Butte, in the hollow of my hand. Nothing in it could faze or frighten me. The skyscrapers had become something attractive and beloved, and the quick fire of the alcoholic things, absinthe, vermouth, chartreuse, had run a thousand times, a negative passion, in my veins. In short, on the altar of the exquisite vampire I had offered up, madly and gladly, what was left of the first half of my youth. I am conscious as I sit here, in the chaste silence of West Park street, in my blue and white room, of but just entering on the second half of my youth - which is a fuller half than the first, if less radiant; light-hearted and care-freer, if less innocent - and by those tokens I fain would haste with it to where the North and East rivers wash the glittering shores of the Isle of Treacherous Delights - to lay it upon the same broad altar, already piled high with a million like gifts.

There is nothing at all in New York that is not fascinating to those who love it. For them there is poetry in every seething subway station, in every low-down Italian, with his banana cart on the Third and Fourth avenue corners, in the Siegel and Macy and Wanamaker department stores, as well as in the wonderful shops on the avenue, in the vaudeville theaters, and even in the piano-organs that awaken the echoes and the dwellers in the apartment buildings on the side streets. To them the look of New York is beautiful. No turreted castle overlooking a desolate sea could show more picturesque than the Flatiron building at sunset, with the dying lights on its battlements, and the Twenty-third street mob, like scurrying insects, at its base. And close to it is another thing of beauty which to me typifies the spirit of all New York - the great bronze Diana of St. Gaudens, which rests a-tiptoe on the Madison Square tower. She suggests youth in its gay and triumphant freedom.

But, however, it's not for those chaste delights alone I'm longing in the midst of West Park street's remote gloom. One can not live on even Flatiron buildings, and Diana, though she's inspiring, is not satisfying to the emotions she rouses. Besides, she's bronze.

But the quality that is so distinctively New Yorkish, and which Butte-Montana conspicuously lacks (having in its place the deadly thrall we all wot of), is the quality of deep and intimate humanness. It is that and not the glitter which makes people, after a half-year of living in it, fall so abandonedly in love with New York; it is that which makes New York people think there's no other town in the world. They may tell you it's the glitter of the gay white way, or the cafes, or the theaters, or the Fifth avenue parade, or what not, but those are only the delectable setting. It's the subtle freemasonry among the millions, the silent recognition and understanding of each other's humanness and the half suggestion of intimacy that one feels toward all or any of the persons one meets and passes on Broadway - it's that that's all the glitter and enchantment of it. And, too, it's that together with the glitter of the white way that is the most alluring and treacherous and annihilating of all the attributes of the vampire. In truth, it is that quality that is the vampire. For it's intimacy with human beings and all that it betokens - the exchanging of bits of one's personality for bits of another's, the idiosyncrasies of friend-ship, the nerve-racking experience of being in love, the hypnotic effects of one personality upon another, the utter throwing to the winds of all one's reserves of body and soul before the compelling magnetisms of some, and the lesser intoxication of knowing one's domination of others - it is all these things that devour flesh and blood and nerve. They eat their way from the outer wall that guards the crude human being to the inmost keep of the citadel. One's loves and friendships have effects on one's slim young body and one's wayward mind that are more malignant than cocaine and more subtle than absinthe. But it's all so exquisitely and poetically and seductively worth while. Not one affair of the heart - and even friendships with me seem to be affairs of the heart - that New York has given me, though they left me, times, battered, stung, wounded, a bundle of frazzled nerves - not one would I exchange for any non-human treasure that life could bring. If there's one tenet that I cling to with sincerity and faith, it's that which enjoins absolute freedom of action, to follow not the precepts but the impulses, to grasp one's heart's desires, to emulate the surging voice of all New York in its wild cry, "More Life, More Life!" - to turn everything outward, to let slip all one's emotions, all one's glimmering passion, all one's dormant lights-o'-love.

That's what you do in New York. And it's that that makes the deadly thrall of Butte seem deadlier and the stillness of West Park street more deep. No solitary cell at Sing Sing could rival my little blue and white room at this moment for aloofness, for there's no such thing as human intimacy in this young, young town.

I did not know that when I lived in Butte before I had myself no intimate friendships, but I knew that I was entirely abnormal, anyway. But since I've been gone from it I realize that the people in Butte are all abnormal in that they form no real intimacies. They are as shy as wild sea-fowl with each other, and absolutely dead-locked in iron-bound personal isolation. They have what they call friendships, and there are little clubs of women who foregather, and people take drinks together and that - but with it all they are not, they seemingly can't be, intimate with each other. They think they exchange bits of their personalities, when they are really exchanging only talk. They exchange kisses and hand-clasps and even lingering caresses, but all in the deadly thrall way. I idly wonder as I sit here whether there would be anything intimate about even the doing of a murder in Butte. "But no," I think to myself, "there would be more of passion, let loose, in New York in a mere brushing together of finger-tips, or in gazing into eyes across a little table, than in anything that's done in Butte. It's the way you do them in New York."

Butte's way is without doubt the wiser of the two, but what's that to do with it? Butte's way makes for more strength in that since one turns nothing outward, one's resources are husbanded, but what's the use? What do we do with our strength after we husband it? There's no development where there's no intimacy. One barely begins to live only after one has rubbed hard against at least two live people, with nerves in their finger-ends and lights in their eyes.

I have in Butte two deadly, thrall friendships - or are they a love and a friendship, I don't myself quite know - upon which I've been bold enough, since I've been back, to try out the methods in favor on and hard-by the white way. It's fascinating to watch their effects, which are to one-third perplex, one-third frighten, and one-third allure. I get nothing of the kind myself in return, since the wild sea-bird shyness is fast upon them and I have all the advancing to do, but, withal, I have at least the pleasure of making two people writhe at the unusualness, in Butte, of friendship in the nude.

But pungent though it is, it is not a wholly satisfying pursuit and the half-lenient gods, after all, do not limit me to those two. There are one or two people in Butte who have themselves lived on the Isle of Treacherous Delights. I find they know the game as it's played there, and they go to it with a recognizing, if shy, eagerness. But - this is Butte-Montana, where the on-lookers make scarlet mountains of drab mole hills - and when all's said I believe I, M. MacLane, am the one citizen Butte will ever have who is absolutely undisturbed and undeterred by the whispering tongues. Contempt is the word which correctly pictures my attitude toward them. And contempt is the correct attitude to maintain. Why should they judge me? Why should any one judge any one else? Which brings me back to little old New York, where no one judges any one else. How much better to be living than slowly drying up inwardly. How much better to be in New York, where people are really let live. How I long at this witching hour of midnight, with the staid quietness of West Park street oppressing me, and at the threshold of my second half of youth, to feel once more the lips of the vampire very close against mine.

On the corner of Fifth avenue and Twenty-sixth street, close to where the bronze Diana stands, poised against the blue, is the Cafe Martin, where the Dry Martini is more palely golden than anywhere else on the Isle, where the people are more attractive and all the delights more bewitchingly treacherous. It has been the scene of more new and well nigh insane adventures for me - and a million other feminine youths - than probably any cafe could be outside London. It is swagger, extremely French (for America), and cordial in its welcome to unescorted women before the bell tolls six in the evening. The place is so pallidly, prettily decorated, the music is so thin and sensuous, the women such high wrought things. It is consequently crowded with them from lunch-time until then. There are also men to be sure - at about four in the afternoon, when one type of the masculine absinthe-drinker of New York assembles to steep its sodden soul in anise. But the restaurant which looks on the Avenue is mostly filled with women, such a picturesque crowd, with a freedom of mood upon them which is remarkable even in New York. They are nearly all young women - (but New York women are still in the throes of youth at five-and-forty) - there are artists, writers, chorus-girls, vaudeville people, *habitues* of Bohemia, *dilettantes* of all sorts - all the loose young feminine fish in New York. It is the one cafe on the Isle wherein the crowd is not specialized - where that most fascinating, most complex, most unexplainable of human beings, the New York young woman, may be seen in the mixed aggregate. In that the Martin is unlike the Knickerbocker, up at Forty-second street, the center of the Rialto and the haunt of the moneyed but unaristocratic theatrical people, or the Cafe des Beaux Arts, frequented chiefly by the high-browed followers of the arts, or Rector's, beloved of the refined *demimondaines*, or Churchill's, loved of the unrefined ones, or Sherry's, the feeding-place of the swagger, or the Waldorf, where the ungrammatical and heavily upholstered inhabitants of Pittsburgh feel at home, or Maria's, the resort of the not-too-successful *litterateurs*, or Jack's, where the hippodrome ballet nightly grazes. Any or all of those types are to be seen at Martin's, whereas they would be unlikely to find themselves at any two of the others.

What a picture of youth it is at the Martin, at four in the afternoon! - a picture of tired, tired youth, women like crushed lilies or half-wilted jonquils. They are all in the clutch of the vampire. The mark of the vampire is upon their delicately-rouged and faintly-drooping lips, in the glint of their all-knowing eyes, upon their insolent brows and in the movements of their slender hands. Their hearts and bodies are weary from the ceaseless glitter of the world and from their endless pursuit of Pleasure - a Pleasure like an *ignis fatuus* that is always a little way beyond, that never, never waits. I have seen it myself around corners, behind doors, at the top of flights of stairs - always beyond, never in my hands or by my side. I have sat, times, in the Martin, with some delectable companion, twirling the stem of my absinthe glass with my thumb and finger and with my chin on my hand, and looked about at the gay-hearted company and wondered if they knew they had never caught up with the *ignis fatuus* Pleasure, and never would - and if they did that the flavor of the Grape would become wormwood on their lips, and the daylight shadowed, and the music stilled.

But no, assuredly they never think of it at all. The generality of the amblers down the primrose path are happily not given to introspection. That is a seething curse peculiar to those to whom the birth-stars are not kind, with whom it plays perennial mischief. And if one is both lured by the primrose path and, too, given to introspection - so much the more grievous the curse - so much the more.

For as one sits here, in the aforesaid silence, it comes over one like a cold, distracting breath, and the look of all of life makes one but shudder. One's longing for the Isle of Delights falls away like a mantle - that mad utter folly, that dedication of all things to life at its last and utmost tension, that picture of the flower-faces, of tired youth, in the Cafe Martin - float across one's mind with a suggestion of blackness like death itself.

One wants no human intimacy either in the marts of New York or the little by-ways of Butte. One sees one's portion in an aloofness and isolation far beyond what even Butte can give. For the having fed at the flesh-pots in the Isle of the Delights one pays a heavy, heavy reckoning - and to introspection that does it all. It once made the Delights more seductive, and it now makes the heavy reckoning so much the more heavy - so much the more, and -

"The Flower that once has bloomed forever dies."

New York or Butte-Montana, is it worth while - or isn't it? I ask me, with my hands pressed upon my eyes.

"The Borrower of Two-Dollar Bills - and Other Women"

Butte Evening News · 15 May 1910

I, of womankind and something-and-twenty years, have by this time con-cluded that those gay buccaneers, the citizens of Butte, whose victims are the set-apart individualities in their midst, are going to put their own peculiar con-struction upon every thing one writes, say what one may to prevent it, which being the case, it's only to let them go ahead and do it. When I find I can not stem a tide I instantly stop trying and move aside with as much of good grace and light-hearted contempt as may be - and I let the wild water rush upon its way. Even though it's a matter one cares about much - still, it's to give but the shrug of a shoulder and to let all effort in the contrary direction die at its birth. When you come right down to it, I am fond of those gay buccaneers, the citizens of Butte. I should prefer that they understood me, rather than to in some ways misunderstand so profoundly as they do. But they never will. No, they never, never will. It's to let it pass. They will in particular misunder-stand some things about this article and the side of me it reveals. I care about it, but, well - *un haussement de m'epaule,* and forever my love to the citizens of Butte. The men I have met and known more or less intimately in my seven years of experience have far outnumbered the women and have been far easier to know and classify and manipulate and manage. But for some inexplicable reasons the women I have known and loved have been the crucial incidents in my life, the real and informing events. They have been alike my staunchest friends and my worst and bitterest enemies - the stars of my night and the murky pools and the pitfalls and snares about my feet. Women have always been, since the days of the Anemone Lady, more interesting to me than men, because they're more complex, more subtle, fuller of delicate incongruities and illusions, harder to understand. Two-thirds of all the women in the world, some consciously and some unconsciously, have the same feeling toward their own kind. There are millions who conventionally marry some worthy and agreeable husband and are happy with him in a perfectly sane and bromidic way - but the while to their woman friends, possibly without knowing it, they give all their poetry, all their imagination, their subtlety, their intricate complexity, their mental concentricity and fascination, and their tenderness of heart. And there are many women who recognize and admit the charmed fact. It is not wonderful. What every woman knows is that each and all of us are cursed with vulnerable fragile bodies, and vulnerable sensitively-sincere hearts which together bring, often and often, an anguished durance so poignantly real as to be the dominating factor of life with us, and yet so remote as to be beyond thought and analysis - beyond everything but feeling, and of which men have not the most shadowy conception. In the plainest language women could tell it in, it will be to men as Greek and Sanskrit; not even the men poets (with - who knows? - the exception of that most wonderful of them all, Robert Browning) know the inner voice of women. Not even Elizabeth Browning, as deeply woman as poet, could write the thing itself, though in her life and in the feeling of her poems it speaks fatally, heartbreaking, albeit with a restrained passion-flower sort of quiescence. It is this thing that to two-thirds of all women is the silent unseen tie that binds.

At that I shall but picture a few hybrid women who have been my friends and half-friends and passing acquaintances in New York of the Treacherous Delights. Women do not come in types except physically and in other outward seeming - each of them is mostly a personality and an individuality unto herself. Outwardly two women, or a dozen, may be of the same type - their bodies may have the same kind of garnishment as to clothes and coiffures and grooming, but inwardly they differ as the poles. One may be a settlement worker and another a kept woman; one may be a cloak model and another a club woman; one may be a plain crook and another a trained nurse - and yet be of one physical and mental caste. Caste - which has nothing to do with class - is possibly the subtlest distinction by which we differentiate human beings, and at first blush we make the mistake of thinking it a matter of breeding and environment and education. It is a long mistake. Caste, as the people of the world are measured, is caste of our physical equipment and the effects of our subsequent lives upon it, combined with the much or little of mental adroitness, which is not mentality, we may develop. It's a fascinating bit of work to determine that subtle distinction of caste among the people one knows, particularly women, and particularly in New York where women are the pervading spirit - the duchesses, the town princesses, the Beloved of the Town; a little nation of Nell Gwynns.

I have not known so many of them as of men, but still, during my last two years in New York, life seethed with women. They were one's companions in the apartment houses where one lived, at matinees, in tea rooms, at the Cafe Martin, in the shops, on Fifth avenue at the ends of the afternoons, on Broadway always, at the apartments of friends - in all the highways and byways. If you're an unattached young woman living alone in New York, and markedly a free-lance, you'll meet up with a million other unattached women. They color up your life and mean adventure - in the day-light and the dark. During my last months in New York I had an apartment - four and a half green-and-white rooms - with a young woman with whom I had once been good friends, but with whom I then maintained but a semi-intimate aloofness suitable for the sharers of apartments. Experienced livers in New York apartments - it's probably of all modes of living the most checkered and highly-seasoned - will tell you that the unwisest thing you can do is to take an apartment with any one you're fond of. My friend, a girl a year or two younger than I, who looked like an angelic child, but was in reality a little demon for tempers and furies, and as variable and false as the shade of the light-quivering aspen, with two divorced husbands and a meteoric career in her offing - had her own friends and I had mine. And the women (to say nothing of the men) who were likely to ring our telephone bell at any hour of the day or night were variegated indeed. When the bell rang for me it might be the Borrower of Two-Dollar Bills, the Logical Thief, the Morose Manicure Girl, the Golden Weeper, the Literary Woman, the Chorus Girl, the Young Russian Anarchist, the High-browed Actress, the Piquant and Passionate Pursuer, the Devilish Sub-Editor of the *Woman's Home Companion*, the Red-Headed Fisher of Men, the Fluffy Slob, my Friend in the Face-Fixing Business, the Discontented Marryer of Husbands, the Pink-and-Blue Dilettante, - or one of many more. When you consider that they all lived their lives, not as we do in Butte, Montana, with a deadly thrall and a wild-sea-bird shyness upon us, but as they do in New York, with absolute freedom and abandonment of emotion and nerve - you may infer that at least one's life had color. Seventeen minutes being one's time on the stage, one can picture but a few of them.

The Borrower of Two-Dollar Bills I met first in the Cafe Martin. I was sitting alone one afternoon behind that interesting door labeled "Smoking-Room Pour les Dames," upstairs, when there ambled over to me a half-beautiful woman of perhaps seven-and-thirty, in a black princess gown of a swagger cut and a black turban of the *chicest,* but with an indefinable air of subtle vagabondage about her. She had a complexion and skin of a lustrous softness and large sea-green eyes, and dusky hair artistically done, and she was in that state of goodfellowship which betokens recent libation - not too much, but some. "Kiddo," remarked this personage, "do you happen to have an extra Milo on you? I'm dying for a puff." I didn't have a Milo, but I lassoed Felice, the maid, and got her a box - her personality promised entertainment. She sank down upon a divan with one black suede foot on a taboret, and "lit up" - and spoke with a certain lack of reserve. "You're probably thinking, 'Gee, what a crust!' but as I said, I'm dying for a puff, and between you and me I'm absolutely strapped - I haven't even the price of one of these." I expressed a proper regret, which led the conversation into how extremely easy it is to be "strapped" in New York. "My God!" said the subtle vagabond, "for eighteen years I've never been able to see an hour and a half into my future, and yet I've lived - and always within a cab-whistle of Forty-second street and Broadway, at that. Me for the Rialto. I started in vaudeville, when vaudeville was punk, and then I did the choruses, and then I understudied Edna May for three years. I've earned the living wage, all right - but what's a living wage in New York? Besides, I've always been too strong on the liquor. Gee, I'm never happy if I'm not half soused all over - and now I've got a profession that almost makes ends meet." "And what's that?" said I. "I live by borrowing two-dollar bills all over the island and Brooklyn and Jersey City, wherever I can. Some days a few and some days a lot, but always some." "But," said I, "I should think you'd soon get to the end of your tether, and the works shut down, sort of." "Oh, not at all," said the Borrower, airily. "New York is a big place. Everybody in New York at two dollars a throw would mean a fortune, wouldn't it? Of course I don't know quite everybody, but at that it's a fertile field. I almost make ends meet. New York's certainly a big place." "But why limit each touch to two dollars?" I inquired. "Kiddo," said the Borrower, "because I don't want the populace forever at my heels. If they threw good money after a bad lady, wouldn't they be apt to follow her up? But who's going to follow up a two-dollar bill? It's a real profession - and let me again remind you, New York's a big place. I'll tell you a lot about it - if you happen to have the price of a couple of drinks on you." Unfortunately I had. It led to an acquaintanceship and almost constant companionship which lasted seven weeks and led me into the twilit mazes of life as it's led by the genus parasite. The Borrower of Two-Dollar Bills was one who lived for her physical senses alone. She had no friendships, though plenty of companions, and her one heart-interest had been years in its grave. She lived but to pamper and satiate her senses - she was held in a desolate bondage of the body which made even me feel like an ethereal sprite from a higher plane. But her effect upon me was like that of a blasting devitalizing south wind. There are many like her in New York.

The Literary Woman - I just knew her in Boston - a friend of mine for years, a girl of about thirty, with a pallid husband who was a secondary interest, her first being her work, which was short stories, for which she had made a distinct market. She was rather beautiful in a foreign-looking way, with a small svelte body, a complexion of rose-and-bronze, and eyes like hazel-colored half-glacial windows to her mind. She had spasmodic warmths of heart (I was, and am, fond of her), but I should hate to be wholly dependent on one of her ilk for the light o' love. This her line of talk:

"MacTrey, I don't know just how you look at it, but to me the two most worthwhile things in God's world are Fame and Freedom. If I were to be granted three wishes this instant, this instant I should say: Fame, Freedom, and the ability I feel in me now to appreciate them absolutely to their last pitch. I know I'll never be free - I'll always be held down by a hundred fetters, because I'm afraid. But I fully intend to be famous, if it isn't till I'm fifty. I've made me a short-story reputation in four years, by just keeping on hammering my typewriter and bucking the literary game. As for you, MacTrey, I don't quite get your attitude, and perhaps you'll say it's none of my business, but I can't help thinking you're squandering and dissipating your life on these experiences of yours - you seem to pay so high and to such an insatiate piper. In your place, what wouldn't you do? You've proved you're not afraid of anything the world can hand you and you've got, at an age which seems to me just like being a little girl, your own particular niche of fame. With that you might do anything - you might make even this big flinty New York sit up and rub its eyes and stare till they dropped out - you could put it all over the two million other sulphites. But instead of that you madly flit about after silver-and-scarlet butterflies. For what you have only to stretch out a languid hand and take, I'd give my useless soul for." "Jane," said I, "don't be a bore. Let's go over to Keith's and see Yvette Gilbert, she goes on at three. She has an exquisite French sort of pathos about her which will take your mind off me." "Yes, I want to see her," she replied, "I want to study her type a little. It's distinctly European. But I'd like still more to give you a much-needed spanking." A good sort, the rose-and-bronze, but if you ask me, a sort which misses the pink honey of life. There are many like her in New York.

The Devilish Sub-Editor of the *Woman's Home Companion*. She and I were pals-at-arms, and occasionally at daggers drawn, for six months. She had black, dead-looking hair, wonderful Nile-green eyes, a battered young body - she was about eight-and-twenty - and a clever and cynical mind. I was first attracted toward her by the delicate incongruity of her being on the staff of the *Woman's Home Companion* - herself would have fitted into the home-and-fireside with the facility and appropriateness of a billy goat. She was one of the crookedest pals I've ever had (which is putting it strong). She never told the truth when she could get away with a lie, and she drank whiskey, she drank absinthe, she "shot" cocaine occasionally, she took a form of deadly nightshade, and she played fast and loose, not only with her own emotions but with other people's. At twenty-eight she looked all of forty, and she had a fancy for dressing like a Lithuanian peasant woman - in a dark green kirtle and skirt with a white bodice. She and I met every noon, on the corner of Thirty-fourth street and Sixth avenue, and walked over to a Turkish Restaurant and had luncheon. "I love this place," said the Devilish Sub-Editor, "for a variety of reasons, and though we discovered it together I shall keep on coming here alone, even after you have begun to hate me, cherie. There's so much about it that's satisfyingly decadent and suggestive of death. This mysterious salad, perchance, is made from the green things which grow on poets' graves, and those white hyacinths - Monsieur the Headwaiter surely purchased them early this morning from one who took them from the dead body of a snow-maiden who died in her innocence. To eat this white, white flesh of the suckling pig is like eating one's own baby garnished with sugared cherries. The coffee is a heavy drug, and this ridiculous wine, for its warm, mild taste and its fiery effects, might be the blood of Sappho. And the people - look at those at that corner table, five of them, with white faces - I'll lay you three bob that the pupils of their eyes almost overlap the irises and are blacker than night - fine people, sitting eating and yet, as they sit, dead - dead. Drink up, MacTrey, and we'll pledge their deadness in another pint." She filled me with mirth as long as her crookedness didn't turn in my direction. But still, as a human being she was not a complete success. There are many, very many, like her in New York.

The Golden Weeper - my friend and daily companion for several months, during which time I had more tears, reproaches, recriminations, threats, jealousies, tempers, and general uproar of emotion spilled over me, like a glittering cascade, than life has contained for me before or since. I was very fond of her, and am yet, for the game abandonment with which she threw herself into all her affections. She was a charming young thing, a year or two younger than I, with golden hair and golden eyes, a slim young body and lips of startling redness. She played a harp in vaudeville and sang in a voice sweet as jessamine, as a vocation, and for pleasure and pastime she made a fine art of friendship. She made it altogether too fine an art - she would split hairs and snatch at straws, and trifles as light as air were things to be argued over for half a week without sleeping. And I - I matched her at it - we waded together in a delightful river of silliness. She lived up at Eightieth street with a most ineffectual mother whom she had completely dominated at the age of two years, and ever after. The Golden Weeper was likely to come to call on me at any hour whatsoever, by preference three in the morning. A ring at our bell some rainy night and I would go to the door (three being the conventional hour than otherwise) to find her standing in the dim light of the apartment-house hall in a pale green evening frock and a white cloak. "You," said I - "all these blocks in the rain! Come in - what is it now?" "No, I can't come in," said the Golden one. "I've come to ask you if you still love me." "You know I do," said I. "In fact I told you so at eleven o'clock this morning." "But I saw you at four o'clock this afternoon and you didn't say so then, and you looked at me only twice, and your manner was cold at that," said the Weeper. "Because you spent too much time talking to that LeMonte woman," I made answer. "Well, what could I do - you were simply eating that little Lloyd - I had to talk with somebody," said the Weeper. "And I talked to Lloyd," I said, "which is different from eating her, because she was the only one there who was friendly toward me. The rest of them didn't like me, and you joined with them, and yet you call yourself my dearest friend." "I didn't join with them," said the Golden Weeper; "you always say that - but I tell you, once and for all, you'll not have another chance." And, presto! a flood of golden and temporary tears de luxe. "If you think to start anything in the sympathetic line, with me, by weeping," said I, "you're making a deep mistake. You weep a deal too easily and too often." "Have I said I wanted to start anything?" said the Golden one; "and tears of mine have nothing to do with you." And so on and on. The gray dawn crept in at darkling skylights and we would still be standing at the door of the green-and-white apartment engaged in what was to us a fascinating cross-purpose. An ardent child of impulse, the Golden Weeper, and in New York there are many, many like her.

There are many, many of all ilks in New York. They move in deep and shallow waters. But in the deeps or the shallows they are all, and with it all - just human: the same in Butte-Montana.

"A Waif of Destiny on the High Seas"

Butte Evening News · 22 May 1910

The thing I went in for during my all-too-brief sojourn in New York was not to improve my erratic mind and my slim, young body, but to fill them both to the gunwales with life, to have them beaten and tossed about and played with by the long swishing waves and wild white-capped breakers which roll over Manhattan with each sun's rising and setting. And if the cold gods had conspired together to that end I could not better have had my wish. I was borne along on the tumbling waves like an unmoored and rudderless cat-boat - a waif of destiny on the high seas. And all about were crafts of every known shape, from light-riding white-sailed ships, aflutter with pennants, to low rakish craft which flew the black flag. And 'twas many and many a one of them that ran across my bows.

You can go to New York for a variety of reasons: to study something - anything, from settlement work to the stock-broking game; to earn money or to spend it (it's a particularly good place for the latter purpose); to market your wares or to commit suicide; to turn your wits into money or to learn to poetically poison your body by way of the delicate pallid-tinted vices of the day. But my hope when I went there was that I might get local color - not to write with, but to swathe myself in - I wanted to gather up great lumps of it and throw it into my unquiet life, to make it of vermilion and indigo. I wanted to mix with something seething and vast and human and detailed. And as I always do what I want to do, if the road lies straight before me - or even if it's crooked, yet accessible - I got what I wanted from little old New York. The unhuman aloofness which once was mine New York knocked off me in less than twenty flitting weeks, and for local color - my two perfectly good hands and my slim, young body were fascinatingly stained with it, in all the wonderful tints and tones, in a twelve-months' time. Here and yet, in the fastnesses of Butte-Montana, I look at my finger-tips and I see a little rose-glow of passion on them: the local color of the town of Treacherous Delights. And it will not rub off. It will never rub off.

Of three elemental things which lure humanity, the lure of the wild, the lure of the blood, and the lure of seething cities, it's the lure of seething cities which is the last winner out. The lure of the wild - back to Nature, and that - is strong, but at best a spasmodic thing. Our love for it hardly outbids our love for beds to sleep in, looking-glasses to look in, and silver forks and white serviettes at dinner. The lure of the blood is indeed passing strong - a pleasure of the chase (or the chased), an enchantment, a seduction, an intoxication, all washed in the same white-burning fire and born of the same red instinct. It moves the world, but at that, following forever at its heels, are tawdry emotions of remorse, regret, dark humors, malcontents - and always there's the fatal element of satiety, the drop too much which can make wormwood of gold honey. But the lure of seething cities we have always with us. Their civilizations are as down cushions between our slim, young bodies and the rough surfaces of the world. The uncounted variety in them forfends satiety, and their infinite humannesses are the all-magnetic thrall that, while we contemn it, leads us to them, and back to them, and holds us in a quiescent bondage. It were better, as everybody knows, to live in New York and be knocked about and battered and bruised and seared, and by those tokens to be gifted with one spark of charity for one's kind, than to be deadlocked in a remote New England town, hedged in by puritanic and subtly immoral precepts, and with a large distrust of things human, like a worm in the bud, gnawing forever at one's soul.

The women I knew in New York were not, for the most part, an elevat-ing influence - and all that tiresome stuff. They were something human to be liked, studied as piquant articles of *vertu*, loved, and made friends of. There are women in New York who go in for cults - religious, mental, psychological, scientific - what not? - till they're blue in the face, or at least in the vitals, but who have not reached so high a plane, from any viewpoint whatsoever, as a hash-slinger who meets misfortune gamely and is on the level with her pals. I associated with a lot of women, friends and half-fiends, whom I didn't in the least approve of, but at that I don't entirely approve of anybody - myself, or the citizens of Butte. If I like people, that's enough for me - approving of them be damned, as I used to say in my first book. (From people, by the way, of whom I do entirely approve, kind Devil deliver me.) But this article is to picture a few live ladies I have met, so it's to have at them - as many as one has space for, culled from among those captioned: the Logical Thief, the Morose Manicure Girl, my Face-Fixing Friend, the Discontented Marryer of Husbands, the Kind-hearted Landlady, the Fluffy Slob, the Pink-and-Blue Dilettante, the Red-Headed Fisher of Men.

The Fluffy Slob - a fat blonde person, with very white hands, very pink, shiny nails, very yellow hair, very glad clothes, and a very noticeable lack of brains - was my next-door neighbor in the last New York apartment-house but one that I lived in. She barely knew she lived. She had a white poodle, even fluffier than herself, and a black maid who regulated her life. It was the maid who put her to bed at night, hauled her up in the morning, sat her down to her food, and girded up her loins when she went forth on the highways. She was one of those vague people who float along on the high-tides of life without effort and without volition - to whom the whole scheme is naught but eating, sleeping, and the donning of gay raiment. She was a most lazy creature - too lazy even to pronounce her words correctly. And thus the Fluffy Slob: "But if you really wanta know a nice gen'leman, you wait till you meet my gen'leman frien'. My gen'leman frien', he comes Friday nights, and we have a good, quiet, comfortable time. On Friday night I don' care for the theater, and I don' care to stick around the restaurants, and I don' care to go out in a taxi - I just wanta sit down and have a talk with my gen'leman frien'. His manners are so restful - you hardly know you're entertainin' a gen'leman when he's there - he's that soothin'. You yourself seem to have such noisy frien's - I hear you in there sometimes. And so I just wantcha to meet my gen'leman frien'." And one Friday night I did meet the gen'leman frien'. He was, indeed, all that she had said. If the Fluffy Slob was barely conscious of living, her gen'leman frien' went her one better - he had all but passed away. He was pallid, white-haired, silent - a very ghost of a gen'leman frien'. Yet I dare say he had his uses in this bright world - he suited the Fluffy Slob right down to the ground. And there are many, many like her in New York.

The Red-Headed Fisher of Men was a half-friend of mine and a marked contrast to all fluffy slobs and other tame birds. She was a dazzler - a high-flier and a very beautiful woman - with slenderness and grace and hair like burnished copper shining in the sun. Her way of entering a room was like that of the duchesses of one's dreams, and her speaking voice was the most seductive I have ever heard. It rivaled Mrs. Fiske's, in Mrs. Fiske's great moments. And with all this equipment the Red-Headed Fisher was nothing more and nothing less than a blackmailer, and her prey was Wall Street brokers. She used occasionally to have a cup of tea and a cigarette with me, and an afternoon's visit. And thus the Red-Headed: "Well, it may not be ethics and it may not be morals, but if I see a man with a pair of eyes in his head and a large account in a bank, I've just naturally got to have my toll out of it. The easiest thing in the world, believe me, Mary MacLane, is to blackmail a broker. They seem to lose their heads and then you've got them. They always have wives and fearfully respectable families and that makes them insanely cautious - so cautious they defeat their own purpose. But after all, it isn't because they're so very respectable, or so very cautious, that I find them an easy prey - it's because I myself - I say it without vanity - am so very handsome. I have lived, and lived well, on my looks alone since I was twelve years old. There's hardly a broker in Wall Street who wouldn't object to it being known that I visit his office, simply because I'm good looking and so well got up that everybody who knew it would suspect the 'ulterior motive.' So, as I say, it's the easiest thing in the world - a half-hour's perfectly innocent conversation in a broker's office, and either he gives me as much money as I ask for - I'm wise enough not to demand too much - or I make things generally very nasty for him by simulating intimacy and telling a few wonderful lies. Of course," added the Red-Headed, "unless one is very, very beautiful it doesn't work. But I know I'm beautiful - I have to know it - just as you know you're brainy, and Maude Adams knows she's magnetic." "You're certainly a stunner," said I, "and awfully clever, and a good fellow and altogether delectable - a rose o' the world. But your business seems to me a very rotten business to be in - you must have terrible moments." "Oh, yes, of course," she replied, "but who hasn't terrible moments? They're all in the day's work. I also have a very good living. I make men pay even for the privilege of admiring me - and so they should, what?" Rose of the world she surely looked, but she surely looked also a fisher of men. And like her, too, there are very, very many in New York.

My friend in the Face-Fixing Business - a plump bit of flotsam-and-jetsam, aged about five-and-forty, upon whom the untoward fates had wrought their wandering will for all of thirty brazen years. The world was her oyster and she either was constantly opening it by the hard brass of her kind of philosophy or having her fingers pinched and snapped by the sharp-edged and strong-muscled bivalve when it proved beyond her. She was heavily built, smartly garbed in black tailored suit, and endowed with a strongly marked appetite for food. If of her own purchasing the food took the form, perchance, of low-browed pork-chops, of some one else's it covered a wide range, from mallard duck to Mumm's. In two thick-padded, patchouli-scented rooms in Twenty-third street, just off the Avenue, she conducted the business of putting anything from a thick layer of complexion to an entire new face on a large and somewhat shady clientele of female women. I first knew her in the life-time of her husband (who was the manager of Armless Wonders and Oriental Dancers and other unpleasing things) between whom and herself cups, plates, and saucers flew at meal-times with startling regularity and fury. Once a cup, which she aimed at her husband, went unusually wide of the mark and hit me beneath the ear with quite some force. From which time she and I were the best of friends. It was several years ago in Boston, and when I saw her again in New York her husband had been gathered to his long house and she was doing faces for a livelihood. She had an apartment up at Ninety-sixth street and thither I went every Monday night to take dinner with her. The dinner was sent in from a cafe and served by an antique deaf woman, "not quite all there," to quote popular rumor, who acted as intermittent hand-maiden for seven other apartments in the same building. And thus my Face-Fixing Friend: "Now, Mary MacLane, if I seem to chuck in the eats for awhile instead of talking to you, just you remember I'm a poor working girl with a pelican's appetite. If you'd all day been doing over the maps of the rankest lot of plucked fowl that ever blew home from a week-end up the country, you'd know what honest hunger is. Here's the viands, so go to it, 'bo. Bring along that drawn-butter, you devil" - to the antique who presently sauntered nonchalantly in with it. The edge of the pelican's appetite having been removed, she proceeded. "If you ever think, Mary MacLane, of throwing away your little old pen and going into the face-fixing business, take a tip from me and gently refrain. I've been in several lines, but this certainly has them all nailed to the mast for showing up the kinks in the characters of ladies. I was in the hair-shampooing business for a while - I went up and down the Island dragging a living out of the tangled heads of the populace - and some nifty menages did I get into, my word. But that was nothing to what I get in this business. While I'm busy with my little trowel, laying on complexions, they're busy handing me out their raw inside histories. Bring the salad, you vampire. Yes, they tell me everything they know, and I hate it. It makes me feel as if I got only the lungs and livers and gizzards of life, and none of the white meat. But they seem to think I like it. Today a woman, whose complexion looked as if it had been eaten off her by a wild-cat, came in to have it put on again, and if she didn't give me one bad hour then I never had one. She gave me the complete story of her past, dating from about a day and a half before her birth (which it seems was premature and not entirely unconnected with her father's having eloped with the parlor-maid) up to that hour. Her family seem to have been visited with about every known affliction from cholera infantum to delirium tremens, and from very weak minds to very strong passions - and your face-fixing friend had 'em spread all over her. And, of course, it's me for the sympathetic every time. If they don't get their money's worth of sympathy out of me, besides their complexions, they think they're cheated. If I could do one or the other alone, I would not mind. But when it comes to renovating maps badly damaged by Manhattan orgies and sympathizing all over the place besides - it would tell on a mule's constitution. Open another bottle, you jade. But there are three distinct advantages in the business, after all. It saves me the necessity of paying good money to the vaudeville theaters, the moving picture shows, and those phoney clinics 'for women only.'" Thus my Face-Fixing Friend like whom, even, there are several more in New York.

The Pink-and-Blue Dilettante: she was one of those astounding creatures to be met with, among the followers of the various arts, who strive madly to be original and unusual. The Pink-and-Blue was a girl of twenty-six, pretty, but rather colorless, with a yearly income of about three thousand dollars, which enabled her to be original up to the handle. She owned but two frocks at a time, a pink one and a blue one both made of liberty silk, which for some reason always looked appropriate. They looked like evening frocks in the evening, and yet at seven in the morning they seemed the nicest and girlishest of morning dresses. And at seven o'clock every Tuesday morning she came to call on me. She knew that that was as midnight to me, and she herself went to bed at any time between six in the evening and six in the morning. But seven o'clock and Tuesday morning invariably found her leaning over the foot of my little brass bed, in either her pink or her blue frock, and with her own special sort of conversation which she paid out without a smile and without a change of voice or face: "Daughter of Eve, I am come to drag thee from the arms of Morpheus back into this world of Pink Things. See, I have brought thee for breakfast a love apple," - laying a pale tomato on my white blanket - "rouse thee and eat it. I myself rose with the lark and performed three tasks: I made an inkwell out of a felt slipper; I killed my canary and ate it; I wrote an obscene letter to Lyman Abbott. Very presently I shall boil a ham. My grandfather's sister came an hour ago to visit me. I gave her the yellow bottle of salad dressing to play with and came away. A loathly object, she. But served in the form of veal pie she might pass. Once I wrote a monograph on how to make soup from corset-laces. Couldst do better, my pink pet, and write on how to make a veal pie from a great-aunt? Eternity itself might be fashioned out of a dead mouse, a rubber eraser, a postage stamp, and an umbrella. I crave a veal kidney. I must go. As I pass through your outer room I shall steal your brass snuff-box." Upon which I bounced out of bed and rushed after her to rescue my brass snuff-box - for the Pink-and-Blue quite meant what she said. A struggle for the snuff-box, and I was left gasping and bruised on the floor with the outer door closing on the Dilettante and the box. "That's the confoundest class of persons New York has to show," I thought to myself, as I crept back to bed. And New York can show many like her.

The Kind-hearted Landlady was a half-friend of mine who kept a lodging-house up-town and whom I liked to go and take a cup of tea with now and again, for being both kind-hearted and a landlady in New York struck me as being a very delicate incongruity indeed. She was a brow-beaten looking woman in a black wrapper, whom every ring at her front bell made start up like a frighted dear. She may have been laying up for herself treasures in heaven, but she assuredly laid up none in New York. Her kindness of heart, added to her being a landlady, meant a houseful of perpetually "broke" people who never paid their rent and were never turned out in the street. Consequently hers was an extraordinary little household, kept up on nothing a week, and with a very thick atmosphere of indebtedness always hanging over it. Said the Kind-hearted Landlady: "They not only can't pay their rent - they can't buy their food. So they want me to board them. I tried it for a week but, Lord, they ate me out of house and home - and me with nothing to show for it but a new sheaf of bills. And the gas-man came and threatened to jerk the gas range right out from under my pots and kettles - I was cooking dinner - if I didn't pay the gas bill. They own the stoves, you know. Well, he didn't do that, but he turned off the gas - and there was I with a half-cooked dinner, not a light in the house, not two coppers to buy a candle with, and a raft of hungry people sitting around in the dark. Just think of it - not the price of a tallow candle among twelve grown people." "Goodness," said I, in an inward spasm of mirth, "why on earth didn't you run out and pawn something?" "Pawn!" shrieked the Kind-hearted. "It's a pipe you don't really know what a New York lodging-house is if you suppose there was anything left to pawn with when we'd got this far. We'd have pawned our false teeth if we could. I thought I couldn't stay in this business when I started in, but I find I can't get out. I seem to have adopted eleven people, and I can't keep them and I can't throw them away. It's an awful life." Thus the Kind-hearted Landlady - and I believe there's not another in New York.

New York or Butte-Montana, as I have remarked before, they are all, and with it all, - just human: the fascinatingest thing in the world.

"The Autobiography of the Kid Primitive"

Butte Evening News · 3 April 1910

Far be it from me, in the insolent intrepidity of my youth, to make anything like excuse or exculpation to anybody who walks the earth, particularly the citizens of Butte. For I do what I do, and I write what I write, absolutely without let or hindrance, and with naught but high scorn for those who question it. If it's liked or if it's not liked - what boots it? If they line up with the javelins - what's that to me? Inside of me are good and sufficient reasons for what I do and what I write, and that's enough. The public's one privilege anent the matter is to cherish their own opinion. I don't expect them to change it, and a pox o' me, as they say in early English dramas, if they can make me change mine. Still, even that being so, I fain would say here this: If I seem mostly to write about myself for the citizens of Butte to run and read, it is not because of egotism and vanity, or because I'm fond of myself. I have but just my share, my human share, of egotism and no more, and no one who knows me ever saw my thousand faults with a clearer eye or a colder judgment than I do - my word upon it. And as for being fond of myself - Gramercy! (to quote again from the aforesaid dramas) - my chief feelings toward me are exasperation with a large "E," bewilderment with a large "B," and despair with a large "D." But I'm fascinated by myself because I'm always fascinated by live persons, and I am the live person I know most about. Of course, people don't admit it, but it's nonetheless evident that to each person the most fascinating thing in life is herself or himself - and next to that we are interested in other personalities. The pictures I have made of my personality have been the most real writing I have done. It was real. It was alive. And it happens to be a field that I have all to myself. Other writers lack the courage, or the audacity, or the gameness, or something, to turn their search-lights inward and write of what they see - and unless they make their fictional characters very striking and original indeed, the reading public will none of them. There are many, many novels published every year, clever ones, written by clever people, that are still-born or strangled at birth - never heard of - merely because they are fiction after all, and not reality. But the red Mary MacLane book, in some ways a far lesser thing than many of the still-born novels, was simply eaten up from the day it was published until two or three years later - it drew instant blood from the newspapers, the public, Anthony Comstock, and the vaudeville stage - not for its cleverness, or its originality, but because it was no little masquerade of fictional characters, but a live portrayal of one live young woman. I would myself give nearly anything in the world if some one else would write that sort of book - for the enthralling pleasure I should have in reading it, in feeling the heart-beats beneath the words.

Before I have done I shall, perhaps, write for the *Evening News* about such things as the condition of the roads, or the height of the Big Butte, or the look of the highlands, or the color of the sunsets - and lo, the people who condemn me for egotism and all, will be the first to cease reading it. I know human nature and the citizens of Butte well enough to be convinced of that.

Meanwhile, however, I still, in the present page, write of M. MacLane. If you're bored with it, gentle readers, then pray do not read further. Send the papers to the grocer's boy.

Though now I'm indeed of womankind and something-and-twenty years; though I've been cast by the heels out on the hard-paved highways of life; though I've had every possible experience that a young woman can have - except one or two; though I have had all of New York to be reckless in - yet there was a time when they were all far impossibilities, when life was largely mystery and battle, when "green fields and running brooks" were all my surroundings, when the pomps and vanities of this wicked world were all far removed from me; in short, there was a time when I was seven years old.

There are people who will tell you that we do not change with the going of years - we only develop. It might be, and I suppose that I, at seven, was the embryonic M. MacLane of now. But an even half of my character is different as day from night from the character of the hard young villain who was myself at seven, and the other half seems to me the same as it then was, without the development. But you can never tell about those things. The perspective and the view point alter so much that there's no certain comparison.

But my recollections of me at seven, and of the setting of my life, and of my own outlook upon it are as vivid in my memory as if 'twere all yestere'en. And yet so remote am I, a complex young woman, from the Primitive Kid of seven that it's as if I were making a picture of some other child.

The Primitive Kid lived in Minnesota, the land of the little lake, the gopher, the hazel nut, and the Norwegian hired girl. It was on the outskirts of a little town - a large gloomy-looking house, surrounded by oak trees, poplars, and balm-o'-Gileads. I can see the trees now on a sultry August afternoon, with a tense stillness upon them, with not a movement of leaf or whisper of branch, and a mysterious fearsomeness in their presence, and I can see the same trees just before sunset, lashing to and fro in the fury of a thunder squall, now looking like black masses of tangled foliage, and anon, lit up by terrific flashes of lightning in which each leaf-vein seemed picked out in silver-point lightning, such as is hardly known but in that region. And there were hedges of wild roses, pink-blooming in June, and a kitchen garden, and a corn field, and two brackish little ponds on our five acres, and stretches of bird-haunted woods. And the air from the wind-swept hillsides came laden with anemone and was exceeding sweet, and the subtle perfume of the meadows was rosemary, and the wet places in spring-time were a-bloom with blackthorn. Green grew the rushes on the shores of the little ponds and winding and devious were the hidden pathways in the woods. Also there was a great red barn where the wrens built their tiny houses over the sliding door and the swallows their mud nests under the eaves. And there was a horse or two and a cow or two inside it, and two spotted pigs in their pen back of it, and a chicken house at the side. It was full of nooks to play in and its possibilities were greater than if it had been a "fretted palace with music in th'enameled walls."

We were three who played and quarreled frantically together within its red portals. I, aged seven; Jim, my brother and henchman, aged five; and a chronic playmate and neighbor of ours, named Henrietta, aged six. I was a slim, tanned, pig-tailed person in a faded gingham frock reaching not quite to my knees - the same being handed down from my sister, whose cast-off, outgrown, faded summer-before's wardrobe meant tight detestation to me. I looked, on general principles, rather too much like a Shanghai rooster to be quite beautiful. Also I was insufferably arrogant and proud-stomached - a leader and a tyrant. Jim, my henchman, was an equally slim and somewhat freckled individual, plaid-kilted and glengarry-bonneted, a craven soul if ever there was one, whose keeper I seemed to be (very much against my will), whose lickings I had to take, whose business in life was four-flushing. And his sense of humor was a weird and astounding thing. But let me add for him that his four-flushing was done with extreme cleverness, that he was a faithful henchman and in crucial moments a game loser. That he was scared to death of a good, strong mosquito, hawk, or a humming bird in a rampant state, and would turn tail and run like a deer from an infant garter snake, that he had no imagination whatsoever, and was unable to project his mind so much as four minutes into the future, that he believed absolutely everything that was told him, by anybody - these were points in his makeup perhaps more to be pitied than censured. It is not to condemn him now for his defects. Say rather that as a henchman he was perfect. As for Henrietta, she was too oft the scapegoat of us both. She was a smooth, rather plump, yellow-haired fluffy personage, afflicted with a weak will and an erratic mother. She had shapely legs, a round pink and white face, and a quite unholy passion for brown sugar. She was not so craven as the Henchman - she had far more temper and enterprise - what is technically known as "spunk" - but she was by nature a grafter, was Henrietta, with too much the spirit of the genus tight-wad upon her. Still she was a not unfascinating companion and no raid on the pantry, braving the fire of that arch enemy the hired girl, was a real success without Henrietta on picket duty - albeit she did require infinite brown sugar as her reward. Failing that from the raid she would sell out both the Henchman and me to the Arch Enemy for one lump of it.

As we were of the vintage of the late '80s, when Harrison was President, the three of us - Henrietta, the Henchman, and I - wore our hair in a thick breastwork of "bangs" across our foreheads, the feature which would be most noticeable in us could we fare forth now. For the present-day fringe on boys is but the pallid ghost of the amazing bangs of '88. Mine was straw-colored, Henrietta's hay-colored, and the Henchman's a neat chocolate brown.

It remains but to describe the hired girl, who was a poignant factor in our lives. She was a person who chewed gum without ceasing and had teeth which were very, very false - quite the falsest teeth I have seen before or since. She wore her hair in a sort of tight cylinder above her forehead in what was then known as a "French twist" - and she had an arm like a sledge-hammer and a voice like a foghorn. She used to sing a mournful ballad about a butcher's boy whom she had loved not wisely, but too well. Her classic name was Ida, and she concocted strange pies which came out of the oven looking rather black. Her ruling passion was not for brown sugar but for laying out in the barrel-stave hammock under the trees and dozing there, oblivious to pies and all the other mundane things - with the possible exception of woodticks. Follows is a hypothetical bit of a diary such as I might have written at seven had I been able to write at all - which I couldn't, not having been sent to school till eight - and had I possessed a vocabulary. I had plenty of ideas and plenty of analytic introspection in those days, but a limited erudition. So the vocabulary and the diction and the idiom of the hour in the following bits of diary must be more or less those of my present day.

*

Fergus Falls, Minnesota
Aug. 13, 1889

This is Tuesday. The hired girl is ironing in the kitchen. I want my bean blower off the window sill, but I don't dare go after it, and it's no use sending Jim. He would bungle and be sure to let her see him going out with it. She would instantly take it and smash it, because I hit her in the ear with a kidney bean. Besides, she is still mad over the dead toad we dropped in the churn. To pay me for that what does she do but go and gobble up my half of the peach turnover. She is a devil. But I'll be even with her yet. The last time she ate pie off me I had Jim go upstairs and spit in her hat - the one with the gilt bunch grass on it. He did it. No, she doesn't get the start of me. While we are waiting for Henrietta we'll go and play in the barn. It is nice in the barn. I would rather be there than in the house any day. I like to be with the horse. He is a nice horse and we feed him lots of oats. Then we bring him ever so much water, nearly a tubful, in the wooden pail, and he drinks it all up through his nose. Then he makes a noise inside like an engine just starting. And when the hired man comes in he says, "What the deuce've you young brats been feeding this horse today? You want to give 'im the heaves?" I'm sure it's not we that's giving him heaves, if he gets any. We never give him anything but a few oats and a little water. The hired man is crazy. He is a good healthy horse. I wish he would have a colt this summer - a Shetland pony one. So does Jim. But no such luck. We have wished that for years, and he has never had a colt yet. I see Henrietta coming so I guess we'll go over by old man Causs' garden to play. Their melons are getting ripe.

Aug. 14

We had such a delightful time yesterday afternoon. There wasn't much doing over at old man Causs' in the way of melons - old man Causs was at work in his garden. So we came home and I tried to get Henrietta to go and get the bean blower. But no chance. She couldn't see any brown sugar in it, and besides she's even more afraid of Ida than I am. While we stood looking at the Arch Enemy from the wood shed off the kitchen a bright thought came to me. I had a match in my pocket that I had found under the stove, and it came over me in a flash what a dandy idea it would be to light it and set fire to the hired girl, and just burn her up. No sooner said than done. She was standing with her back to us ironing and chewing gum, and I softly lit the match on the doorsill and said to my henchman: "Here, Jim, you take this and slip up behind her and light the bottom of her dress - and don't let her hear you or see you." Jim was delighted. Jim is no good at all in laying plans or bringing them, unaided, to fruition. But as a serving man I think he has no equal. My plans always make an instant hit with him, moreover - he knows by long experience that they seldom fail to furnish prolonged entertainment for him and Henrietta and me. So he took the match and, slipping up on the hired girl, he held it to the bottom of her calico dress. He held it till a little blue blaze was well started, while Ida continued ironing and chewing in happy oblivion, and Henrietta and I watched from the wood shed door. I can see now the little blue blaze turning yellow and getting larger. I can see the Arch Enemy suddenly leave off her ironing - and eke her chewing - and with a flat-iron in her poised hand begin to sniff the air and exclaim: "Something's burning." I can see Jim - Jim, who like the perfect fool he is, knew no more than to first set a hired girl on fire and then go and tell of it - I can see Jim, pleased at being able to convey useful information, pointing out to her the source of the burnt odor. I can see her glance follow the direction of Jim's pointing finger and herself suddenly become aware of the location of the blaze. And I can see her, with the iron in her hand, begin to whirl round and round and round, like a kitten chasing its own tail, in a very vain effort to catch the fire. The heavy flat-iron lent her a momentum which she otherwise lacked, and she spun around like a human teetotum, while the Henchman, with the burnt match still in his fingers, and his eyes popping out of his head, stood back, rooted to the floor with astonishment at the antics he had caused, and Henrietta and I looked on with excitement and pleasure from the wood shed. The hired girl brought matters to a quick terminus by sitting down abruptly in the water pail, which stood beside her table - and, of course, the fun was over. The Henchman made a hurried exit at my behest and we all three retired to a safe sequestered nook to talk it over. For about two minutes, we had one grand time. The Arch Enemy, with a flat-iron at one end of her and a fire at the other, doing a frenzied waltz around the kitchen, with fright writ large on her countenance, was a sight which brought keen delight to us and one we rarely witnessed. Henrietta even forgot to require brown sugar, and she, like me, took an artist's impersonal pleasure in the neat unusual form of our revenge. It was well worth the loss of my half of the peach turnover. She'll think twice before she eats another off me, I guess.

Aug. 15

What do you think of this for news? Today the Frankberg kid, the little one, came and offered to fight me. He shook his fist in my face and called me a low-down blackguard. Now, I don't take that from anybody, and it was hardly a minute before the fight was on. I had only Henrietta, the Henchman, Milly Wessberg, and Georgie Lee lined up behind me, while he was being backed up by the entire Norwegian Sunday school. But I didn't care. I knew what the outcome would be. He had something on me in weight and reach, and that's all. My wallop is known for as much as a mile around here, to say nothing of my left hook, and everybody knows how quick I am on my feet. He came in for punishment and went home, after between two and three rounds, a bloody-nosed and beaten kid. The Norwegian Sunday school, if it had had it in mind to move in an armed phalanx on Henrietta, the Henchman, Milly Wessberg, and Georgie Lee, changed its mind and followed him. The yelling on both sides beat anything that has ever been heard before in this vicinity. Ida put her head - with her gum in it - out the kitchen window and remarked in no uncertain terms that if we didn't all shut up and clear out she'd give us all something to yell for. This may have had a little to do with the retreat of the phalanx and the Frankberg kid - but something tells me that he won't soon call me a low-down blackguard again. I don't know what is a blackguard. It sounds to me like a turnip or something of the sort.

Aug. 16

Life is so dull here. There's positively nothing interesting to do. This afternoon my brother Jack brought home some fish that he had caught, and one was a horned-pout, which Ida and the family rejected as food. So Jim and I and Henrietta took him and put him in the rain barrel in the hope that he would entertain us by coming to life and swimming. But he wouldn't. So we took him out and tied a pink ribbon very tight around his waist - so tight that his eyes looked prominent - and brought him into the house to show the family. But if they were uninterested in him as a fish, they were still less interested in him as the wearer of a sash. Ida was told to take him out and dispose of him. I last saw him in the warm embrace of the cat. His sash was the worse for wear. It's so difficult to find anything amusing to do. Henrietta went home in despair and in search of brown sugar, and the Henchman and I went upstairs by the back way and rummaged awhile in Ida's.

Aug. 17

The Henchman, Henrietta, and I went up the hill back of the barn to play today. We had a good time, though nothing happened. Jim was mad because he had to wear his red suit that's got all the pockets ripped off. If he had to wear what I do he might have something to rew about. Dolly must have used the one I've got on today to play run-sheep-run in the back pasture in. It does not look like a hand-me-down merely - it is more like an heirloom. Henrietta had about a peck of brown sugar that she had lifted off the grocery wagon while it was standing at our gate. And Jim and I took a package of figs that the grocery man had left on our kitchen table. He was busy talking to Ida at the side door. Every time he comes to her and says, "Well, how's my best girl today?" And she says, "Go along with you, you pelican." The grocery man says that to everybody's hired girl. We knew Ida had not missed the figs when we got to the top of the hill because we could hear issuing from the kitchen -

In Jer-sey - town
Where-I-Once-Did-Dwell
Lived a butch - er's-boy
I-Loved-Too-Well.
Oh, what a fool - ish, fool-lish joy
To - wreck—my - life
For-A-Butcher's-Boy!

We sat down on the windy hilltop and had a feast. Henrietta, who would willingly pawn her soul for an ounce of brown sugar, for once had almost as much as she wanted of it. I had some matches and I brought the hatchet and the buggy whip so we could cut it up and smoke it. I cut off a short piece like a cigar, and so did Henrietta, but the Henchman, thinking doubtless that if a short one would taste good a long one would taste better, hacked off a piece about a foot long and smoked it - with very much difficulty. It was manual labor, but Henrietta and I didn't have so far to draw in the smoke, so we got along better. But a buggy whip cigar is rather strong. We laid ours down after about five minutes and filled in the time with conversation. Jim had already laid his down and laid himself down beside it. He keeled over in a pale, red-kilted heap. It was the figs as much as anything, I guess. He looked figgy. But he got over it presently.

"I," said Henrietta, "am going to be a hired girl when I get big." "I'm going to be a pirate," said the Henchman, instantly.

They asked me what I was going to be, but I have no wish except to grow up into a grown woman and to get away - away, to the other side of the horizon, where I'm sure are wonderful things that glitter and dazzle - to break the chrysalis, to be free: the desire of the moth for the star.

*

I have had my wish.

"The bird of time has but a little way to flutter," and alack, the bird even then was "on the wing." I have got to the other side of the horizon and seen and touched the wonderful things. And it's to never, never return. Much farther off now is the day of the Primitive Kid than ever was the horizon at that time. I think of Henrietta as the companion of another life, and wonder where she is. In me rises a hope that the gods have been kind to her, and that their largess included limitless brown sugar. And I wonder what fates gathered in the hired girl, and whether they battered her, and "who's kissing her now." As for the Henchman - vanished, gone. Back of me as I write sits what once was he - with a volume of de Maupassant and a pipe, and a measure of contempt and indifference in his philosophy that rivals even mine. He is not indeed a pirate, but it's possible he is a henchman - of another color.

I mix me a mental cocktail - of the gin of introspect, the vermouth of retrospect, and the subtle bitter of unshed tears - and I drink it to the memory of: Henrietta, the Henchman, the Hired Girl, and me.

NOTES

BIBLIOGRAPHY

14. *To The Devil* - This dedication was cut by the publisher.

15. *peripatetic* - Ref. to Aristotle, whose thrust is akin to м's emphasis upon sense-experience, logical analysis, friendship, and self-realization. м plays upon the (now questioned) tracing of his philosophy's nickname to his known habit of strolling as he taught - *peripatein* means "to walk about."

15. Marie Bashkirtseff - Russian painter and diarist (1860-1884), died of tuberculosis in Paris. Bashkirtseff's posthumously-published diary was well-known in its day for the writer's unabashed egotism.

15. *Byron of* - His incomplete epic in the tragicomic *ottava rima* scheme was famed for its irony and vastness of scope. Goethe called it "a work of boundless genius."

18. *germs of intense* - Poss. from story in Cicero's *Tusculan Disputations* (orig. in Phaedo's *Zopyrus*): as rendered by Nietzsche, "A foreigner who knew about faces once passed through Athens and told Socrates to his face that he was a *monstrum* - that he harbored in himself all the bad vices and appetites. And Socrates merely answered: 'You know me, sir!'" (*Twilight of the Idols*, trans. Walter A. Kaufmann).

20. *sulphur smoke* - Smelters operated within Butte's city limits.

24. *ozone* - In this usage, archaic term for wind-freshened rural air; thus, Ozone Park, Queens, New York (*c.* 1882) and Ozone, Tennessee (1896).

24. *Bacchantes* - Female Dionysus-worshippers in Euripdes' play *The Bacchae.*

25. *of shade* - From the poem "The Meeting of the Waters" by the Irish musician, poet, popular entertainer (and friend of Byron's) Thomas Moore (1779-1852): *Sweet vale of Avoca! how calm could I rest / In thy bosom of shade, with the friends I love best, / Where the storms that we feel in this cold world should cease, / And our hearts, like thy waters, be mingled in peace.*

25. *memory is possession* - From the prelude to the poem "Regret" by the English novelist and poet Jean Ingelow (1820-1897): *It is true / That we have wept. But O! this thread of gold, / We would not have it tarnish; let us turn / Oft and look back upon the wondrous web, / And when it shineth sometimes we shall know / That memory is possession.*

28. *blue* - Prob. *Pulsatilla patens* ("Eastern pasqueflower," "prairie smoke"), poss. *Anemone blanda* ("Grecian Windflower"), both of fam. *Ranunculaceae* (buttercup); *P. patens* (sometimes incl. in genus *Anemone*) is a Montana-area native (indeed, is Manitoba's provincial flower - a sub-species is S. Dakota's state flower) and prized for its blooming near Easter (whence "pasqueflower"); *A. blanda* is native to Lebanon,

Syria, SE Europe, and Turkey, but is also known as "Blue Anemone" (as was *P. patens* in Montana in early 20th c.).

28. *to rejoice* - From the 1864 free-love novel *Victoire* by Mary Clemmer (1839-1884, also known as Mary Clemmer Ames): *Be faithful to thyself and to all that ever was thine. Thy friend is always thy friend. Not to have or to hold to love, or to rejoice in, but to remember.*

31. *when Omar* - From the third stanza of the introductory poem by the Irish politician and author Justin Huntly McCarthy (1859-1936) to his translation of *The Rubaiyat of Omar Khayyam* (1889): *Alas for me, alas for all who weep / And wonder at the Silence dark and deep / That girdles round this little Lamp in space / No wiser than when Omar fell asleep.*

31. James Whitcomb Riley (1849-1916) - American Midwestern writer, best-seller in his time, known as "The Hoosier Poet" and "The Children's Poet"; tended to the humorous or sentimental; contributed to the creation of regional literature in the US.

31. *tragedy to* - From aphorism attrib. to English antiquarian, litterateur, and politician Horace Walpole (1717-1797): *Life is a tragedy to those who feel, and a comedy to those who think.* (Attrib. at times to Molière.)

32. *vile dust* - Prob. from Sir Walter Scott's "Lay of the Last Minstrel" (pub. 1805): *High though his titles, proud his name, / Boundless his wealth as wish can claim; / Despite those titles, power, and pelf, / The wretch, concentred all in self, / Living, shall forfeit fair renown, / And, doubly dying, shall go down / To the vile dust, from whence he sprung, / Unwept, unhonoured, and unsung.*

33. Jacques - From Shakespeare's *As You like It* II:1 (spoken by the First Lord at the Forest of Arden): *The melancholy Jaques grieves at that, / And, in that kind, swears you do more usurp / Than doth your brother that hath banish'd you.*

33. *dropsical* - From "dropsy," an archaic term for edema.

33. *of green* - From the poem "Afoot" by the Canadian author Sir Charles G.D. Roberts (1860-1943), known as "the Father of Canadian Poetry": *Comes the lure of green things growing, / Comes the call of waters flowing - / And the wayfarer desire / Moves and wakes and would be going.*

33. *Law of Compensation* - From Emerson's *Essays: First Series* (1841).

34. Anne "Ninon" de l'Enclos (1620-1705) - French courtesan and wit.

34. Olive Schreiner (1855-1920) - South African novelist and feminist; wrote *The Story of an African Farm* (1883) and *Woman and Labour* (1911).

35. *pathetic* - The modern contemptuous/ridiculing sense (which dates from the 1930s) must nowhere be applied to M's use of the term.

41. *Give thyself* - From Charles E. Norton's rendering (c. 1896) into English of J.B. Nicolas' French translation of *The Rubaiyat* (1867): *Give thyself to joy, for grief will be infinite. The stars shall again meet together at the same point of the firmament; but of thy body shall bricks be made for a palace-wall.* Paragraphing appears to be M's.

41. *this be* - From a song ref. to in, or a direct quote from, the novel *Sir Jaffray's Wife* by English author Arthur Williams Marchmont (1852-1923): *For answer, he kissed her again. / "Have I made you happy, Jaffray?" she asked, after a long pause. / By way of answer this time, he hummed the snatch of a song, "If this be vanity, vanity let it be," an old teasing trick of his, when she had seemed to look for a compliment from him.*

42. *conceiving but* - Poss. ref. to Descartes, specifically his argument that mind and body are two substances since they may be clearly and separately conceived. (If so intended, M ironically inverts and extends the argument in a passage of sensualism.)

42. *heart with* - From the final stanza of Wordsworth's poem "I Wandered Lonely As a Cloud" (pub. 1807): *For oft, when on my couch I lie / In vacant or in pensive mood, / They flash upon that inward eye / Which is the bliss of solitude; / And then my heart with pleasure fills, / And dances with the daffodils.*

42. *meeting of* - Where the rivers Avonmore and Avonbeg meet to form the Avoca is called the Meeting of the Waters.

42. *never to* - From Shakespeare and Fletcher's *Henry VIII* III:2: *There is, betwixt that smile we would aspire to, / That sweet aspect of princes, and their ruin, / More pangs and fears than wars or women have: / And when he falls, he falls like Lucifer, / Never to hope again.*

43. Henry James (1843-1916) - American-born writer, regarded as a central figure of 19th-century literary realism.

43. William Dean Howells (1837-1920) - American realist author and literary critic; nicknamed "The Dean of American Letters."

43. *"Goo-Goo Eyes"* - Ref. to song "Just Because She Made Dem Goo-Goo Eyes" (1900), lyr. John Queen, mus. Hughey Cannon.

43. Maria Louise Pool (1841-1898) - American author, pub. by M's publisher Herbert S. Stone's predecessor company, Stone & Kimball; M was unaware that Pool had died several years earlier; para. was del. in published ver.

44. Eugene Field, Sr. (1850-1895) - American writer best known for his children's poetry and humorous essays.

50. *plungers* - Gamblers.

50. *box rustlers* - Prostitutes who worked the curtained upper boxes of theatres.

50. *impossible women* - Prostitutes; there may also be some Lesbian signaling to the term.

50. *beer-jerkers* - Barkeeps who drew beer in saloons.

50. *biscuit-shooters* - Waiters or waitresses (incl. Harvey Girls, of the respectable railside dining establishments of Fred Harvey) or camp cooks.

51. *four-in-hands* - Ref. to carriage with four horses and a single driver.

52. *grass widow* - Euph. for a not-respectably-single woman: *e.g.* divorced, separated, an ex-mistress, mother of an illegitimate child, or parted from husband for a protracted time.

52. *of sprouts* - Difficult, prolonged course of instruction or treatment.

54. *stalled ox* - From Proverbs 15:17: *Better* is *a dinner of herbs where love is, than a stalled ox and hatred therewith.* (King James)

54. *among thieves* - From Luke 10:30, but M reverses gender: *And Jesus answering said, A certain man went down from Jerusalem to Jericho, and fell among thieves, which stripped him of his raiment, and wounded him, and departed, leaving him half dead.* (King James)

56. *little folding* - From Proverbs 6:10: *Yet a little sleep, a little slumber, a little folding of the hands to sleep* (King James)

58. Nora Perry (1831-1896) - American journalist, poet, writer of children's stories.

58. *with reluctant* - From Longfellow's poem "Maidenhood" (pub. 1842): *Standing, with reluctant feet, / Where the brook and river meet, / Womanhood and childhood fleet!*

58. *Hildegarde Graham* - Ref. to popular series of girls' novels (1889-1897) by Laura E. Richards (1850-1943) known as The Hildegarde Series; neither the series nor any volume in it bears the title that M gives.

58. *What Katy Did* - Girls' book by Susan Coolidge (pseud. of Sarah Chauncey Woolsey, 1835-1905).

65. *are heavy* - From Matthew 10:28: *Come unto me, all ye that labour and are heavy laden, and I will give you rest.* (King James)

65. *the waters* - From the first stanza of Charles Wesley's influential hymn "Jesus, Lover of My Soul" (pub. 1740): *Let me to Thy bosom fly, / While the waters near me roll, / While the tempest still is high. / Hide me, O my Saviour, hide, / Till the storms of life be past; / Safe into the haven guide; / Oh receive my soul at last!*

67. *little more* - From stanza 39 of Browning's "By the Fireside" (written 1853): *Oh, the little more, and how much it is! / And the little less, and what worlds away! / How a sound shall quicken content to bliss, / Or a breath suspend the blood's best play, / And life be a proof of this!*

67. *the people* - From Job 12:2: *No doubt but ye are the people, and wisdom shall die with you.* (King James)

70. *Cashmere* - Common archaic term for Kashmir. M poss. read in Byron's friend Thomas Moore (*cf.* n. 25 p 175): *Who has not heard of the Vale of Cashmere, / With its roses the brightest that earth ever gave, / Its temples, and grottos, and fountains as clear / As the love-lighted eyes that hang over their wave* (from "Lalla Rookh," pub. 1817) or the New England poet George Bancroft Griffith (1841-?): *With its cincture of snows lies the wonderful plain / That the paladin formed when the dragons were slain; / 'Tis the Hindoo's delight; and the poets endear / By their songs of its beauty, the Vale of Cashmere* (from "The Vale of Cashmere," apparent 1st pub. *Granite State Monthly*, Oct. 1881, p 17).

70. *Lethe* - In Greek mythology, Lethe was one of Hades' five rivers; those who drank of its waters forgot all.

70. Charles Kingsley (1819-1875) - British university professor, priest, historian, novelist; poem has variant texts - ver. given here is that in the orig. printing.

73. Archibald C[lavering] Gunter (1847-1907) - Popular American playwright and widely-read self-published author and magaziner.

73. Albert Ross (pseud. of Linn Boyd Porter, 1851-1916) - American novelist.

74. *mere vile clay* - Not, evidently, a literary quotation.

76. *two thieves* - Poss. ref. to a set of Rembrandt drypoints of the subject in various stages of finish.

78. *deferred and* - From Proverbs 13:12: *Hope deferred maketh the heart sick: but when the desire cometh,* it is *a tree of life.* (King James)

79. *servant a* - From 2 Kings 8:13: *And Hazael said, But what, is thy servant a dog, that he should do this great thing?* M may also have had the echo at 2 Samuel 9:8 in mind: *And he bowed himself, and said, What is thy servant, that thou shouldest look upon such a dead dog as I am?* (King James)

79. *song of* - Poss. from *A Modern Ideal: A Dramatic Poem* - an early work (1886) by Sidney Royse Lysaght (1860-1941), an Irish writer who also worked in the iron industry: *The kind and wonderful voices, / They speak the truth of existence, / Truth, the wonder of wonders, / They show us the soul of all things, / They touch the shadow and semblance, / And set the reality free; / They sing the song of the world that is / To the music of what might be.*

80. Charlotte Corday (1768-1793) - French patriot, assassinated revolutionary leader Marat while he bathed; was executed.

80. *If to do* - From Shakespeare's *Merchant of Venice* 1:2: *If to do were as easy as to know what were good to do, / Chapels had been churches, and poor men's cottages / Princes' palaces.*

84. *gall and* - Wormwood and gall are paired at numerous points in the Bible, but in the King James that phrase appears only in Deuteronomy 29:18: *lest there should be among you a root that beareth gall and wormwood.*

85. *and Haidee* - Beautiful Moorish-Greek girl who found Don Juan cast ashore, restored him to animation, and became his lover.

86. *timothy-grass* - *Phleum pratense*; European perennial grass that has spread through the US since Colonial times; important in some nutritious animal feeds, *e.g.* for horses and rabbits.

87. *health and* - From the hymn "Sweet the Moments, Rich in Blessing" (orig. James Allen, 1757, ed. Walter Shirley, 1770): *Sweet the moments, rich in blessing, / Which before the cross we spend, / Life and health and peace possessing / From the sinner's dying Friend.*

87. *winds with* - From Milton's "Ode on the Nativity" (1629): *The winds, with wonder whist, Smoothly the waters kiss'd;* "whist" is an archaic form of "quiet" or "silent."

87. *blew, and* - From Matthew 7:25: *And the rain descended, and the floods came, and the winds blew, and beat upon that house; and it fell not: for it was founded upon a rock.* (King James)

88. *nearer my* - From the hymn "Nearer, My God, to Thee" (1841) by the English poet Sarah Fuller Flower Adams (1805-1848); based on Genesis 28:11-19.

89. *air was over* - From second stanza of the poem "Great, Wide, Beautiful, Wonder-

ful World" by the English author, reporter, preacher, and renowned nursery-poet William Brighty Rands (1823-1882): *Great, wide, beautiful, wonderful World, / With the wonderful water round you curled, / And the wonderful grass upon your breast - / World, you are beautifully drest. // The wonderful air is over me, / And the wonderful wind is shaking the tree, / It walks on the water, and whirls the mills, / And talks to itself on the tops of the hills.*

91. *Dr. Johnson* - Samuel Johnson.

91. *Our Young* - Prominent children's magazine; it merged with *St. Nicholas* in 1874, so the volume M was reading was decades-old.

91. J[ohn] T[ownsend] Trowbridge (1827-1916) - American author and editor; his Jack Hazard novels (1870s) were a popular boys' series; one was *Doing His Best* (c. 1873).

92. *Lucy* - From Wordsworth's "Lucy Gray - Or, Solitude" (1888): *You yet may spy the fawn at play, / The hare upon the green; / But the sweet face of Lucy Gray / Will never more be seen.*

92. *are old* - Seventh stanza of Lewis Carroll's nonsense poem "You Are Old, Father William" in *Alice's Adventures In Wonderland* (1865): *"You are old," said the youth, "one would hardly suppose / That your eye was as steady as ever; / Yet you balanced an eel on the end of your nose - / What made you so awfully clever?"*

100. *the other* - From the refrain in the hymn "Rest for the Weary" by the Irish-born American professor and minister William Hunter (1811-1877): *There is rest for the weary, / There is rest for you. / On the other side of Jordan, / In the sweet fields of Eden, / Where the tree of life is blooming, / There is rest for you.*

100. *thorns* - From Matthew 7:16: *Ye shall know them by their fruits. Do men gather grapes of thorns, or figs of thistles?* (King James)

103. *the beasts* - From Psalms 49:12: *Nevertheless man being in honour abideth not: he is like the beasts that perish.* (King James)

103. *brave thing* - As the ed. has located no earlier appearance, phrase appears to be from *A Practical Grammar of the English Language* (Van Antwerp, Bragg & Co., New York , rev. ed. 1878, p 215) by Ohioan educator and writer Thomas Wadleigh Harvey (1821-?).

104. *cometh not* - A refrain in Tennyson's poem "Mariana" (1830) about the char. in Shakespeare's *Measure for Measure*.

104. *The Mill on the Floss* - 1860 novel by George Eliot.

106. *sweet-fern* - Deciduous flowering shrub, *Comptonia peregrina* (monotyp.); leaves give pleasing odor when crushed; tends to grow in dry, sandy areas, esp. amid pines; native to eastern North America, extending west to Minnesota.

109. *for bread* - From Luke 11:11: *If a son shall ask bread of any of you that is a father, will he give him a stone? or if he ask a fish, will he for a fish give him a serpent?* (King James)

113. *sweet-flags* - *Acorus calamus*, also known as "calamus"; lofty wetland perennial, used in fragrance-making and archaic medicine; native to areas in various continents, incl. the northern US and southern Canada.

114. *eats its* - Poss. from article "James Russell Lowell," *Southern Review*, Oct 1875 (no author given but employs editorial "we"): *It may be as a cause, or it may be as an effect; but falseness of expression, and falseness in principle, are indissolubly associated. Like sentimentality in feeling, cant in religion, affectation in manner, it is sure to be a superficial malady, which is either a sure indication of the unsoundness within, or else, after a time, it eats its way inward, poisoning, finally, the very springs of life.* All previous uses the ed. has located relate literally to fungi, larvae, etc.

115. *L'Envoi* - From older French poetry, in which a brief separate line or verse at the end states the theme or dedicates the piece to a specific person.

*

120. *weary* - Popular quot. of Walter Horatio Pater (1839-1894), English writer and critic, infl. upon the Aesthetics, esp. Oscar Wilde; from his seminal *Studies in the History of the Renaissance* (1st ed. 1873), re. da Vinci's *La Gioconda*: *Hers is the head upon which all "the ends of the world are come," and the eyelids are a little weary. It is a beauty wrought out from within upon the flesh, the deposit, little cell by cell, of strange thoughts and fantastic reveries and exquisite passions.*

120. *Phyllis* - At present, an untraceable ref.

124. *have only read* - An odd claim even if M were being provocative, in light of M's knowledge of Bashkirtseff's work in *I Await* and having two pictures of the Russian diarist in her room (*cf.* p 96); ed. suggests a reporter's or shorthand recorder's mishearing of M's speaking in past tense: *I had only read two or three entries in her journal, but I knew that.*

125. *Cyrano* - Ref. to Edmond Rostand's play *Cyrano de Bergerac* (1897).

*

127. *and vanities* - M is incorrect: from the Catechism in the Church of England's 1689 *Proposed Book of Common Prayer*.

128. *sloe-eyed* - Having slanted or dark blue to purpling black eyes; from the small dark fruit of the blackthorn.

128. *vineyard* - From Isaiah 5:1: *Now will I sing to my wellbeloved a song of my beloved touching his vineyard. My wellbeloved hath a vineyard in a very fruitful hill.* (King James)

129. *flesh-pots* - From Exodus 16:3: *And the children of Israel said unto them, Would to God we had died by the hand of the* LORD *in the land of Egypt, when we sat by the flesh pots,* and *when we did eat bread to the full; for ye have brought us forth into this wilderness, to kill this whole assembly with hunger.* (King James)

129. *Solomon* - From the Sermon on the Mount.

129. *purchased sea air* - Ref. to charities that gave vacations to New York's poor youth, *e.g.* The Fresh Air Fund (founded 1877).

129. *equipages* - Ref. to a carriage inclusive of its horses and attendants.

130. *Bailey's* - Then as now an exclusive private beach club; owned by the Spouting Rock Beach Association.

131. *the brave* - From the first stanza of the poem "Alexander's Feast" (1697) by John Dryden: *None but the brave / deserve the fair.*

131. *small and old* - Trinity Church, constr. 1720s, Episcopal; attended by prominent families; Washington's having attended in 1781 is a local oral tradition.

132. *the little rift* - Ref. to Tennyson's poem "Merlin and Vivien," part of his large elegiac cycle *Idylls of the King* (pub. 1856-1885): *It is the little rift within the lute, / That by and by will make the music mute, / And ever widening slowly silence all.*

*

133. *old, old* - From Dickens' *Dombey & Son* (serial pub. 1846-1848): *The golden ripple on the wall came back again, and nothing else stirred in the room. The old, old fashion! The fashion that came in with our first garments, and will last unchanged until our race has run its course, and the wide firmament is rolled up like a scroll. The old, old fashion - Death!* M alludes to this passage several times in her early work; the close of her second book, *My Friend Annabel Lee* (1903), is an extended homage.

133. *the ten-thousandth* - Prob. from Deuteronomy 7:9: *Know therefore that the* LORD *thy God, he is God, the faithful God, which keepeth covenant and mercy with them that love him and keep his commandments to a thousand generations* (King James)

134. *minds are they* - From Matthew 5:4: *Blessed* are *they that mourn: for they shall be comforted.* (King James)

134. *that soft tale* - A literary phrase which appears in several sources in the early 1800s, *e.g.*, "The Lady of the Lake" by Sir Walter Scott (pub. 1810), M's likely source.

134. *mills of* - A widespread alteration of Longfellow's translation (1845) of Friedrich von Logau's poem "Retribution" (1654): *Though the mills of God grind slowly, yet they grind exceeding small.*

135. *bay-tree that* - Prob. from Psalms 37:35: *I have seen the wicked in great power, and spreading himself like a green bay tree.* (King James)

135. *duck* - Cotton linen fabric, classically unbleached white in color.

136. *Trinity* - Episcopal church at intersection of Broadway and Wall St. in lower Manhattan; first building constr. 1698; third (and present) building finished 1846; 281-foot spire was city's tallest point until the New York World Building (finished 1890).

137. *lame, the* - Popular phrase based on Luke 14:21: *So that servant came, and shewed his lord these things. Then the master of the house being angry said to his servant, Go out quickly into the streets and lanes of the city, and bring in hither the poor, and the maimed, and the halt, and the blind.* (King James)

137. William Andrews Clark, Sr. (1839-1925) - One of Butte's three "Copper Kings," politician; reputedly deeply corrupt; among the richest men in American history; de facto founder of Las Vegas, Clark County, Nevada.

*

138. *of my stocking* - Prob. money, poss. secreted high-value cards.

138. *jade* - Slang for nag, old woman, or prostitute - here, prob. cocky or disreputable.

139. *accouchement* - Fr.: confinement, esp. laying in, before childbirth.

139. *shocked Butte* - Ref. to various unlikely rumors of her behaving with shocking rudeness to Butte high society ladies at a tea, luncheon, or evening party; Atherton (1932, p 491) repeats one such.

140. *plaisance* - Fr.: pleasantness.

140. *rounder* - Slang, several meanings; here, prob. one who "makes the rounds" from drinking establishments to prisons to flophouses and then repeats the cycle; term is colored by other meanings: itinerant worker on railroads (thus unprosperous and work-worn, of the lower class), and a criminal or hustler.

140. *swissesse* - Briefly-fashionable hairdo with one or several curls dangling behind the ear.

140. Thomas Joseph "Sailor Tom" Sharkey (1873-1953) - Irish-born heavyweight boxer active 1893-1904; considered one of the sport's great punchers; his eponymous bar on 14th St. was famous for a time.

140. *of a deadlock* - Ref. to price of Butte's then-primary export, copper, being down; copper's nominal tonnage price is illuminating: 1906 - $524; 1907 - $441; 1908 - $291; 1909 - $289; 1910 - $284; 1911 - $277 (per *http://minerals.usgs.gov/minerals/pubs/historical-statistics/ds140-coppe.pdf*, accessed 30 September 2014).

140. *cabs* - "Sea-going cab" was slang for: a yacht, a small launch, and recklessly or rapidly driven taxi; "deep" seems M's addition - perhaps for "deep in(to) the night."

140. *roadhouses* - Slightly disreputable drinking establishments located just outside city limits on secondary or primary roads, thus often unmolested by authorities; some offered gambling and, at times, prostitutes.

140. *Mercury* - Center of Butte's prostitution district.

141. Carrie Nation (1846-1911) - Teetotaler; famed for carrying an axe wherewith to wreck bars.

142. Ann O'Delia Dis (or Diss) Debar - (born Ann O'Delia Solomon, var. Salomon, 1849-?) - Notorious American spiritualist/con artist with numerous pseudonyms; influenced by Theosophy; served several terms in prison.

142. Elinor Glyn (1864-1943) - English screenwriter and novelist; wrote the successful sex novel *Three Weeks* (1907); popularized the concept of "It" - magnetic appeal of a charismatic personality.

142. Cecilia Loftus (1876-1943) - Scottish music hall performer/vaudevillian.

142. Alice Lloyd (1873-1949) - English vaudeville and music hall performer; sister of Marie Lloyd.

142. Marie Lloyd (1870-1922) - English vaudeville and music hall performer; sister of Alice Lloyd; called "Queen of the Music Halls."

142. Vesta Victoria (1873-1951) - English music hall singer.

142. *'alf* - Ref. to trad. English drinking mixture of any two of ale, beer, and twopenny (the strongest, so called because 18th c. cost was two pence per quart).

*

144. *eke* - Archaic: also.

147. *and that* - Slang of the time; meant "all of that" or "and so on."

149. *ignis fatuus* - Lat. "foolish fire": will-o'-the-wisp.

149. *the Grape* - Ref. to *The Rubaiyat*; alcoholic products and their source in the fruiting berry have deep meaning in other Sufi poets, *e.g.* the in-turned, complexifying Rumi and the extroverted, senses-celebrating Hafiz.

*

150. *un haussement de m'epaule* - Fr.: "a shrug of my shoulders."

151. *cloak* - A live model of feminine attire for purchases in stores; strict standards of proportion and fitness were enforced.

151. *caste of our* - The ed. has changed the original's "a waste" to "caste" as a likely compositor's error.

151. Eleanor "Nell" Gwyn (alt. Gwynn, Gwynne, 1650-1687) - Comic actress of Restoration England, Charles II's long-term mistress, mother of two of his sons.

152. *Milo* - Popular "Egyptian"-style cigarette made in US.

153. Edna May (born Edna May Pettie, 1878-1948) - American musical actress in Edwardian era, noted for comedy; as May was pretty, often featured on postcards, the Borrower indicates her attractiveness in youth.

154. *MacTrey* - An otherwise-unexplained nickname; *cf.* p 155; also *cf.* Pruitt, Elisabeth

(ed.): *Tender Darkness: A Mary MacLane Anthology*, Abernathy & Brown (Belmont, Calif.), 1993, pp 193-194 for extended discussion.

154. *sulphites* - Cf. *ibid.*, p 194.

154. *Yvette Gilbert* - Ref. to Yvette Guilbert (name usu. Americanized with dropped "u," 1865-1944); French actress and cabaret singer; as M indicates, noted for working pathos into her acts.

154. *Woman's Home Companion* - Highly successful US magazine (1873-1957); shared publisher with *Collier's* and *Farm and Fireside*; M may be alluding to the latter with "the home-and-fireside."

154. *kirtle* - Middle Ages garment, sim. to a tunic.

155. *than night* - Ref. to mydriasis, either due to cocaine use or withdrawal from opioids, *e.g.* morphine or heroin.

156. *LeMonte* - Untraceable ref.; poss. pseud., or poss. ref. to woman connected with singer Signor Lemonte [*sic.*], part of traveling troupe Ferullo and His Band (AKA Ferullo's Band); for Sig. Lemonte as band member *cf. Racine Daily Journal* (Wisconsin), 12 Oct 1908, p 2; for Ferullo's Band in New York City *cf.* Joseph Gigante Coll., Wisconsin Music Archives listing at UW-Madison, at *http://music.library.wisc.edu/ wma/papers/gigante/gigante.htm* (accessed 30 September 2014).

156. *that little* - Alice or Marie Lloyd.

*

157. *settlement* - Movement (1880s-1940s) begun in Great Britain aimed at overcoming class divisions by creating integrated community residences containing people of lower and middle classes that were funded by upper class people; Jane Addams' famed Hull House in Chicago was inspired by earlier British examples. cf. p 151.

158. *hash-slinger* - Cook in cheap restaurant.

158. *captioned* - M's articles on women bore captions prominently listing her monikers for the women she would portray.

160. Maude Adams (born Maude Ewing Kiskadden, 1872-1953) - American stage actress who had immense success, particularly with J.M. Barrie's plays; was the first Peter Pan on Broadway.

160. *rose o' the world* - Prob. ref. to Yeats' poem "The Rose of the World" (1893); first stanza: *Who dreamed that beauty passes like a dream? / For these red lips, with all their mournful pride, / Mournful that no new wonder may betide, / Troy passed away in one high funeral gleam, / And Usna's children died.*

160. *a fisher of men* - Ref. to Matthew 4:19 and Mark 1:17.

161. *go to it, 'bo* - Popular phrase; evidently alludes to having set a plate of food before a hungry hobo.

162. *silk* - Printed by firm founded by Arthur Lasenby Liberty (1843-1917); noted for fresh floral designs.

162. Lyman Abbott (1835-1922) - American clergyman and religious writer.

*

164. *what boots it* - Archaic phrase: "what profits it"; appears in, *e.g.* FitzGerald's translation of *The Rubaiyat*: *Ah, fill the Cup: - What boots it to repeat / How time is slipping underneath our Feet. / Unborn* TO-MORROW, *and dead* YESTERDAY, / *Why fret about them if* TO-DAY *be sweet?*

164. *anent* - Regarding, about.

164. *Gramercy!* - From Old Fr.: *grand merci* - "great thanks."

164. Anthony Comstock (1844-1915) - Crusading United States Postal Inspector, founder of the New York Society for the Suppression of Vice.

165. *fields and running* - Poem, and eponymous volume of poems (pub. 1893), by James Whitcomb Riley.

166. *grew the* - Prob. ref. to folk song "Green Grew the Rushes, O."

166. *glengarry-bonneted* - Ref. to trad. Scottish hat.

166. *four-flushing* - From poker: one who boasts emptily or bluffs failingly.

167. Benjamin Harrison (1833-1901) - 23rd US Pres. (Mar 1889-Mar 1893).

167. *straw ... hay* - Cf. p 90 - M appropriates from Thackeray.

169. *teetotum* - Spinning top used in gambling; mentioned in Lewis Carroll's *Through*

the Looking-Glass.

169. *little one* - George W. Frankberg (1882-1937); in 1910, was lawyer in Fergus Falls; late in decade would be elected Mayor and in 1932 would be a delegate from Minnesota to Republican National Convention.

170. *horned-pout* - North American fish (*Ameiurus nebulosus*); also known as brown bullhead or mud cat.

170. *rew* - Syn. for "row" - in v. form, "to raise a scandal or conflict over."

170. *peck* - US and British dry measure equivalent to 8 dry quarts.

170. *pelican* - Slang term of various meanings; one is "a hearty eater"; another (from Fr.) "a dressy courtesan"; here, poss. a non-specific term of opprobrium or term for a male who hangs around looking to catch women.

171. *butch - er's-boy* - A text highly variant to known versions of the old ballad "A Butcher's Boy," which itself has numerous variants, *e.g.* in first lines: *In Jersey City where I did dwell / A butcher's boy I loved so well* and *In London city, where I did dwell. / A butcher boy I loved right well.* The version M gives is abbreviated, suppresses the suicide of the abandoned maiden, and has lines not recorded elsewhere. *Cf. http:// en.wikipedia.org/wiki/The_Butcher_Boy_(folk_song)* (accessed 30 September 2014).

171. *desire of* - From second stanza of Shelley's poem "One Word Is Too Often Profaned" (pub. 1822): *I can give not what men call love; / But wilt thou accept not / The worship the heart lifts above / And the Heavens reject not: / The desire of the moth for the star, / Of the night for the morrow, / The devotion to something afar / From the sphere of our sorrow?*

171. *time has* - From FitzGerald's translation of *The Rubaiyat*: *Come, fill the Cup, and in the Fire of Spring / The Winter Garment of Repentance fling: / The Bird of Time has but a little way / To fly - and Lo! the Bird is on the Wing.*

171. *who's kissing her* - Ref. to song "I Wonder Who's Kissing Her Now" (1909), lyr. Hough *&* Adams, mus. Howard *&* Orlob: *I wonder who's kissing her now, / I wonder who's teaching her how, / Wonder who's looking into her eyes, / Breathing sighs, telling lies; / I wonder who's buying the wine, / For lips that I used to call mine. / I wonder if she ever tells him of me, / I wonder who's kissing her now.*

This is the most extensive survey of writing by and about Mary MacLane undertaken to date. Much of her own writing was feature work done on commission for newspapers, and as such was never collected or indexed systematically. Undoubtedly, more of her work is simply awaiting disovery - in the pages of old newspapers. There was, *e.g.*, not a hint of the existence of the *Chicago Sunday Tribune*'s "Mary MacLane Says - " until a clipping of it surfaced during the editor's research in the Newberry collection.

Similarly - because the secondary literature on her was not collected or tabulated as it appeared over the years - there is more writing *about* MacLane still to be discovered and catalogued.

This bibliography, then, is by no means exhaustive. It may be taken instead as an outline of MacLane's oeuvre, an indication of her impact upon the press and public of her time, and an index to published references both during her lifetime and after, made as complete as present knowledge permits.

The editor has relied upon Lipson's, Wheeler's, Mattern's, and Pascoe's valuable bibliographic work (see citations below) for information on items that could not be personally inspected.

Page numbers and publishers' names have been provided where possible.

WORKS OF MARY MACLANE

MacLane, Mary Elizabeth. Untitled editorial on literature and censorship. *Butte High School Leader*, January 1898. (Only known from an excerpt printed in *New York World*, 13 July 1902, p 7; all copies of the *Leader* from MacLane's years as editor are said to have been destroyed by a fire at the Butte High School.)

———. "Consider Thy Youth and Therein." Editorial on stoicism. *Butte High School Leader*, Spring 1899. (Excerpt printed in *New York World*, 13 July 1902, p 7.)

———. "Charles Dickens - Best of Castle-Builders." High School oration. (Only known from reprint in *Butte Miner*, 13 May 1899, p 8.)

———. *The Story of Mary MacLane - by Herself*. Herbert S. Stone & Co., Chicago, April 1902. (British edition published by Grant Richards, London, November 1902. Foreign-language editions not yet located. Microfilmed in 1980 by Microfilming Corp. of America for inclusion in the Gerritsen Collection of Women's History.)

———. "Mary MacLane at Newport." *New York World*, 24 August 1902, Sunday magazine, p 1.

———. "Mary MacLane at Coney Island." *New York World*, 31 August 1902, Sunday magazine, p 1.

———. "Mary MacLane on Wall Street." *New York World*, 7 September 1902, Sunday magazine, p 1.

———. "Mary MacLane in Little Old New York." *New York World*, 14 September 1902, Sunday magazine, pp 6-7.

———. "On Marriage." *New York World*, 9 November 1902, Sunday magazine, p 5.

———. *My Friend Annabel Lee*. Herbert S. Stone & Co., Chicago, 1903.

———. ["Four Years Later."] Associated Sunday Newspapers syndicate, early 1906.

(12000-word autobiographical essay on MacLane's life and thoughts in the years after publication of *The Story*; copy not yet located, but letters to M.E. Stone (Newberry collection) confirm publication.)

———. ["Caruso in the Metropolitan."] Untitled, almost certainly unpublished feature article giving impressions of Caruso in Aida and of the opera-goers. (Written in January 1909 for the *New York Evening Journal*; MS in Newberry collection.)

———. "The Second Story of Mary MacLane." *Butte Evening News*, 23 January 1910, p 9.

———. "Mary MacLane Soliloquizes on Scarlet Fever - and Other Things." *Butte Evening News*, 20 March 1910, p 9.

———. "Mary MacLane Meets the Vampire on the Isle of Treacherous Delights." *Butte Evening News*, 27 March 1910, p 9.

———. "The Autobiography of the Kid Primitive." *Butte Evening News*, 3 April 1910, pp 9-10. (Subsequently syndicated; appeared in, *e.g.*, *Morrison's Chicago Weekly*, 19 January 1911.)

———. "Mary MacLane Wants a Vote - For the Other Woman." *Butte Evening News*, 17 April 1910, p 9. (Subsequently syndicated; appeared in, *e.g.*, the *Chicago Sunday Tribune*, 20 November 1910, under the title "Mary MacLane Believes in Woman [sic] Suffrage, But She Would Never Vote for a Fat President.")

———. "Men Who Have Made Love to Me." *Butte Evening News*, 24 April 1910, pp 9, 10. (Subsequently syndicated; appeared in, *e.g.*, *Morrison's Chicago Weekly*, 2 February 1911.)

———. "Butte Society - 'The Lady in Green Tights.'" *Butte Evening News*, 1 May 1910, p 9.

———. "The Latter-Day Litany of Mary MacLane." *Butte Evening News*, 8 May 1910, p 9. (Subsequently syndicated; appeared in, *e.g.*, the *Indianapolis Sunday Star*, 12 February 1911.)

———. "The Borrower of Two-Dollar Bills - And Other Women." *Butte Evening News*, 15 May 1910, p 9.

———. "A Waif of Destiny on the High Seas." *Butte Evening News*, 22 May 1910, p 9.

———. "The Big Fight 'Has Something Doing.'" *Butte Evening News*, 3 July 1910, p 9.

———. "Woman and the Cigarette." *Morrison's Chicago Weekly*, 9 February 1911.

———. "Mary MacLane Says - " *Chicago Sunday Tribune*, 10 September 1911, Part VII, p 1. (Clipping in Newberry collection; may be one of a series.)

———. *The Story of Mary MacLane - By Herself - New Edition With a Chapter on the Present*. Duffield & Co., New York, 1911. (Contains a lengthy autobiographical appendix on MacLane's life since *The Story's* original publication.)

———. *I, Mary MacLane: A Diary of Human Days*. Frederick A. Stokes, New York, 1917. (Microfilmed in 1980 by Microfilming Corp. of America for inclusion in the Gerritsen Collection of Women's History.)

———. *Men Who Have Made Love to Me*. Screenplay for Essanay Studios, Chicago, 1917. (Based on the *Butte Evening News* feature article. It dramatized six of MacLane's love-affairs. The film was produced in late 1917 with MacLane starring as herself, edited to 90 minutes in length over either seven or eight reels, and released nationally in January 1918. *Cf.* Mattern pp 31-32 and Brownlow pp 30-33. Further information is contained in files at the Film Study Center of the Museum of Modern Art and in the Library of Congress. Neither the screenplay nor a print of the film has yet been located.)

————. "Mary MacLane on Marriage." *Chicago Herald*, 24 June 1917.

————. "The Movies and Me." *Photoplay*, January 1918.

————. (Letter.) "Notes and Queries" department, *American Mercury*, October 1925. (Responds to a reader's request for information on her present doings.)

————. *The Story of Mary MacLane*. Jonathan Cape, London, 1981. (Photo-duplication of 1902 Stone edition, with an introduction by Michael Yocum.)

————. *The Story of Mary MacLane*. Reprint Services, Irvine [California], 1991. (Photo-duplication of 1902 Stone edition.)

————. *I, Mary MacLane: A Diary of Human Days*. Reprint Services, Irvine [California], 1991. (Photo-duplication of 1917 Stokes edition.)

BOOKS MENTIONING MARY MACLANE

Atherton, Gertrude. *Perch of the Devil*. Frederick A. Stokes, New York, 1914, pp 37, 173.

————. *Adventures of a Novelist*. Liveright, New York, 1932, pp 490-492.

Burlingame, Merrill K. and Toole, K.R. *A History of Montana*. Lewis Historical Publishing Co., New York, 1957, vol. II, p 286.

Brooks, Van Wyck. *The Confident Years: 1885-1915*. Dutton, New York, 1952, pp 319-320, 469.

Brownlow, Kevin. *Behind the Mask of Innocence: Sex, Violence and Crime - Films of Social Conscience in the Silent Era*. Alfred A. Knopf, New York, 1990, pp 30-33, 514-515.

Canfield, Mary Cass. *Grotesques and Other Reflections*. Harper & Bros., New York, 1927, pp 48-60. (Essay on *I, Mary MacLane*. Orig. appeared as "Mary MacLane and the Apparent Agonies of Introspective Pathology," under the by-line "Peter Savage," in *Vanity Fair*, June 1917.)

Derleth, August. *Still Small Voice*. Appleton-Century, New York, 1940, pp 58-59. (Biography of MacLane's *New York World* interviewer, Zona Gale.)

Doran, George H. *Chronicles of Barrabas - 1884-1934*. Harcourt-Brace, New York, 1934, pp 29-30.

Faderman, Lillian. *Surpassing the Love of Men: Romantic Friendship and Love Between Women From the Renaissance to the Present*. William Morrow, New York, 1981, pp 299-300.

————. *Odd Girls and Twilight Lovers: A History of Lesbian Life in America*. Columbia University Press, New York, 1991, p 113.

Ferlinghetti, Lawrence and Peters, Nancy. *Literary San Francisco*. City Lights Books, San Francisco, 1980, p 92.

Foster, Jeannette Howard. *Sex Variant Women in Literature*. Vantage, New York,

1956. (Reprinted by Diana Press, Baltimore, 1975.)

Garland, Hamlin. *Companions on the Trail*. Macmillan, New York, 1931, p 147.

Hall, Dr. G. Stanley. *Adolescence: Its Psychology, and its Relations to Physiology, Anthropology, Sociology, Sex, Crime, Religion, and Education*. Appleton, New York, 1904, vol. I, p 559-560; vol. II, p 629.

Katz, Jonathan Ned. *Gay American History*. Meridian, New York, 1992. (Rev. ed.; orig. pub. Crowell, New York, 1976.)

Kittredge, William and Smith, Annick, eds. *The Last Best Place: A Montana Anthology*. University of Washington Press, Seattle, 1991. (Reprints passages from *The Story* and *I, Mary*.)

Kramer, Sidney. *A History of Stone & Kimball and Herbert S. Stone & Co*. University of Chicago Press, Chicago, 1940.

Mencken, H.L. "The Butte Bashkirtseff," in *Prejudices - first series*. Alfred A. Knopf, New York, 1919, pp 123-128.

Richards, Dell. *Lesbian Lists*. Alyson Publications, Boston, 1990.

Ross, Ishbell. *Ladies of the Press*. Harper, New York, 1936, p 419.

Rudnick, Lois Palken. *Mabel Dodge Luhan: New Woman, New Worlds*. University of New Mexico Press, Albuquerque, 1984, pp 139-140.

Spacks, Patricia Meyer. *The Female Imagination*. Alfred A. Knopf, New York, 1975, pp 6, 166, 171-180, 182, 184, 189, 192, 205, 218, 250, 316, 317.

Truitt, Evelyn M. *Who Was Who on Screen*. R.R. Bowker & Co., New York, 1977, p 293.

Workers of the Writers' Program of the WPA in the State of Montana. *Montana - A State Guide Book*. Viking Press, New York, 1939, p 103.

————. *Copper Camp: Stories of the World's Greatest Mining Town - Butte, Montana*. Hastings House, New York, 1943, pp 1, 257-258.

BY-LINED ARTICLES, ESSAYS, AND REVIEWS

Anonymous. "Mary MacLane as a High-School Friend Knows Her." *Butte Evening News*, 30 January 1910, p 9.

Chapin, Peter. "The Devilish Mary MacLane." *Montana Standard*, 6 June 1981, pp 2, 19.

Eastman, Barrett. (Review of *The Story*.) Originally appeared in the *Chicago Journal*; reprinted in the *Anaconda Standard*, 10 May 1902.

Faderman, Lillian. "Lesbian Magazine Fiction in the Early Twentieth Century." *Journal of Popular Culture*, vol. XI [1978], p 800.

Fuller, Henry B. "Unquenchable Fires." *The Dial*, 2 May 1917, pp 400-401.

Gale, Zona. "The Real Mary MacLane." *New York World*, 17 August 1902, Sunday magazine, pp 1-2.

Hancock, Helen M. "For Your Program." *Exhibitor's Trade Review*, 19 January 1918, p 595. (Suggested promotional copy for *Men Who Have Made Love to Me*.)

Heath, Marion. (Review of *The Story*.) Originally appeared in the *Chicago Journal*; reprinted in the *Anaconda Standard*, 10 May 1902.

Heap, Jane. (Review of *I, Mary MacLane*.) *The Little Review*, April 1917.

Hill, Edwin C. "The Human Side of the News." King Features Syndicate, 1938.

Irwin, Grace Luce. "Current Books - Mary MacLane is not Exciting." *Overland Monthly*, September 1902, p 237.

Irwin, Inez Haynes. "The Life of an Average Woman." *Harper's Bazaar*, May 1912, p 281.

Kerfoot, J.B. (Review of *The Story*.) *Life*, 26 June 1902, p 546.

Maguire, John. (Review of *The Story*.) Originally appeared in the *Anaconda Standard*; reprinted in *Red Lodge Picket*, 9 May 1902, p 4.

Mattern, Carolyn J. "Mary MacLane: A Feminist Opinion." *Montana: The Magazine of Western History*, Autumn 1977, pp 54-63.

McQuade, James. (Review of *Men Who Have Made Love to Me*.) *Motion Picture World*, 28 January 1918, p 525.

Mencken, H.L. "The Cult of Dunsany." *Smart Set*, July 1917, p 138.

Miller, Barbara. "'Hot as Live Embers - Cold as Hail': The Restless Soul of Butte's Mary MacLane." *Montana: The Magazine of Western History*, September 1982, pp 50-53.

Milne, Peter. (Review of *Men Who Have Made Love to Me*.) *Motion Picture News*, 2 February 1918, p 734.

Monroe, Harriet. "Fire of Youth." *Poetry*, June 1917, p 154.

Page, Ada. "Mary Goes Back to Sand and Barrenness." *Overland Monthly*, November 1929, p 345.

Parsons, Louella. "On Movies." *Chicago Herald*, 25 January 1918.

Pascoe, Peggy. Unpublished undergraduate essay on Mary MacLane, written at Montana State University. (Title page evidently missing. Identified by Butte-Silver Bow Public Library as written before 1982. Copies in Butte-Silver Bow Public Library and Montana Historical Society collections.)

Paul, John. "A Young Messalina Out of the West." *New York Times*, 10 May 1902, p 314. (Review of *The Story*.)

———. "Mary MacLane Again." *New York Times*, 5 September 1903. (Unsigned review of *My Friend Annabel Lee*.)

Risley, R.V. "The Story of Mary MacLane." *The Reader*, November 1902, p 96.

Roberts, Nesta. "Breakout from Butte." *London Times Literary Supplement*, 10 July 1981, p 792. (Review of Jonathan Cape reprint of *The Story*.)

Smith, Patsy. "Among the Women." *Variety*, 8 February 1918. (Article on *Men Who Have Made Love to Me*.)

Terris, Dr Virginia. "Mary MacLane - Realist." *The Speculator*, Summer 1985, pp 42-49.

Tinee, Mae. (Review of *Men Who Have Made Love to Me*.) *Chicago Daily Tribune*, 25 January 1918.

Wheeler, Leslie A. "Montana's Shocking 'Lit'ry Lady.'" *Montana: The Magazine of Western History*, Summer 1977, pp 20-33.

Woodward, Helen Beal. "Dear Diary - Will Secret Scribblings Bring Fame to a New Marie Bashkirtseff or Mary MacLane?" *Mademoiselle*, April 1943, pp 98-99, 154-156.

UNSIGNED ARTICLES, EDITORIALS, REVIEWS

Butte Miner. "Girls Who Graduate - Three of the High School Class Delivered Orations Yesterday - The Subjects were Interesting - Miss MacLane Talked of Dickens - Miss Conway Spoke of Germany's Contribution to Civilization and Miss Knowlton Told the Story of Virgil and Dante." 13 May 1899, p 8. (Contains MacLane's "Charles Dickens - Best of Castle-Builders.")

Butte Miner. (Article on Butte High School's graduating class.) 3 June 1899.

Chicago Record-Herald. (Review of *The Story*.) 26 April 1902.

Butte Miner. "Orders for Thousands of Her Weird Book - Miss MacLane's Book Causing a Sensation in the Literary World." 27 April 1902.

New York World. "The Story of Mary MacLane - by Herself - A Very Remarkable Book That Has Just Come Out of Chicago." 27 April 1902, Sunday magazine, p 1.

New York World. "'I Love Devils,' says Genius Mary." 28 April 1902, p 12.

The Missoulian. 29 April 1902, p 4.

Butte Intermountain. 30 April 1902.

Butte Miner. 30 April 1902, p 9.

Great Falls Tribune. 30 April 1902.

Butte Miner. "The Story of Mary MacLane - Views of Jeanette Gilder." 1 May 1902, p 4.

Butte Miner. "Our Peculiar Mary MacLane - Jeannette L. Gilder Criticizes Her in New York Herald - More Extracts Given - Thinks She is Mad and that Books and Paper Should Be Put Out of Reach Until She is Restored." 1 May 1902, p 5.

Great Falls Tribune. 2 May 1902.

Anaconda Standard. 4 May 1902.

Butte Miner. 4 May 1902.

Great Falls Daily Tribune. 4 May 1902, p 10.

Helena Independent. 4 May 1902.

Red Lodge Picket. 9 May 1902, p 4.

Butte Intermountain. 16 May 1902, p 4. (Newbro Drug Company's advertisement for its Mary MacLane highball - "with or without ice cream, cooling, refreshing, invigorating, devilish, the up-to-date drink.")

Butte Tribune-Review. 17 May 1902. (Report from Kalamazoo, Michigan of the suicide of Frances Goodrich Stout, a young girl made "morbidly mad from the reading of Mary MacLane's book in the nude.")

Butte Intermountain. 20 May 1902.

Butte Intermountain. "'Our Mary' Talkative." 24 May 1902, p 5.

Butte Intermountain. (Editorial.) 2 June 1902, p 4.

New York World. "Prof. Triggs Enthuses Over Mary MacLane." 28 June 1902, p 7.

The Critic. (Review of *The Story*.) July 1902, pp 7-8.

New York World. "Mary MacLane to go to Radcliffe College - Before Starting to School She Will Visit New York with the 'Anemone Lady.'" 1 July 1902, p 2.

New York World. "Mary MacLane Busts Home Ties." 8 July 1902, p 3.

New York World. "Chicago is a Bore to Mary MacLane." 9 July 1902, p 12.

Butte Intermountain. "Our Little Mary MacLane Will Outgrow It." 12 July 1902, p 9.

New York World. "Look Out! Here Comes the 'Anemone Lady' - Also Mary MacLane." 13 July 1902, Sunday magazine, p 7.

Helena Independent. "Mary MacLane Mops Floors of Hostess." 14 July 1902.

The Missoulian. 15 July 1902.

New York World. "Mary Will Skip New York." 15 July 1902, p 1.

New York World. (Editorial comment.) 15 July 1902, p 6.

New York World. "She's a Genius of Poetic Woe - Ida Monroe, The Latest Poetess of Passion - New York Produces a Composer that Beats Butte's Wonder a Block - She Discovers Herself Good and Hard - Samples of her Poems as She Reels Them Out on Paper Bags." 15 July 1902, p 5.

New York World. "'Ho for New Yor-r-k!' Now Says Mary MacLane." 16 July 1902, p 2. (With cartoon of Alderman Timothy Sullivan holding in hand his proposed resolution inviting MacLane to New York City and to address the Board of Aldermen "on the new literature of the new West and why the East needs it.")

New York World. "Mary MacLane Slips Into Boston - Dodged All the Reporters and Camera Sharps on the Trip." 21 July 1902, p 4.

New York World. "Mary by 'Devil' Meant 'Ideal.'" 22 July 1902, p 2.

New York World. "Folk Out in Butte are Best of All." 23 July 1902, p 4.

Missoula Fruit-Grower. 25 July 1902, p 4.

The Literary Digest. "A Montana Marie Bashkirtseff." 26 July 1902. (Quotes reviews of *The Story* from the *Chicago News*, *Washington Post*, *St Louis Mirror*, and New York's *Commercial Advertiser.*)

New York World. "Mary MacLane - What Do You Think?" 21 September 1902, Sunday magazine, p 5.

New York World. "What They Think of Mary MacLane - Opinions by Readers of Her Articles in the World's Sunday Magazine." 28 September 1902, Sunday magazine, p 5.

New York World. "Echoes of Mary MacLane - More Letters from World Readers." 12 October 1902, Sunday magazine, p 8.

New York World. "The Love Story of Mary MacLane's Sister." 2 November 1902, Sunday magazine, p 5.

London Times Literary Supplement. "List of New Books and Reprints." 7 November 1902, p 335. (Review of *The Story.*)

Butte Intermountain. "Eloise Larsen of Chicago, Victim of MacLaneism - Head of Local Mary MacLane Society Arrested for Stealing a Horse." 4 December 1902, p 10.

Chicago Record-Herald. 29 August 1903.

Butte Miner. (Review of *My Friend Annabel Lee.*) 3 September 1903, p 4.

The Reader. (Review of *My Friend Annabel Lee.*) October 1903.

Butte Evening News. "Mary MacLane in the Shadow of Death - Butte Authoress Dangerously Ill at her Home on W. Park Street." 29 January 1910.

Butte Evening News. "Mary MacLane Improving." 30 January 1910, p 1.

New York World. "Still Seeking Her Devil, is Mary MacLane." 18 March 1910. (Clipping in Newberry collection; page number not recorded.)

Thermopolis Record [Wyoming]. "The Celebration is Now in Full Swing - Thermopolis' Railroad Days are Proving to be of Exceptional Merit." 23 June 1910, p 1.

Thermopolis Record. "Mary MacLane Says - " 30 June 1910, p 1. (Interview.)

The Atlantic Monthly. (Advertisement for *I, Mary MacLane.*) April 1917.

The Little Review. (Advertisement for *I, Mary MacLane.*) April 1917.

Anaconda Standard. "I, Mary MacLane is Her Latest Book." 13 April 1917.

New York Times Book Review. 15 April 1917, p 133.

Anaconda Standard. "Mary MacLane Lays Bare Her Soul." 22 April 1917, p 8. (Review of *I, Mary MacLane.*)

Montana American. "Miss MacLane's Book." 27 April 1917. (Review of *I, Mary MacLane.*)

The Bookman. "Chronicle and Comment - Mary MacLane." June 1917, p 421. (Review of *I, Mary MacLane.*)

Montana Newspaper Association. Newspaper insert, mid-September 1917. "Mary MacLane Will Act Her Story for Movies." (Clipping in Montana Historical Society collection.)

Chicago Tribune. (Arthur Berthelet, director of *Men Who Have Made Love to Me*, interviewed.) 21 October 1917.

Motography. "Pick MacLane Cast with Care." Vol. XII, no. 5, p 226. (Late 1917 or early 1918.)

Exhibitor's Trade Review. (Distributor's film-trade advertisement for *Men Who Have Made Love to Me.*) 15 February 1918, p 392.

Wid's Daily. (Review of *Men Who Have Made Love to Me.*) 17 January 1918, p 873.

Variety. (Review of *Men Who Have Made Love to Me.*) 1 February 1918.

Moving Picture World. (Film-trade information on, and tips for promoting, *Men Who Have Made Love to Me.*) 2 February 1918, p 722.

Montana Newspaper Association. Newspaper insert, 4 February 1918. "Mary MacLane in the Movies." (Clipping in Montana Historical Society collection.)

Fergus Falls Daily Journal. "Mary MacLane Now in Court" 28 July 1919, p 6.

Montana Newspaper Association. Newspaper insert, 4 August 1919. "Mary MacLane in Court for Debt." (Clipping in Montana Historical Society collection.)

OBITUARIES

Boston Evening Transcript. 7 August 1929, pp 1, 7.

Butte Daily Post. 7 August 1929.

Fergus Falls Daily Journal. "Mary MacLane, Former Fergus Falls Writer, Dies." 7 August 1929, p 1.

Montana Standard. 7 August 1929, pp 1-2.

Chicago Daily Tribune. 8 August 1929, pp 1, 3. (With back-page publicity still from *Men Who Have Made Love to Me.*)

Detroit News. 8 August 1929.

Fergus Falls Daily Journal. "Mary McLane [*sic*] is to be Buried in Fergus Falls." 8

August 1929, p 1.

New York Times. "The Paths of Glory." 8 August 1929, p 24. (Obituary editorial.)

New York Times. "Mary MacLane, Author, Found Dead." 8 August 1929, p 25.

United Press International. "Dies as 'Gods' Fade - Lovely Pagan Mary MacLane, Who Wrote of Men and Passion, Finds her 'Damning Tomorrow.'" 8 August 1929. (Clipping, apparently from a Chicago newspaper, reproduced in Mattern p 62.)

Chicago Daily Tribune. 9 August 1929, p 24.

Fergus Falls Daily Journal. 9 August 1929.

Montana Standard. 9 August 1929.

New York Times. "To Bury Mary MacLane." 9 August 1929, p 17.

Chicago Daily Tribune. 11 August 1929, p 18. (With back-page photo of MacLane's brother James and their mother at the funeral service.)

New York Times. "Mary MacLane's Funeral Today." 11 August 1929, p 27.

New York Times. "Simple Services for Mary MacLane." 12 August 1929, p 19.

Fergus Falls Daily Journal. 14 August 1929.

Time. 19 August 1929, p 53.

The Chicagoan. 31 August 1929. (Untitled obituary editorial; copy in Newberry collection.)

MISCELLANY

Great Falls Tribune. (Article on MacLane's father, James W. MacLane.) 1 June 1889.

Fergus Falls Journal. (Obituary of James W. MacLane.) 1 August 1889.

Fergus Falls Weekly. (Obituary of James W. MacLane.) 1 August 1889.

Fergus Falls Weekly. "As Ever Sadie." (Undated obituary of James W. MacLane. Mentioned by Lipson p 7.)

Who's Who in America. MacLane's first entry appears in 1902 ed.; is reprinted and and updated irregularly thereafter until her death. (A summary entry appears in *Who Was Who in America*, A.N. Marquis & Co., Chicago, 1943, vol. 1, p 764.)

Weber, Joseph and Lew Fields. *The Story of Mary McPaine.* (Vaudeville parody of *The Story*; held the stage for some time at New York's Broadway Music Hall. Script not yet located.)

Life. "Intensity." Cartoon caricature of MacLane from the mid-1900s. (Undated photocopy in the editor's collection.)

American Mercury. August 1925, "Notes and Queries" department. (Letter from a reader.)

Fergus Falls Daily Journal. "'Flatboat' McLane [sic] Plied the Red." 25 June 1972. (Article on James W. MacLane's role in the early development of Minnesota.)

Lipson, Phil. "Mary MacLane Bibliography." Seattle, 1970s. (Unpublished.)

McAllister, Ada. *Abandoning Mary.* Unpublished play based on MacLane's life 1890s-1910. Written late 1980s, produced irregularly thereafter. (Copy in Butte-Silver Bow Public Library collection.)

*

THIS
BOOK HAS
BEEN SET IN
ADOBE GARAMOND
PRO, A FONT BY ROBT.
SLIMBACH SPECIFICALLY
FOR DIGITAL TYPESETTING.
PERSONAL INSPECTION OF C.
GARAMOND'S ORIGINAL PUNCHES
INSPIRED A DESIGN FAITHFUL TO THE
ORIGINAL ROMAN TYPE, WHICH
TRADITIONALLY HAS BEEN
PAIRED WITH THE MORE
SLOPED, ENERGETIC
ITALICS CUT BY
R. GRANJON.

*

BOOK
DESIGN
HAS, IN YEARS
RECENT, DEPARTED
FROM CLASSICAL STRICTURES
AGAINST TYPOGRAPHICAL WIDOWS
AND ORPHANS. GIVEN THE NATURE
OF THIS TEXT, THE DECISION WAS
MADE TO HOLD RIGIDLY TO
PAGEBLOCK GEOMETRY
AND PERMIT WIDOWS
AND ORPHANS
FREELY.

*

* COMING NEXT *

Mary MacLane - a 19-year-old diarist from the early 20th century, still influential today - was the first of the modern media personalities. Now, her whole story is being told in a series of books from Petrarca Press.

On the heels of the successful launch of a 600-page anthology, *Human Days: A Mary MacLane Reader*, we are proud to announce 2015 release of two new books in our MacLane Series: *Mary in The Press: Miss MacLane & Her Fame* and the first-ever complete study of MacLane's life, career, and influence, *A Quite Unusual Intensity of Life: The Lives, Works, and Influence of Mary MacLane*.

Mary in The Press provides, for the first time, more than one thousand pages of interviews, news stories, reminiscences, attacks, opinions, plaudits, personal letters, cartoons, photographs, and more - almost all unseen for a century. With a detailed introduction and lengthy footnotes and bibliography, this mammoth two-volume edition unfolds for the first time the enormous controversy - and adoration - over the writer a forthcoming PBS documentary calls "The First Woman of the Twentieth Century."

A Quite Unusual Intensity of Life goes beyond the usual biography to unfold Mary MacLane's inner and outer worlds; the people she knew and loved; her influences, and her influence on the future; her life outside of writing as a gambler extraordinaire and silent film writer/star; the inner secrets of her unique, still-compelling literary style - and much more.

Michael R. Brown, foremost MacLane scholar in the world today, says of these two books: "This is the other half of Mary's story, and it's taken decades of research to tell it. She gave herself totally in her writing, and the world's slowly remembering now. These are the books I wish I'd had at my side when I read those first words, thirty years ago."

Check http://marymaclane.com for exclusive content, updates, and all news about the ongoing discovery of Mary MacLane. For publication information and pre-ordering for *Mary in The Press* and *A Quite Unusual Intensity of Life*, email groupmail@petrarcapress.com or dial 530-566-6615. ISBN and SAN information forthcoming.

*

Adobe Garamond Pro * Body: 11.5 pts, lead: 12 pts. * Notes: 10 pts, lead: 11.175 pts. * Page: 6in. x 9in. * Margins: top 1 in., bottom 1.375 in., inner 0.91 in., outer 0.7213 in. Text width 4.3687 in. * Normal indent: 0.1667 in. * Fleuron from LTC Vine Leaves